HANS STADEN'S TRUE HISTORY

The Cultures and Practice of Violence Series

Series Editors:
Neil L. Whitehead, University of Wisconsin, Madison
Jo Ellen Fair, University of Wisconsin, Madison
Leigh Payne, University of Wisconsin, Madison

The study of violence has often focused on the political and economic conditions under which violence is generated, the suffering of victims, and the psychology of its interpersonal dynamics. Less familiar are the role of perpetrators, their motivations, and the social conditions under which they are able to operate. In the context of postcolonial state building and more latterly the collapse and implosion of society, community violence, state repression, and the phenomena of judicial inquiries in the aftermath of civil conflict, there is a need to better comprehend the role of those who actually do the work of violence—torturers, assassins, and terrorists—as much as the role of those who suffer its consequences.

When atrocity and murder take place, they feed the world of the iconic imagination that transcends reality and its rational articulation; but in doing so imagination can bring further violent realities into being. This series encourages authors who build on traditional disciplines and break out of their constraints and boundaries, incorporating media and performance studies and literary and cultural studies as much as anthropology, sociology, and history.

HANS STADEN'S
TRUE HISTORY

An Account of
Cannibal Captivity
in Brazil

Hans Staden

Edited and translated by
Neil L. Whitehead and
Michael Harbsmeier

Duke University Press   Durham and London   2008

© 2008 Duke University Press

All rights reserved.

Printed in the United States of America on acid-free paper ∞

Designed by Heather Hensley

Typeset in Adobe Garamond Pro by Tseng Information Systems, Inc.

Library of Congress Cataloging-in-Publication Data appear on

the last printed page of this book.

CONTENTS

List of Illustrations

VII

Preface

IX

Acknowledgments

XIII

Introduction

XV

*The True History and Description of a Country
Populated by a Wild, Naked, and Savage Man-munching
People, situated in the New World, America . . .*
By Hans Staden

I

Appendix

147

Notes

151

Bibliography

181

Index

197

LIST OF ILLUSTRATIONS

(Captions have been added by the editors; none appear in the original text.)

Map

Indigenous groups of the Coast of Brazil in 1557,
after Hans Staden, figure 3   xiv

Figures

1. Sete Katu   5
2. Navigators & God's Providence   18
3. Map of Brazil   19
4. Departure from Lisbon   22
5. The Battle with the White Moors   24
6. A Storm with St. Elmo's Fire   25
7. The Defense of Iguaraçu   28
8. The Battle with the French at Buttugaris   29
9. The Passage from Seville to São Tomé, Guinea   31
10. Arrival in Brazil, near Shipwreck in Supraway   33
11. A Providential Arrival at Santa Catarina   36
12. Shipwreck off São Vicente (Upaunema)   41
13. Tupiniquin and Portuguese try to rescue Staden   43
14. Staden is Captured   48
15. The Bound Animal   52
16. The Weather Shaman   53
17. The Arrival at Uwattibi—Aprasse Dance   56

18. The Dance with the Arasoya — 57

19. The Speech of Konyan Bebe to his Hopping Food — 63

20. The Attack of the Tupiniquins — 65

21. The Angry Moon — 66

22. Death and Curing — 70

23. The Tupiniquin Trading with the Portuguese — 77

24. The Death of the Carijó Slave — 80

25. The Maria Ballete refuses Staden — 83

26. Meyen Bipe War Camp — 85

27. The Pursuit of the Tupiniquins from Brikioka — 86

28. The Treatment of Captives at Meyen Bibe — 88

29. The Dance with the Captives at Occarasu — 90

30. Weather Shamanism and The Cross — 93

31. Weather Shamanism and The Fish — 94

32. The Attack on a Portuguese Ship at Rio — 100

33. The Catherine de Vatteville's Providential Voyage — 101

34. Tupinambás — 106

35. Palisaded Village — 110

36. Fire Sticks — 111

37. Ini—hammock — 111

38. Fishing — 112

39. Weather Shamanism and The Cross (ii) — 115

40. Preparation of Drink by Women — 118

41. Male Adornment — 120

42. The enduap—worn in war and feasting — 120

43. The tammaraka — 124

44. Induction of the Captive—Aprasse Dance — 130

45. The Dance with The Arasoya — 130

46. Iwera Pemme — 131

47. The Women Drinking and Feasting — 133

48. The Women Adorn and Carouse with the Captive — 133

49. The Dance with Iwera Pemme — 134

50. The Women Carouse with the Captive — 134

51. The Women Taunt the Captive — 135

52. The Dismemberment of the Flayed Body by The Men — 135

53. The Women's Feast — 136

54. The Youngsters' Feast — 136

55a. The Armadillo—Dattu — 138

55b. The Possum—Serwoy — 139

PREFACE

Hans Staden's *Warhaftige*[1] *Historia und Beschreibung eyner Landtschafft der wilden, nacketen, grimmigen Menschfresser Leuthen in der Newenwelt America gelege* (Marburg, 1557) is a fundamental text in the history of the discovery of Brazil, being one of the earliest accounts we have of the Tupi Indians from an eyewitness who was captive among them for over nine months, as well as offering a highly detailed description of the nature of early Portuguese enclaves in the region of Rio de Janeiro. The work also dates to a point in time when the Portuguese presence in the region was directly challenged by the French, who had been visiting the Brazilian coast for the trade in brazil wood since at least the 1520s. In this context both French and Portuguese attempted to recruit and maintain native alliances, making knowledge of the indigenous population much more than a disinterested ethnological issue. Staden's account therefore also hinges on the way in which this intercolonial conflict played into his situation as a captive of the Tupinambá,[2] allies to the French. In this way the work, although chiefly famed until now as a text on Tupian cannibalism, is no less important for appreciating the nature of European colonialism in Brazil and how that context was significant for the emergence of various ethnic and national antagonisms in Europe. In fact the issue of cannibalism, although obviously prominent in Staden's text and its accompanying visual illustrations, is by no means the only matter of contemporary interest to historians and anthropologists—how and why this should be so is part of the purpose of the introductory essay to explain.

It therefore needs to be emphasized at the outset that Staden's *Warhaftige Historia* has become a key reference in the resurgent debate on cannibalism and its discourses;[3] a debate that had its very origins at the moment of the text's production, such as in the speculations of Michel de Montaigne, who also conversed with Tupi people brought as living exhibits to France, as well as in the way the idea of Brazilian cannibalism was used to mediate European controversies about the eucharistic cannibalism of Jesus Christ in Christian religions of the period.

So too, Staden's text has a particular significance in contemporary Brazil as both a source for Oswald de Andrade's inspiration for a distinct Brazilian modernism—termed the *antropofagista* movement—and for the visual reinterpretation of the woodcuts in the *Warhaftige Historia* by Candido Portinari—the Brazilian "Picasso." A more popular legacy for the *Warhaftige Historia* is also evident in the production of children's literature based on Staden's story—Manuel Lobato's *Aventuras de Hans Staden* has gone through eleven editions and been in print since 1927—making Hans Staden somewhat analogous to Davy Crockett as an icon of the "wild frontier." There are also renderings of Staden's account in contemporary Brazilian cinema, notably by Nelson Pereira dos Santos in 1974 but also as recently as 2000 in a film by Luiz Alberto Pereira.

Despite this cultural genealogy there has not been an English-language version since Malcolm Letts's edition of 1928, and only two versions in modern German since Fouquet's edition in 1941.[4] While accurate transcription and translation of Staden's text are therefore the bedrock of this edition it is also our aim to make the text intellectually and aesthetically accessible to contemporary audiences.[5] This means that we aim to alert the reader to the anthropolgical and historical aspects of Staden's text in the light of modern scholarship on both colonial Brazil as well as still-living Tupian peoples. Our critical introduction therefore brings new perspectives to this text, particularly ethnographic experience of ritual anthropophagy, as well as literary and ethnological critique of travel writings and its genres.[6]

Undoubtedly part of the continuing importance of Staden's text is precisely the way in which it relates to current debates on knowing or interpreting others distant in both cultural space and historical time, and the issue of cannibalism vividly highlights ideas of such difference. It is therefore crucial to note that it was the issue of observation, not of cannibalism, that was taken up in the introduction to Staden's work by Johannes Dryander, a professor of medicine at the University of Marburg, where the work was first published. As such the *Warhaftige Historia* is perhaps uniquely important among the class of early colonial documents more generally, not for the representations of savage cannibalism, for which the work is currently notorious, but for the way it broaches questions of observational epistemology, as well as the meanings of captivity and cultural difference. Nonetheless, the appearance of the cannibal sign in an early and highly intense form through Staden's text can hardly be denied, but it is important to remember that this reflects European concerns and anxieties of the time, and the relevance, if any, of Staden's observations to the reconstruction of past cultural practices of the Tupi will be part of the task of the Introduction to explain.

ACKNOWLEDGMENTS

This work has had a long gestation and the intellectual support and encouragement of our colleagues has been invaluable. In particular we would like to thank Peter Hulme for suggesting the collaborative project and Stuart Schwartz's consistent enthusiasm for its outcomes. We trust that the text that follows meets those expectations. We would also like to thank Nils Holger Berg for assistance in making this translation.

Gordon Brotherston, Antonio Curet, Jose Rabasa, Lucia Sà, Kevin Terraciano, and Lee Wandel all deserve particular thanks for their interest in this work. Presentations given at Stanford, the Chicago Field Museum, UCLA, and the University of Wisconsin were invaluable for the comments on the editorial strategies we have pursued, and thanks are due both the organizers and audiences.

We would also like to thank Walter Schiffner of the Wolfhagen Museum for organizing a conference in 2007 celebrating the 450th anniversary of the original publication of Staden's account where the comments of encouragement of a variety of Staden scholars from Germany, France, and Brazil were invaluable. This was also the occasion for the celebration of a new translation of Staden's text into modern German and Portuguese by Franz Obermeier, Joachim Tiemann, and Guiomar Carvalho Franco (2006). We refer the interested reader to the detailed comments contained in the notes to this critical philological edition as well as in the Introduction and its exhaustive bibliography.

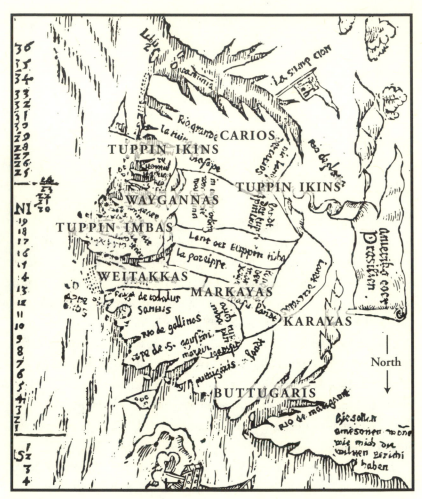

Indigenous groups of the Coast of Brazil in 1557, after Hans Staden, figure 3.

INTRODUCTION

I. The Warhaftige Historia *in Context*

1. THE TEXT OF THE *WARHAFTIGE HISTORIA*

The *Warhaftige Historia* itself originally comprised one hundred and seventy-eight folios and fifty-five woodcut illustrations and a map. The first edition was published in Marburg on Shrove Tuesday in 1557 by Andres Kolben at the sign of the Clover Leaf. A second printing by Kolben in the same year omitted the map of Brazil and its native peoples that appears in the first printing (EA I: 88).[1] Another edition with two printings also appeared in that year, in Frankfurt, but the original woodcuts, likely done under Staden's direct supervision since his figure regularly appears in the scenes, were replaced by utterly irrelevant pictures of Turkey and the Levant; the map was also omitted.[2]

The Marburg woodcuts are a vastly underappreciated aspect of the text—possibly because they only appear in their entirety in the first edition and they were evidently a source of inspiration for the reworking of the Staden material for presentation by Théodore de Bry (1592) in his collection of voyages. Since this later work was also issued in Frankfurt we might assume that it simply supplanted the original Staden material, because of both the better reproductive quality of the de Bry graphics and their greater accessibility as part of a widely disseminated compendium of travel, colonization, and ethnological description.

There have been numerous subsequent editions[3] of the *Warhaftige His-*

toria in both Latin and Dutch as well as German; an Antwerp edition as early as 1558 and again in 1563, and in Amsterdam in 1595, as well as versions by Théodore de Bry in 1592 and 1593 (EA I: 88). There were ten further editions between 1605 and 1630, in either Latin or Dutch (EA:II: 915). Six of these editions issued by B. Janszoon in Amsterdam and three editions were issued by J. J. Bouman in Amsterdam in 1655, 1656, and 1660 (EA III: 658), reflecting the colonial presence of the Dutch in Brazil during the period 1625 to 1654. Staden's account was also included in collections of voyages by Johann Gottfried in 1655 and Johann Wynkelmann[4] in 1664 (EA III: 658). Three further Dutch editions were published in 1679, 1685, and 1686 in Amsterdam and Utrecht (EA IV: 683), and two more out of Amsterdam in 1701 and 1714, with two editions appearing in Leiden in 1706 (EA V: 574) and one out of Amsterdam in 1736 (EA V: 819). There was then something of a lull in the outpouring of editions until the first French translation, made in 1837[5] followed by a modern German edition in 1859 edited by Karl Klüpfel[6] and the first Brazilian edition in 1900, edited and translated by Alberto Löfgren and Teodoro Sampaio,[7] to celebrate the quatercentennial of the discovery of Brazil. The first English-language translation was made by Albert Tootal for the Hakluyt Society under the editorship of Richard Burton (1874), who was British consul to Brazil in the early 1870s. There have been numerous translated and facsimile editions[8] since then but only one other English translation made by Malcolm Letts (1928).

The text, comprising two distinct parts, the (I) *Historia* and the (II) *Beschreibung* of fifty-three and thirty-six chapters respectively, and to no lesser extent its illustrations,[9] is undoubtedly a touchstone for all those who consider the Brazil shore in the sixteenth century, and this is despite the fact that the French- and Portuguese-language sources have dominated the representation of the Tupi and in particularly the rites of cannibalistic incorporation they practiced. Clearly there are good reasons for this interpretative emphasis on the French and Portuguese materials, including the breadth of commentary through time, the overtly ethnological ambitions of their authors, who were relatively educated and literate, their accessibility, and the fact that they were the product of a set of political, military, and economic relationships more enduring than personal encounter. Nonetheless, Staden's highly personal account was born of a very distinct and intense experience that lasted just over nine months and in this sense was the more properly ethnographic, understood as a dialogic and sustained encounter, than the priestly ethnologies, understood as principally synthetic and second-hand.

However, Staden's text is not without the imprimatur of ethnological, if not liturgical, approval, for the account of his captivity itself is preceded by an "Introduction" by one Dr. Johannes Dryander.[10] The endorsement is given by Dryander since he had known Staden's father for "upwards of fifty years": "And since the proverb says that the apple always tastes of the tree, one can expect Hans Staden, the son of this honorable man, to resemble his father in virtue and piety" (Dryander's introduction 4). However, it is more than a simple endorsement, for Dryander also says that he was asked by Staden "to revise it and where necessary correct it."[11] The introduction thus deals with a number of matters, principally the probity of Staden's testimony; the cultural and epistemological status of eyewitness accounts of the strange lands (largely by analogy to the way in which astronomical knowledge is established contra theology); Staden's motives for publishing his account as being pious rather than vainglorious; the power of prayer and trust in God to produce deliverance and redemption; and the duty of those so redeemed to communicate this to their fellows. Dryander notes that Staden was verbally interrogated in his presence by Philip, Landgrave of Hesse,[12] to whom Staden also dedicates the book. Staden himself chooses to quote Psalm 107, which opens with the lines "They that go down to the sea in ships, that do business in great waters: These see the works of the Lord and his wonders in the deep . . . ," underlining the profoundly religious approach with which Staden mediated and represented that experience, the significance of which will be taken up later in this introduction.

Dryander also presumably involved himself in the production of Part II of the *Warhaftige Historia*, which is essentially an ethnological appendix to the "direct" testimony of Staden himself which composes Part I. The intellectual context and wider relevance of the ethnological aspects of Staden's text are further discussed below, but it is useful to first rehearse the central features of the testimony of Staden himself before proceeding to discuss these more general implications.

2. THE TESTIMONY OF THE *WARHAFTIGE HISTORIA*

Little else is known of Hans Staden aside from the story of his captivity in Brazil. From the preface of Johannes Dryander we learn that his father was born and grew up in the same village, Wetter, as did Dryander and later moved to the town of Homberg, where Hans Staden then claimed to have come from. Until the 1950s nobody seems to have cared much about the identity and family of the pious "gunner," "soldier," and "adventurer" who after his two voyages to the New World settled in the nearby small town of Wolfhagen. During the preparations for celebrating the four-hundred-year anniversary of the *Warhaftige Historia*, however, a number of local historians began to search for more material in the archives for the purpose of the "systematic genealogical and sociological exploration of the Staden family."[13] Most of the results of these endeavors, all published in a special issue of the journal *Hessische Heimat* in 1956, deal with the Staden family more generally rather than the famous traveler, who probably took part as a soldier in the Schmalkaldic War of 1546–47, but even his father's name remains unknown. Two, and later three, archival documents, however, do tell us a little more. According to the first of these, soon after the publication of the *Warhaftige Historia* Staden must have started a career as a powder maker because, as of June 4, 1558, he had not yet paid back the equivalent of two tons of saltpeter to the owner of a powder mill in Marburg, Hans Kampfer, with whom Staden had served as apprentice (Ruppel 1956: 5). Two other documents are more closely related to the *Warhaftige Historia* since they both are letters by its author dedicating his book to the recipients, Count Wolrad II and Count Philipp Ludwig II. The purpose of these two letters seems to have been to ask for financial support or perhaps some sort of appointment. More interesting, however, seems to be the fact, which Gerhard Menk more recently has pointed out, that apparently neither of the two letters was written by Staden himself.[14]

Staden was in Lisbon in 1547, where there was a German commercial colony, in hope of finding employment as a ship's gunner. He set sail in June of that year on a ship transporting convicts, which had orders to attack any French interlopers off the Brazil coast. He reached Pernambuco in January 1548 (*Warhaftige Historia* I, chaps. 1–5) and then returned to Portugal in October 1548 but sailed again in March 1549 on a Spanish vessel that was part of a new expedition to Rio de la Plata. Unfavorable weather broke up the fleet, which was partially reunited at the Portuguese colony of Sao Vicente (Santos). Here the Portuguese were allied with the Tupiniquin, which meant that the Tupinambá to the north were hostile to their settlement, the Tupinambá in turn being allied with the French. Staden was persuaded to stay in Portuguese service for a further two years, acting as a gunner in a new Portuguese fort to the east of Sao Vincente on the island of Sao Amaro, opposite the existing fort of Brikioka. It was during this period that he was captured by the Tupinambá and the bulk of his text describes the events leading up to this episode and his subsequent captivity.

While out hunting in the vicinity of the fort, Staden was surprised by a party of Tupinambá warriors. Stripped naked and beaten, Staden was immediately carried off by his captors (figures 14, 15) toward their settlement of Uwattibi (Ubatúba). Given his treatment and the words of his captors, it was apparent that he was destined for sacrifice — *kawewi pepicke* (*Warhaftige Historia* I, chap. 18) — as a prisoner of war. However, his two years of service in the fort had given him opportunity to learn the Tupi language and this was to serve him well. As Staden candidly tells us: "At this time I knew less of their customs than I knew later, and I thought to myself: now they are preparing to kill me" (*Warhaftige Historia* I, chap. 22).

Staden at least had the wit to understand that if he were to be taken for a Portuguese he would almost certainly die and so he begins what is to be an interminable struggle to play off the fact that he was not a Portuguese but a "German," or, more precisely, from Hesse in Germany, and so should be exempted from the cycle of political revenge between Portuguese and Tupinambá. To that end, and notwithstanding his positive identification by a Tupinambá captured in a Portuguese and Tupiniquin raid and enslaved to the Portuguese at Brikioka,[15] he attempted to persuade a French trader who was living four miles (*staden*) from Uwattibi to vouch for the fact that he was not Portuguese:

> Then they took me to him, naked as I was, and I found him to be a youth known to the savages by the name Karwattuware. He commenced to speak to me in French, which I could not well understand, and the savages stood round about and listened. Then when I was unable to reply to him, he spoke to the savages in their own tongue and said: "Kill him and eat him, the good-for-nothing, for he is indeed a Portuguese, your enemy and mine." This I understood, and I begged him for the love of God to tell them not to eat me, but he replied only: "They will certainly eat you." (*Warhaftige Historia* I, chap. 26)

Staden was abandoned to his fate; "the savages said only: 'He is indeed a true Portuguese. Now he cries. Truly he is afraid to die'" (*Warhaftige Historia* I, chap. 26). He was duly prepared to be ritually killed but a timely attack of toothache, which his captors tried to remedy by a forcible dental extraction, led him to refuse food and he grew correspondingly thin, although they "threatened that if I do not eat and grow fat again they would kill me before the appointed day" (*Warhaftige Historia* I, chap. 27). Questioned as to the disposition of the Portuguese, Staden suggested that it was the Tupiniquin who were planning to attack his captors. When this prediction came true, not only was Staden's status as a possible prophet-shaman established but he also reluctantly joined them in defending Uwattibi against the Tupiniquin attack (figure 20). Following this prophetic event Staden went on to suggest, when asked one night why he looked at the moon so intently, that the moon was angry with the Tupinambá (see figure 21). This proved, whether by luck or judgment, to be a most culturally effective observation since it produced both curiosity and alarm among his captors.[16] When his captors themselves subsequently fell sick this became a further opportunity for Staden to perform as a shamanic healer and, since epidemic disease was ravaging Tupi populations at this time, this must be a highly significant factor in the plausibility given to Staden's acting out of shamanic roles (see figure 22). Staden suggested that he could intercede with his god to relieve the Tupinambá of the sickness that afflicted them. However, this was not initially effective; as Staden tells us, "I went to and fro laying my hands on their heads as they desired me to do, but God did not suffer it and they began to die" (*Warhaftige Historia* I, chap. 34). Nonetheless, the ultimate recovery of the chieftains Jeppipo Wasu, Vratinge Wasu, and Kenrimakui, despite the deaths of other members of their families, meant that "there was no more talk of eating me. But they guarded me closely and would not suffer me to go about unattended" (*Warhaftige Historia* I, chap 24).

Staden thus had ample opportunity and the linguistic abilities to understand and record what occurred around him, and it is this aspect of his text which speaks most strongly to his subsequent commentators. It is notable that both contemporary and subsequent sources may add to and amplify, but do not contradict or undermine, his account of the Tupinambá.

The peculiar new status of Staden also meant the Frenchman, Karwattuware, now was prepared to say that Staden was indeed a "German" and was different from the Portuguese. But despite the offer of trade goods the Tupinambá were not about to give up their strange, and powerful, new prophet-healer. Staden recounts how he observed the cannibalism of other captives (see figure 24) and the frustrating attempts he made to escape with various visiting ships. He also joined them on raids against enemy villages (see figure 27) and observed and commented upon the practice of war and the cannibalism of captives, including Portuguese (see figure 28). Finally, however, Staden was able to parlay his way aboard a French ship, although he nearly died of a serious gunshot wound when they encountered a Portuguese vessel off the Brazilian coast. He finally arrived in Honfleur, France, on February 20, 1555.

The narrative tension at the heart of Staden's text is how his direct experience of the cannibal Tupinambá, which was far more extensive and "ethnographic" than that of other contemporary commentators, threatens to continuously overwhelm the religious and ethnological testament that he, and his ghostly interlocutor Dr. Dryander, wished to make.[17] Thus Staden's captivity among the Tupinambá is used to produce a homily of redemption and faith in which anthropophagic sacrifice is but one of the many tests and redemptive proofs of faith the text offers. This threat of bodily and spiritual dissolution through the visceral certainty of customary cannibalism is not the only test that Staden's god inflicts upon him, and other physical dangers—shipwreck, disease (both epidemic and dental), gunfire, and the perfidy of the French—also loom large as moments in which evidence of Staden's god become manifest.

However, Staden's experience undermines this didactic purpose since the vivid nature of his experiences while captive among the Tupinambá, that is Staden's engagement with actual cannibals, at all points threatens to escape the straitjacket of Christian testimonial and ethnological distancing into which he and Dr. Dryander[18] try to encase it. In this light the text may also be understood as part of Staden's "ritual of return,"[19] which allows both him and us to give meaning and purpose to and to derive cultural illumination from the otherwise "incomprehensible" experience of being captive among the Tupinambá. But before considering the nature of that experience, as it bears on questions of Tupinambá ethnology, and how the resulting text has been used by subsequent commentators, it is necessary to situate the *Warhaftige Historia* in relation to the other more copious and better known accounts of the sixteenth-century Tupi.

3. THE PORTUGUESE DISCOVERY TEXTS

The Portuguese materials have a chronological priority over the description of the Tupinambá and Tupinikin given by Hans Staden. In particular these include the letters of discovery of Pedro Vaz de Caminha and the "Four Letters" of Amerigo Vespucci, which are also among the earliest descriptions of the New World itself and justly famous for that reason. However, although some of the details given by Caminha and Vespucci clearly indicate that Tupi populations were among those described, very little detail, when compared to the richness of the *Warhaftige Historia*, emerges from these accounts. However, the rhetorical association of Brazilian natives and the practice of cannibalism is quickly established, as is the presence of exotic sexuality. Vespucci writes, probably of the northern coasts of Brazil,[20]

> They eat little flesh unless it be human flesh, and your Magnificence must know that they are so inhuman as to transgress regarding this most bestial custom. For they eat all their enemies that they kill or take, as well females as males, with so much barbarity, that it is a brutal thing to mention: how much more to see it, as has happened to me an infinite number of times. They were astonished at us when we told them that we did not eat our enemies. Your Magnificence may believe for certain, that they have many other barbarous customs. (1894: 11)

Vespucci also initiates a startling image of indigenous sexuality,

> They are not very jealous, but lascivious beyond measure, the women much more so than the men. I do not refer to their contrivances for satisfying their inordinate desires, so that I may not offend against modesty. (1894: 8)

but he does indeed refer to their contrivances in a subsequent passage of his third letter:

> Another custom among them is sufficiently shameful, and beyond all human credibility. The women being very libidinous, make the penis of their husbands swell to such a size as to appear deformed; and this

is accomplished by a certain artifice, being the bite of a poisonous animal, and by reason of this many lose their virile organ and remain eunuchs. (1894: 46)

Staden is remarkably silent on such sexuality, and he notes, "The men and women also do as is fitting and do their things in private" (*Warhaftige Historia* II, chap. 20, p. 95) (the original reads: *machen ire sachen heymlich*), which suggests that he may not have had the opportunity to observe much anyway. Vespucci goes on to reinforce the notion of a cannibalism as a subsistence practice, rather than ritual proclivity:

I have seen a man eat his children and wife; and I knew a man who was popularly credited to have eaten 300 human bodies. I was once in a city for twenty-seven days, where human flesh was hung up near the houses, in the same way as we expose butcher's meat. I say further that they were surprised that we did not eat our enemies, and use their flesh as food, for they say it is excellent. (1894: 47)

Absurd and defamatory though these claims appear, the value of Staden's account is that it allows us to reconstruct a cultural context in which such statements may be better understood as the exaggerations and misrepresentations that they are. The sacrifice of children or women with affinal status is thus more clearly explained in later sources, as is the accumulation, through the capture and sacrifice of enemies, of honorific names, which was indeed a way in which an individual may have claimed to have "eaten" over three hundred of his enemies. In the same way the "excellence" of human flesh can be related to the importance and satisfaction of revenge through ritual sacrifice, as much as to any gustatory pleasures.

Vespucci's verifiable voyage to Brazil in 1502 was preceded by that of Pedro Vaz de Caminha, who accompanied and described Pedro Alvares Cabral's foundational discovery of Brazil in 1500 (Caminha 1938). Caminha does not mention "cannibalism"[21] but rather signals "savagery" through the sexualized nakedness of the natives they encounter;

And then they stretched themselves out on their backs on the carpet to sleep without taking any care to cover their privy parts, which were not circumcised, and the hair on them was well shaved and arranged. (1938: 13)

There were among them three or four girls, very young and very pretty, with very dark hair, long over the shoulders, and their privy parts so high, so closed, and so free from hair that we felt no shame in looking at them very well. (1938: 15)

Caminha also highlighted the use of feathers among the Tupi; "The man who befriended him was now well on in years, and was well decked with ornaments and covered with feathers stuck to his body, so that he looked pierced with arrows like Saint Sebastian" (1938: 16) as well as their use of lip-plugs;

They go naked, without any covering; neither do they pay more attention to concealing or exposing their shame than they do to showing their faces, and in this respect they are very innocent. Both had their lower lips bored and in them were placed pieces of white bone, the length of a handbreadth, and the thickness of a cotton spindle and as sharp as an awl at the end. They put them through the inner part of the lip, and that part which remains between the lip and the teeth is shaped like a rook in chess. And they carry it there enclosed in such a manner that it does not hurt them, nor does it embarrass them in speaking, eating, or drinking. (1938: 11)

The subsequent letters of Amerigo Vespucci also mention the use of lip-plugs and other facial piercings set with crystals (Vespucci 1894: 46). The participation of women in violence is also given emphasis by Vespucci, a theme that Staden more accurately illuminates through his precise reporting and which was to play a significant role in the later reworkings of his original account. Vespucci's "Letters" also foreshadow, along with other accounts from the Caribbean (Hulme and Whitehead 1992: 15), the emergence of the idea of New World "Amazons," fully realized in Gaspar de Carvajal's (1934) account of the Francisco de Orellana's first descent of the "River of the Amazons" in the 1540s:

[A]s we jumped on shore, the men of the land sent many of their women to speak with us. Seeing that they were not reassured, we arranged to send to them one of our people . . . a very agile and valiant youth . . . He went among the women, and they all began to touch and feel him . . . we saw a woman come from the hill, carrying a great stick in her hand. When she came to where our Christian stood, she raised it, and gave him such a blow that he was felled to the ground. The other women immediately took him by the feet, and dragged him towards the hill . . . where the women were . . . tearing him to pieces. At a great fire they had made they roasted him before our eyes, showing us many pieces, and then eating them. The men made signs how they had killed the other two Christians and eaten them. (Vespucci 1894: 57–58)

As will be clear from Staden's account and the illustrations that accompany the relevant text (see figures 47–51, 53), the participation of women was a highly important phase in the ritual sacrifice of enemies captured by the men and was the subject of much ideologically freighted comment by external observers (as is discussed below).

The reports of Manoel da Nóbrega, already some fifty years after these first encounters and virtually contemporary with the sojourn of Staden himself, provide some of the most extended accounts of the Tupi. As a missionary resident among them, Nóbrega was in a good position to outline some of the key features of Tupi culture and society. He duly notes their subsistence practices, their political and ethnic divisions, the rules and customs of marriage and birth, the role of the *pagé* and *karai* (shamans and prophets), but he spends no less space reinscribing the cannibal motif;

When they capture someone, they take him to a great feast, with a rope tied about his neck, and give him, for a wife, the daughter of the chief, or whomsoever else he is most contented with, and begin to raise him as they would a pig, until the time for killing him arrives. For this occasion everyone from the surrounding district comes together, for a feast, and, one day before they kill him, they wash him all over, and the following day they carry him away, and put him in a public place, tied by a cord through the belt, and there comes one of them who is very well ornamented and (who) goes through the habits of his ancestors, and, finishing, he who is about to die answers him, saying that he is courageous and not afraid of death, and that he has also killed many of his own, and that he will be revenged by his family, and other things of a similar nature. And when he is dead they cut off his thumb, because it is with this that he looses his arrows, and the other (fingers) they fasten to sticks, in order to eat them when they are cooked and roasted. (1988: 100)

As will be apparent from Staden's account, this in essence is the Tupian form of ritual sacrifice for war-captives, but as Staden's account also made evident for the first time, the context and motivations surrounding this moment of ritual drama were highly complex. As an actor in that drama Staden is of course uniquely placed to comment on these matters in the way no other observers were, then and now. Moreover, accounts such as Nóbrega's were intended as synthetic summaries, an ethnological overview, and so necessarily tended to erase the contingent and particular in order to arrive at a generalized statement of habits and custom. In Staden's case the reason for the description of cannibalistic ceremony was as part of a biographical narrative in which the particularity of his situation and the individual redemption that God chooses to exercise in his favor are central to the form of the work. This does not mean that Staden undertakes no generalizations whatsoever—indeed the later section of the book is just such a synthetic ethnology—but his reflexive narrative of his role in the events from which he derives that synthesis are much closer to the kind of ethnographic ambition of providing contingent context to ethnological judgment that marks modern anthropological writing.

Like Caminha and Vespucci, Nóbrega also signals the erotic and bodily as part of Tupian identity;

They are very attached to sensual things. Many times they asked me if God has a head and a body, and a mother; and as to whether He eats, and how He dresses, and other similar things. (1988: 101)

This theme is also taken up forcefully in the French texts, but the overall conjunction of the material, fleshy, and naked cannibal body with the spirituality of eucharistic sacrifice is a theme that pervades the literature on the ancient Tupi and to which Staden's text vividly contributes.

In this vein the writings of José de Anchieta, from the period immediately after Staden's text was published, broach not just sensuality but also exotic sexuality, as first mentioned by Vespucci:

The hair of others [a kind of centipede] . . . are venomous and provoke libidinous desires. The Indians are accustomed to apply them to their genital parts which incites and intensifies sensual enjoyment: after three days these hairs putrefy: sometimes the prepuce is perforated and the sexual organs infected with an incurable disease: they not only soil themselves with this foulness, but they also defile and infect the women with whom they sleep. (1988: 126)

Anchieta also widens this concern with sexuality to encompass the rules of marriage, incest, and, crucially, the sexuality of sacrifice:

Agoaçā, which is a name common to both men and women, means "lover" or "concubine," and is bestowed upon a man or woman even if they have had sexual intercourse only once; and in this relationship sexual intercourse is indulged in secretly (though everyone does it), and for this reason they call the act *mandaró* (furtive) . . . If a man has a woman well in hand so that she does not go around with other men . . . , they then enter into the category of those they call *Temirecô* . . . They also call the enemy women whom they capture in war and with whom they live *Temirecô* . . . because they hold that real kinship comes through the fathers, who are the agents; and that the mothers are only bags in which the children grow and for that reason the offspring of female captives are always free and regarded as the other members of the tribe; and the children of the women of the tribe, if they have been begotten by captives, are regarded as slaves and sold, and at times killed and eaten, even though they may be their own grandchildren, the children of their daughters, and therefore they likewise copulate with the daughters of their sisters. (1846: 257–60)

Anchieta thus provides, unlike Staden, a very detailed account of marriage practice, crucial to the political and economic functioning of Tupi society. He notes of Konyan Bebe, a central figure in Staden's narrative, that

if the woman happens to be a bold creature, she may leave her husband and take another, which is what they told me happened with the first wife of Cunhābêba, who was the most respected chief of the Tamoyos living in the Yperuig region; she already had a son and daughter of marriageable age, and notwithstanding all this, she deserted her husband and married another man or became his mistress, because he had taken other wives or perhaps just because it was her whim to do so; and other women do the same without arousing the feelings of their husbands. (1846: 256)

Anchieta also hints at how the politics of leadership among the Tupi were affected by the colonial intrusion, while neatly casting suspicion on the French;

> I was told that Ambirem, a great chief of Rio de Janeiro, naturally cruel and blood-thirsty, and a great friend of the French, ordered that one of his twenty wives, who had committed adultery, should be tied to a post and have her stomach cut out with a butcher-knife; and the adulterer, who was his own nephew, stayed away for a while in fear of death. But this appears in all probability to have been a lesson taken from the French, who are accustomed to dealing out such deaths, because no Brazilian Indian would normally inflict such a punishment. (1846: 256)[22]

It is not for another twenty years or so after Anchieta was writing that we get further extensive reportage on the Tupi, this time from a secular source, Gabriel Soares de Sousa. He was writing as a Portuguese colonist resident many years in Brazil and offers a compendious description of the colony.[23] Sousa resided mainly in the region of Bahia to the north of where Staden was held captive. Like Anchieta he was alert to the politics of cultural practice in the period of his residence:

> Even after the Portuguese had populated the Rio Jaguaripe, there was a great meeting of people from the neighboring villages to break skulls on the plaza amid great festivities. The skull breakers took new names. These skulls were taken from a deserted village in revenge for the death of their fathers and relatives. These skulls were decorated with feathers in their guise. There was a big drinking party organized by the Portuguese who wanted the relatives of the dead to get indignant and resentful. The Portuguese were afraid that they might confederate themselves and attack them, but this was sufficient to prevent the move and to make the settlement secure. (1974: 167)

Sousa also "verifies," the erotic and exotic nature of cannibal sexuality:

> They are addicted to sodomy and do not consider it a shame. The one who acts as the male regards himself as virile and they boast of such

bestiality. In their villages in the bush there are such men who keep shop to all those who want them, like prostitutes. . . . They are not satisfied with their penises as nature made them, but many of them expose theirs to the bites of poisonous animals which causes their penises to swell and they suffer for six months during which time their organs change. Their members become so monstrously big that women can hardly stand them. (1974: 172)

He later adds the comparative note: "The Tupina are very addicted to homosexuality, more than the Tupinamba. Those who are active boast about it and they mention this when they recite their praises" (1974: 188).

But Sousa thereby also opens a slightly broader window on Tupian subjectivity, at least with regard to the power of the karai prophet-sorcerers[24] that also was a repetitive feature of missionary accounts, since spiritual conquest was all important to such writers. Sousa says:

These sorcerers are called pagé and if they are angry because a man has refused to give them his daughter or something else which they have asked for they say: "You shall die," which they call "to cast death." These savages are so barbarous that they go to lie down in their hammocks, stunned, and they refuse to eat and of sheer fright they let themselves die and nothing can take from their minds the notion that they could escape from the verdict of the shaman. Certain Indians give their daughters up as wives to protect their own lives. . . . If they have experienced some unpleasantness they get angry to the point of wishing to die. They set out to eat soil, every day a little, until they get lean and swollen over the face and eyes. Nobody can prevail upon them to make them change their minds. They say that they have been taught such a thing by the devil and that he appears to them when they have decided to eat soil. (1974: 175)

But for someone so long resident in Brazil the facts of Tupian war-sacrifice also loom large; Sousa mentions details that are absent from Staden's account, particularly as concerns the subjectivity[25] of the sacrificial executioner:

[A]ll the inhabitants of the village ask the killer to disclose his new name. He shows first some reluctance but he finally tells them. They compose songs based on the motif of the victim's death and on the killer's praises. When the feast and the drinking are over, the killer lays in his hammock as if he were sulking, for a few days, and he refrains from foods that are considered dangerous during such a period. (1974: 181)

Sousa also notes how individual enthusiasms cross-cut ceremonial order, in a similar way to Staden's particular contextualization of Tupian cultural practice:

> There are some of these barbarians who are so blood-thirsty that they cut the genitalia from the dead, men and women, taking them home and giving them to their wives who keep them after they are boiled on the fire and serve them to their husbands during the feasts. They last a long time. They take home the captives secured in battle to be killed on the plaza during ordinary festivities. (1974: 180)

Sousa also provides an extensive description of sacrificial killing[26] but crucially notes that "cannibalism" per se is not the purpose here since:

> They eat it not to feed themselves, but for vengeance. The young people, male and female, only taste it, and the old people are those who are especially fond of it, and they keep part of the roasted meat to be eaten on the occasion of another feast, in case there is no opportunity for another killing. (1974: 184)

A similar observation also appears in an anonymous account from ca. 1584: "All of those along the coast that have the same language eat human flesh, although some individuals in particular never eat it, and have a great disgust of it. Among the Tapuios are to be found many nations that do not eat it, nor kill their enemies, except in times of war" (1844: 438).

Staden likewise nuances our understanding of "flesh-eating" through his detailed account of how and to whom body parts are distributed. This bears importantly on issues of how the cannibal moment is to be understood in Staden, as well as the broader cultural politics of cannibalistic / eucharistic ritual practice and the way in which such notions continue to haunt the Euro-American colonial imagination.

As descriptions and commentary on the Tupi move into the latter part of the sixteenth century there is certainly some further ethnological detail that emerges. But as Tupian societies along the Brazilian coast were in deepening social crisis through demographic losses, due to European disease and political and economic conquest, through increasing dependency and entanglement with the colonial intruders, so the Tupi become a more abstract context for the philosophical and liturgical musings of the commentators. At this point Pero de Magalhães Gandavo makes a statement about the "savages" of Brazil which has become a somewhat hackneyed articulation of the colonial mentality of the time—: "It [the Tupi language] lacks three letters; one does not find in it, namely, F, nor L, nor R, a very wonderful thing, for they have neither Faith, Law, nor Ruler: and thus they live without order, [having besides no idea of] counting, weights or measures" (1922: 85)—although Vespucci writes in his earliest description that "they use the same articulations as we, since they form their utterances either with the palate, or with the teeth, or on the lips:[27] except that they give different names to things."—suggesting clearly that colonial attitudes were themselves historically evolving, as was the significance of language as a comparative anthropological tool.[28]

These scattered and inevitably partial accounts of the Tupi peoples found in the Portuguese texts nonetheless often contrast favorably with the relatively brief (and perhaps derivative) French materials. The extensive and often systematic ethnology of the Portuguese missionaries, as well as the observations of long-term residents such as Sousa, combine to provide an important anthropological resource. However, for various reasons (discussed below), the French texts have attracted a much more substantive secondary commentary; principally because of the way in which they were seized upon by European philosophers and intellectuals, including Michel de Montaigne, Jean-Jacques Rousseau, and John Locke, but also because the French missionaries evangelized the region around the Amazon to the north of Rio de Janeiro in the early seventeenth century, producing very extensive descriptions of Tupi peoples there. The special place of Hans Staden's *Warhaftige Historia* in this literature overall therefore will be much more evident once those French materials have also been reviewed.

4. THE FRENCH DISCOVERY TEXTS

The early French works on the coastal Tupi all date to a relatively brief period in the mid-sixteenth century, deriving from the attempt by Nicholas de Villegagnon to directly colonize the region that their traders had been regularly visiting since the 1520s. Arriving in the Bay of Guanabara (site of present-day cities of Rio de Janeiro and Niteroi) in November 1555, the French fortified a position at the mouth of the bay and named their enclave *France Antarctique*. The nascent colony, despite the prior presence of French traders in the region, was not a success, as Villegagnon failed to negotiate the complexities of native allegiances. This even encouraged rebellion from these "Norman" traders[29] who, according to Jean de Léry, "accommodating themselves to the natives and leading the lives of atheists, not only polluted themselves by all sorts of lewd and base behaviors among the women and girls . . . but some of them, surpassing the savages in inhumanity, even boasted in my hearing of having killed and eaten prisoners" (1990: 128). The rebellion of the traders was suppressed and Villegagnon sought both political and spiritual reinforcement. He wrote to Jean Calvin requesting that pastors be sent, one of whom was to be Jean de Léry. However, the colony already was served by the Franciscan André Thevet and consequently the religious tensions and conflicts of Europe were transposed to Brazil where the native practice of ritual cannibalism became the colonial mirror of theological dispute over the meaning of Christian Eucharist.[30] Villegagnon in fact turned against the Protestant pastors and executed five of them, even as Léry was returning to France (Léry 1990: 218).

This was also the moment of Hans Staden's captivity, as emerges directly in his account, where the disinterest of French traders in rescuing him from his Tupinambá captors constitutes an important element of the narrative structure. It also is the context for some of the most intensely expressed feelings in Staden's text. After Staden manages to return to Europe on a French ship, he is sought out by the relatives of those men who had earlier refused to aid him and who, providentially in Staden's view, were lost at sea on their own return to France. He spitefully assures them that they must indeed be dead since that is God's punishment for their perfidy toward him while captive among the Tupinambá:

> The wives, relatives, and friends of the men came to me and asked whether I might not have seen them. I said: I have indeed seen them. There are godless people on board the ship. I said that I could not care less, where they were. I told them how one of those who was on board the ship . . . , had told the savages to eat me; yet the Almighty God had protected me. Furthermore, I told them that . . . they had

refused to take me in and I had been forced to swim back to land to the savages. This [refusal] nearly broke my heart. They had also given the savages a Portuguese, whom they had eaten. I told them how they had not wanted to show me any mercy at all. . . . Let them come when they want; I will be a prophet unto you: God will not leave such mercilessness and tyranny, as they showed to me in these lands (may God forgive them) unpunished. . . . Furthermore, I told them how good the journey back had been for those who had ransomed me free from the savages—which is also the truth. God sent us good weather and fair winds, and gave us fish from the depths of the sea. (*Warhaftige Historia* I, chap. 53)

Although Staden, Léry, and Thevet are therefore positioned very differently with regard to both the politics of colonialism in the region and the significance of Tupian sacrificial rituals, they are nonetheless united by the figure of the Tupinambá king Konyan Bebe (also rendered as "Cunhambebe" or "Quoniambec"), who figures prominently in the writings of all three authors. Thevet lauds Konyan Bebe in the following terms;

[H]e was the bravest devil in all the land. . . . By his wise comments he showed us the light of virtue hidden beneath his savage upbringing. . . . This man was large and strong, some eight feet (*viz.*) tall, and the hardest, cruelest and most fearsome of all the other kings of the neighboring provinces. He was also warlike for that country and very knowledgeable and experienced in matters of warfare. (Lussagnet 1953: 92)

Thevet also mentions that Konyan Bebe was adept in the use of firearms and in particular relates an incident, illustrated in his 1575 *Cosmographie Universelle* (reproduced in Whitehead 1993a: 216), when Konyan Bebe held two small cannons over his shoulders to fire at his enemies. Léry (1990: lviii) explicitly mocks this iconic incident as an example of the exaggeration and impostures of Thevet as part of the preface to his own work, *Histoire d'un voyage faict en al terre du Brésil*, which contains an extended polemic against Thevet and his lack of ethnographic and theological credibility.[31]

André Thevet, in his earliest[32] work on Brazil, *Les Singularitez de la france Antarctique* (1557), delineated a geography of man eating that located the uncultured "cannibals" to the north toward the Amazon River, and the ritualized "anthropophages" in the orbit of French influence. The former are characterized as cruel eaters of human flesh as a matter of diet, the latter as exponents of certain elaborate rituals of revenge. Not surprisingly, this cannibal cosmography also conforms to the patterns of French trading and military alliances with the indigenous population in the region (Whitehead 1993a). But it is the matter of direct experience which needs special note here, since Thevet, although often lauded as the "first ethnographer" of the Tupi, in fact composed his account, or had others do so, from a multiplicity of second-hand sources.[33] Thevet notes the progress of the cannibal rite in great detail and seems unable to resist an analogy with the preparation of roasting pig in French peasant culinary traditions;

> The women take this poor victim and carry him to a fire, and roast him like a pig, to cook the first layer of skin, then put him on his belly, and cut him lengthwise, across and down the side. Along all their paths they have dug trenches for these meat roasts. They left the backbone and the head connected, after having cut off the arms and cooked them. (Thevet 1928: 248)

Nonetheless, the metaphor is used in a number of other accounts both prior and later than Thevet's. But it is both Léry and Thevet who, in the transliteration of Tupian ritual into something more akin to a witches' Sabbat,[34] suggest that it is the women who are responsible for this culinary practice. Notably Hans Staden and the Portuguese missionaries all are in accord that this actually was an important role for men, as in the distribution of hunted meat.[35]

Elaborate though anthropophagic ritual becomes in Thevet's subsequent account in the *Cosmographie Universelle* (1575) and his manuscript work *Histoire de . . . deux voyages*,[36] it is clear that vengeance is the hermeneutic key to understanding the meaning of the cannibal act, such that description of the careful distribution of the victims' body parts among allies and affines, as well as the embedding of the ritual in myth, becomes central to these later works. For example, Thevet writes of the prelude to the sacrifice:

> The prisoner, seated in their midst, decides what portions of his body they should have after he is killed—until there is no part of his body left undistributed. However, they will not kill him before this act.

Those to whom a small portion of his body is assigned are obliged to contribute in order to fill the needs of their food supply. They do not refuse, because they themselves will suffer sooner from hunger if prisoners are not treated well. The same day, they decide among themselves which one will kill him, who should blacken him with genipap, feather him and paint his face. They decide also, who will take him when he is unfettered; who shall wash him; those who will set fire to his hair and when he is killed, put the fire-brand into his anus— being careful that nothing of the body is wasted. I shall describe in the following chapter their method of killing, and the accompanying ceremonies—as more space will be needed for this. (1928: 241)

However, this ritual and spiritual inflation of the cannibal act to ongoing tragic theater, as recently elaborated by Isabelle Combès (1992), may, in Thevet's case, actually be predicated on the wordiness, or "narrative dyslexia" as Lestringant (1997: 65, 206 n. 55) aptly terms it, of unsorted evidence. The following passage is typical in this regard:

[T]wo sons Tomanendonare and Aricoute, who were of different characters and hated each other. Tomanendonare was a good father and attended to his fields. Aricoute, was a warrior who wanted to conquer other nations and even his brother. Aricoute returned from a raid with the arm of an enemy and threatened his brother. Tomanendonare laughed at him for having brought only the arm of the enemy and not the enemy himself. Aricoute threw the arm against his brother's hut and immediately the whole village was lifted into the sky, the two brothers remaining on earth. Tomanendonare struck the ground with his foot and a fountain sprouted. The water flooded the whole world. The two brothers climbed mountains and there they sought safety at the top of two trees: a pindona and a genipa. In order to know if the world was dry they threw down fruit. From the two brothers the two enemy tribes of the Tupinamba and of the Temimino (Wayanā), have issued. (1575: 913)

Thevet thus provides details of Tupian cosmology and mythology in the *Cosmographie* that appear nowhere else. However, the cultural importance of the sorcerer-prophets, the *Karaiba*, as well as the evil spirits, such as

Aygnan (*Áñÿ*) and *Kaagerre*, who physically beat and oppress the Tupi, are certainly mentioned in most of the other sources, both Portuguese and French, reviewed here.[37]

Montaigne (1580) later collapses this binary geography and restricts the notion of the cannibal (as opposed to anthropophage) to the Tamoio, as constructed by Thevet twenty years earlier and as contemporaneously read by Léry (1578). Montaigne's method is to conjoin the sensationalism of cannibalism with an unexpected eulogy, mimicking another work of the period on the savageries and civilities of the Ottoman Turks, Guillame Postel's *La République des Turcs* (1560). As Lestringant (1997:54–55) wryly notes, this particularization of the cannibal, unlike with Thevet, allows Montaigne to actually conceal the extent of his analytical and descriptive borrowing from Thevet through Léry, and directly from Léry himself.[38]

Since Léry, unlike Thevet and Montaigne, may have a stronger claim to a form of ethnographic engagement with the Tupi, rather than a more distant philosophical or ethnological interest, his work offers the most relevant counterpoint to the account of Hans Staden. In which case it is important to note that he was only twenty-two years old when he went to Brazil, about the same age as Staden. He was there, though not actually living, captive or otherwise, in the huts of the Tupinambás, for about fourteen months in the period 1557–58. However, unlike Staden's, Léry's account of this youthful adventure, *Histoire d'un Voyage* (1578), was only finally published twenty years later, although it was drafted as early as 1563.[39] In the interval he had become a pastor in the church in Geneva, and he was stimulated to write his account, not so much by the original encounter with the Tupi as by the events of later life, particularly his experiences of brutality and cannibalism during the French Wars of Religion.[40] In this way Léry, unlike Staden, writes with hindsight and youthful memory and published his work much later than either Hans Staden or André Thevet. Léry claimed not to have read Staden's work until 1586 and mentions it (favorably) only in the editions of 1600 and 1611 (Whatley 1990: 231, n. 26).

Léry's borrowing from Thevet, despite their theological differences, is more easily demonstrable. In fact Léry actually adds very little new ethnographic evidence but nonetheless vastly enriches the interpretation and symbolic exploitation of that material (Lestringant 1997: 68–69). In his writing the cannibal becomes a universal symbolic and tropic key; the central motivation of vengeance is made systematic through an examination of various aspects of Tupi culture and he clearly allegorizes the act of eating. In this new framework of semiophagy the carnal and spiritual are expressed through the opposition of the raw and cooked. The northerly (or merely distant) bad cannibals, given specificity through the ethnological example of the Ouetacas, practice a cannibalism that shows no exercise of culinary, and so spiritual, art. However, a devolved cannibalism is also threateningly present inside, as well as outside, Tupi social space through the presence and enthusiastic participation of women in cannibal ritual. As a Calvinist pastor Léry was also a witch-hunter of some enthusiasm in Europe (Lestringant 1997: 70), so that the imagery of life-draining succubi and witch cannibalism of the innocent play easily into his representation of Tupian ritual.[41] This misogyny is given further inflection through the facts of Léry's own biography since he personally encountered survival cannibalism during the siege of Sancerre, just before turning to write the *Histoire d'un Voyage*. A family was caught preparing to eat their dead child, a scene to which Léry (1574) was eyewitness. In his account, originally composed virtually on the spot, the ethical tableau is broken down into the criminal and diabolical with the old woman of the house bearing the full weight of Léry's witch-centered view of female corruption.[42] Indeed the trauma of this event, for so Léry represents it, is plausibly to be directly connected to his literary return to the Brazil shore of his youth (Kingdon 1988; Lestringant 1977: 74–80). Here Tupi cannibalism, as a rite of men and controlled and shaped by their desires, becomes acceptable in a way that the female seduction of masculinity and youth was not in Sancerre.

For Léry cannibalism can also symbolize cruelty, usury, and a lack of charity and so, as the meaning of the cannibal sign universalizes, debate over the Eucharist bloats Léry's deployment of the Tupi materials to the point that even Villegagnon, leader of the French colony of Rio de Janeiro during Léry's time there, is identified on account of his Catholic views as a *soi-disant* Ouetaca (see note 36). So if the Tupian cannibal rite recapitulates at all points the Christian Eucharist, to prevent his readers turning away in ethnocentric disgust Léry goes on to detail the unspeakable cruelties of European tyrants—including Dracula, by way of Vlad the Impaler. In this way Jean de Léry deterritorializes the cannibal who thus freed from the Brazil shore still roams the European and American imaginary.

The French historian Frank Lestringant has produced an important body of work on early modern French thinking with regard to Brazil, the Tupi, and issues of religious conflict which serves to underline the continuing relevance of the works of Léry and Thevet among others, just as the work of Hans Staden has retained a contemporary significance for Brazilian culture. Although the wider issue of how the sign of the cannibal, as derived from those early Brazilian encounters, still pervades European thought is further discussed below, Lestringant's discussion of the French texts is relevant to consider here. In particular Lestringant (1997) has recently made his most complete examination of the intellectual genealogy of the cannibal, originating from the French texts concerning the Brazil shore in the sixteenth century and seventeenth century. He has rightly emphasized the way in which the cannibal was a colonial mirror of not just violence but also spirituality. Lestringant sees a progressive degradation of the image and iconicity of cannibals from the initial encounters with the Tupi, propagandized by Michel de Montaigne, to the nineteenth-century show-ground "Kaffirs" observed by Gustave Flaubert (1977: 4). Although Lestringant has much of importance to say on the French sources, especially Jean de Léry (1578) and André Thevet (1558), his overall notion of a progressive degradation in the iconicity of the cannibal actually seems to be belied both generally by the contemporary relevance of the *Warhaftige Historia* which he does not consider at all, and in particular by the re-appropriation of the cannibal sign by the Brazilian modernist movement and in anticolonial and postcolonial movements more generally. Certainly for Staden the cannibal sign is at best ambiguous, since the intellectual connection between Tupi cannibalism and Christian thought is not one of threatening homology, as it is for Léry, Montaigne, or Thevet, but one of analogy with other tests of faith. In this sense the humanity of the Tupi world emerges in Staden's text through comparison with the treacherous French, and his identification with other intended sacrificees, or with the just revenge that is visited upon them,[43] that is despite, not because of, the practice of cannibalism.

For Lestringant (1997) the subsequent degradation in European writings of the humanity of cannibal on the Brazil shore is paralleled by an increasing inability to make sense of the anthropophagic act as it evolves in colonial mentality from sacrificial ritual into merely a response to the poverty of material circumstances or exigencies of survival—a hunger cannibalism defleshed of its cultural meanings. However Lestringant (1997: 6) himself also plays directly into the cultural politics of cannibalism at the present time, ironically calling William Arens a "sensation hungry journalist" rather than an "exact historian" for his "denial" of cannibalism.[44] At the risk of also being "consumed" by this controversy, one should at least note that Arens didn't deny the historical possibility of cannibalism but rather criticized the kind of evidence that has often been advanced to suggest its occurrence. His examination of that evidence itself is not always so reliable, and Lestringant (1997:7) in turn is somewhat credulous in his acceptance of the archaeological evidence of Anasazi cannibalism, a recent example of the way in which the cannibal sign still engages political and cultural passions;[45] and of course the very indeterminacy as to what constitutes "cannibalism," that is, what is to count as anthropophagic, is often the real dispute here. For example, one might say that logically the Tupi were not cannibals at all, not because they were not eaters of human flesh but because such an act was not allelophagic within their own theology,[46] as Konyan Bebe's words to Staden could be taken to imply:

> This same Konyan Bebe had a great basket full of human flesh in front of him. He was eating a leg and held it to my mouth, asking whether I also wanted to eat. I said [to him]: a senseless animal hardly ever eats its fellow; should one human then eat another? He took a bite, saying: Jau ware sche [Jauára ichê]. I am a tiger [jaguar]; it tastes well. With that, I left him. (*Warhaftige Historia* I, chap. 43)

However, the all too easy elision, on the part of Lestringant, of any evidence of mutilation and dismemberment with a supposed demonstration of cannibalism does mean that he is ethnologically ill equipped to recognize possibly significant aspects of the texts he discusses.[47]

Despite this Lestringant (1997:7) has the powerful and important ambition to retrieve the "proud and cruel eloquence" of the cannibal from beneath the weight of commentary of the last two decades (and the intervening centuries). This emphasis on the conjunction of orality and oratory in the cannibal act is certainly consonant with other recent anthropological interpretations,[48] and more generally this intellectual program has the potential to recover the cannibal as an anticolonialist sign, in the manner of the Brazilian *antropofagia* movement (discussed below) as a mark of liberty in the face of colonial oppression. This was also the use of Karipuna (Caräibe) cannibalism in the Caribbean[49] during a later epoch of French colonialism in the seventeenth century (Hulme and Whitehead 1992; Whitehead 1995a). However, Lestringant does not engage the modern Brazilian materials at all, perhaps precisely because the figure of Hans Staden is central to the *antropofagia* movement, suggesting that Lestringant is more concerned with a reinscription of the French legacy in Brazil than he is with the nature of the cannibal sign itself. In tandem with this emancipatory use of the cannibal sign a paradoxical discourse of cannibalism as "unbearable constraint" also emerged in European writings (Lestringant 1977:8), as a mark of an economic and political tyranny that eats up its victims. Cannibalism thus became allegorized, particularly by Montaigne and Léry, as slavery, feudalism, usury, and conquest.[50]

Lestringant (1977:9) also discusses the centrality of the religious debate as to the meaning and form of the Christian Eucharist in the French sources, and it is this aspect that is the starting point for Montaigne's consideration, "Des Canibales" (*Essais*, 1580). For Montaigne, both Tupi and Christian rules of cannibalism are communal, related to the worship of the dead and done in the hope of benefit to the group. But the key question for the differentiation of Catholic and Protestant liturgy then becomes — is this a literal homology present in the moment of transubstantiation or an analogy of spiritual nourishment that replenishes and feeds faith indefinitely? For Montaigne, as a Catholic, the assimilation of the Tupi practice to the Christian belief is an obstacle to the humanistic embrace of the Tupi. Notably it is a question that does not arise at all for Staden. However, Montaigne fails finally to condemn the Tupi precisely because of the parallels in symbolic practice that Léry explicitly elaborates.

Without the possible religious significance of the parallels between Tupian and Christian Eucharist the subsequent fate of the cannibal is to be superfluous and so anachronistic, fit only for eradication, as with that "exterminating angel" Robinson Crusoe (Lestringant 1997: 11). And so the cannibals come to be seen as responding to their bio-ecological conditions, not their culture, or, in the act of erasure that Lestringant (1977: 12) rightly resists, the materiality of their acts is supplanted by the evanescence of a cultural discourse which "shifts the noise of teeth and lips towards the domain of language."[51] Nonetheless, Lestringant provides a perceptive and careful commentary on the major French sources relating to the Tupi of the Brazil shore in the sixteenth century. It has therefore been all the more necessary that the *Warhaftige Historia* of Hans Staden be situated within this kind of commentary for the counterpoint it provides to both the French and Portuguese sources.

II. *The* Warhaftige Historia *and the Spectacle of Violence in Colonial Brazil*

1. TUPINOLOGY AND THE MODERNITY OF CANNIBALISM

[Men] call themselves by the names of wild animals and give themselves many names, but with one distinction: When they are born, they are given one name. They only keep this [name] until they are fit to bear arms and able to slay their enemies, and each man has as many names as he has killed enemies . . . [the women] are named after birds, fishes, and fruits from the trees. When they grow up, they only have one name, but for every slave killed by the men, the women also give themselves another name.
— *Warhaftige Historia* II, chapters 16–17

Given the richness and variety of the early historical sources it is not surprising to find that the secondary ethnological literature on the Tupi peoples has been the context for a range of anthropological discussions generating a considerable literature both within and outside Brazil. Undoubtedly the somewhat happenstance interest in the native peoples of Brazil on the part of one of the leading anthropologists of the twentieth century, Claude Lévi-Strauss, as well as his resulting conscious and public identification with Jean de Léry, has done much to reinforce that phenomenon outside Brazil, although the use of cannibals as an ethnological backdrop for European philosophical thought began with the moment of first encounter itself. Nonetheless the French ethnological tradition in particular has been central in sustaining the figure of the native and indigenous in Brazil as a vivid context for theoretical, even metaphysical, speculation on the nature of humanity. Particularly important to note here are the writings of Hélène Clastres (1975, 1985) and Pierre Clastres (1972, 1974, 1980), who worked extensively with historical as well as contemporary ethnographic materials in developing an account of Tupi-Guaraní worldview. In particular Pierre Clastres's interests in political and economic theory using these ethnological materials can be considered a contemporary echo of the earlier philosophical musings of Michel de Montaigne (1580) and Jean-Jacques Rousseau (1755), for whom also the savage and cannibal were iconic forms of human existence, prompting reflection on the nature of the civilized and the role that violence plays in human affairs.

This French ethnological tradition has also been very influential in contemporary Brazilian anthropology, while the translations of French and Portuguese source materials into English by Alfred Métraux, as well as his contributions to the *Handbook of South American Indians* (1948), also brought the complexity of the Tupi world to the attention of a wider audience. However, Staden's account of the Tupi as a source for historical and ethnological studies has always been somewhat occluded by the sheer volume of other materials. Although early Dutch editions of Staden were numerous, this was clearly related to the Dutch colonial ambitions in Brazil and the way in which his account played into emergent national and religious identities, much as did Léry's writings for French Protestants.[52] By the nineteenth century a renewed interest in travel writing and early travel accounts made Staden's text no less relevant as a striking example of a captivity narrative and the presence, if not priority, of non-Iberian adventurers in the Americas. Richard Burton's 1874 edition of the *Warhaftige Historia* appeared in the first series of works issued by the Hakluyt Society, named for the Anglo-Dutch compiler of the politically inflected collections of stirring travel accounts,[53] while Malcolm Letts's 1928 edition appeared as part of the "Argonaut Series," an Anglo-American publishing enterprise featuring selections of travel accounts, also including two volumes on that other "Anglo-Saxon" interloper into the Iberian colonies, Sir Walter Ralegh. However, neither of these editors was concerned with the ethnological accuracy or implications of Staden's account, although Richard Burton, consistent with his linguistic skills and interest in Arabic, used his introduction to the work as the occasion for some fairly free-ranging speculation on the philological relationships between the major language families of the South American continent.[54] Burton's view of the Staden text itself was partly influenced by his awareness of various editions in which the original visual materials had been supplanted by others "borrowed from some book on Turkey" (1874: xcii) and how redacted and translated versions had, in the manner of the colonial historian Robert Southey[55] in his widely read

History of Brazil (1810), succeeded admirably well in "tearing the entrails out of the work." Nonetheless, in literary terms, Burton viewed the work favorably, albeit with a robustness somewhat tinged with homoeroticism and a vigorous anti-Catholicism, noting,

> Hans Stade [*sic*] would have sunk into the oblivion which shrouds his tormentors, but for the rude, truthful, and natural volume which he has left to posterity. His style, though simple and full of sincerity, is a poor contrast with the graceful and charming garb which distinguishes . . . the later writers. His vile translation of foreign words requires the especial notice of an editor. His piety is essentially that of the age when the Jesuits spat on children by way of baptism. . . . His superstitions are manifold . . . and all his enemies come to a well-merited end. He prophecies in hope of saving his life. . . . In fact, it is curious to mark the narrowness of the border-line between the belief of the Brazilian cannibal and that of the Christian European of the sixteenth century. (1874: xciii)

For more recent commentators the presence of descriptions of cannibalism in Staden's work have been taken to be indicative of its biases and its role as part of a literary, as well as literal, conquest of America. The prevalence of accusations of cannibalism against native peoples on the point of being colonized, as well as the way in which the idea of cannibalism functions to delineate the space of the barbarous and the savage, have induced some to question the authenticity and veracity of Staden's account of the Tupi, as well as raised the possibility that the whole episode, both the account and the journeys which it describes, were actually fraudulent.

The presence of the cannibal in the ethnological record and the anthropological imaginary of Euro-America has recently been addressed directly by William Arens (1979, 1998), and some of the controversies that work has engendered were alluded to above.[56] However, Arens's rhetorical thunder was already present in the work of Herman Melville.[57] As Melville writes in *Typee*:

> It is a singular fact, that in all our accounts of cannibal tribes we have seldom received the testimony of an eye-witness account to this revolting practice. The horrible conclusion has almost always been de-

rived from the second-hand evidence of Europeans, or else from the admissions of the savages themselves, after they have in some degree become civilized.

Whatever the methodological and theoretical benefits of Arens's arguments, which rightly enjoin us to a careful and sophisticated approach to source materials, he clearly erred in his own application of those principles in his reading of the literature on cannibalism from South America, partly because of a limited consideration of the Francophone writings, even though Hans Staden's adventures received close attention. Arens took the view, as with more recent German literary and historical scholarship, that the *Warhaftige Historia* was some kind of fake account, designed only to profit from an assumed European obsession with cannibal tales.[58] Arens essentially makes an argument about the form of cross-cultural external reporting and how that in itself cannot simply be accepted as forensically secure evidence of "cannibalism," rather than making an ethnographically based argument that such a behavior—if it can be adequately defined—never took place. However, this argument need not be taken to imply that no external account of cannibalism—given a clear definition of what is understood by this term—could ever report this phenomenon. The fact that the idea of cannibalism is used so widely in a discursive manner and as a symbolization of human relationships considerably complicates discussion of such reporting and the evaluation of ethnographically encountered claims[59] but does not in itself invalidate them.

Certainly, the use of the textual materials relating to the early period of colonial encounter and the reports of "cannibalism" therein are always problematic, and one cannot dismiss Arens's wider point that anthropology as a cultural expression is no less apt to mythologize its object than any other academic or professional discipline. Arens's examination of the cannibal literature is an exemplary case of this process and, moreover, is not the only example of how anthropology's approaches to gender, race, or warfare may also have been highly prejudicial to the human subjects of those musings.[60]

In this wider cultural context the *Warhaftige Historia* is clearly then a key source and although seemingly minor compared to the copious ethnological productions of Jean de Léry, André Thevet, as well as the extensive discussion of the Tupi in the later missionary literatures,[61] in fact Hans Staden's text also has to be considered critical to an ethnological understanding of the sacrificial rituals of the Tupi. What the *Warhaftige Historia* may lack in terms of the ethnological sophistication and systematics that induced both Claude Lévi-Strauss (1976: 102) and Frank Lestringant (1992: 9) to consider Jean de Léry's text to be the avatar of all Tupian ethnology, Staden's text more than makes good with an equally ethnographic account of a personal and extended experience of the Tupi. This is evident in the way in which Staden's close observation and reporting of his interactions with the Tupi have proved highly relevant to contemporary anthropological understanding, particularly because of how his account reveals the political and social calculation surrounding the anthropophagic ritual performance, termed *kawewi pepicke* by the Tupi—for example, as in the incidents where a sick slave is killed before he has the chance to die of the disease, and in the eating of his diseased corpse, "except the head and intestines . . . on account of the man's sickness" (*Warhaftige Historia* I, chap. 34), which reveal a political context for understanding the largely unappreciated pragmatics of Tupi sacrificial ritual. More generally, the sometimes patient, even hesitant attitudes of Staden's Tupi captors indicate that they were not driven by some structural-functional necessity of their social system. After all, Staden's eventual escape from his captivity is itself proof enough of the contingency of the ritual sacrifice for the Tupi.

At the same time Hans Staden presents a rather frightening figure, despite his captive servile status, and he was by no means resigned at any point to a possible role as sacrificee. His refusal to allow the removal of his beard, his constant questioning of anthropophagic acts, his constant ruses to elude them, and his ambiguous identity in the minds of the Tupi themselves, shown in the way that they get the French trader Karwattuware to make the judgment as to his appropriateness as "enemy," all may have suggested the wisdom of at least postponing his sacrifice. The subsequent performance of shamanic healing power and knowledge of omens may not in themselves have been all that persuasive but combined with other doubts and circumstance became plausible grounds for not hastening to kill Staden. Indeed a number of other prisoners—of less ambiguous origin and status—are summarily dispatched in his presence. Once he is passed from the custody of his initial captors into the hands of Alkindar it at least becomes clearer that the "vengeful necessity" of sacrifice could well be cross-cut by other considerations than desire for the glory of beautiful names or the weight of obligation to the dead.

In the intellectual genealogy of Tupian ethnology the contributions of Brazilian thinkers are substantial and Hans Staden's account plays an often pivotal role in their anthropological interpretations of the Tupi. This is very much the case with the classic article by Florestan Fernandes (1952) in which a functionalist model of Tupian war and sacrifice is elaborated.[62] Notably this work also appeared in French and was first published in Paris, underscoring the importance of the French intellectual legacy in Brazilian anthropology. Although Fernandes's research interests broadened into a wider concern with all aspects of Brazilian society, as well as sociological theory, the work on the Tupi was among his earliest. Since then Eduardo Viveiros de Castro (1992) and Manuela Carneiro de Cunha (1985) have broken out of the functionalist explanations favored by Florestan Fernandes. Their rich and complex works may be seen as complementing, extending, and reacting to the earlier presentations of Fernandes, as well as those of Alfred Métraux (1948), Hélène Clastres (1995), and Pierre Clastres (1987).

For Viveiros de Castro the text of Staden plays a key role in establishing aspects of Tupi cannibalism that are not present or are differently represented in other works, in particular the connection between male provision of sacrificial flesh and female provision of strong beer (1992: 132); the importance of the motive of name-taking, as much as a generalized revenge, in understanding the purposes of warfare and sacrifice (152, 279); the significance of magical rattles, *Tammaraka* (222), particularly in the cultural logic of war and cannibalism (278), as well as the personal construction of self by the Tupi cannibal warrior (271); the classification of the intended victim as a household pet (280); and the notion that, as Staden succinctly puts it, "Their treasures are the feathers of birds" (374 n. 10).

Of course the works of Léry, Thevet, and the others also enable the recuperation of Tupian cannibal practice, but, as Viveiros de Castro acknowledges (1992: 3567 n. 12) it is Staden's testimony in particular that allows latter-day interpreters to escape the sterile vision of Tupi war and cannibalism as merely an intense aspect of a revenge complex. By making the crucial connection between killing and the accumulation of beautiful names, as described by Staden, Viveiros de Castro is able to elaborate the motivations for war and cannibalism beyond the "revenge" model that the chroniclers promoted and that both Métraux (1948) and Fernandes (1952) uncritically adopted. Therefore, there is a valuable ethnological legacy in the pages of Staden's text as a result of the way in which he vividly, even if not systematically, illumines key details of Tupian cultural practice, as the earlier comments of Southey, Burton, and Letts all suggested. Whatever judgment one might make of Staden's attempt to elaborate such insights into an "ethnology" in the second part of his work, it remains the bedrock of his ethnography that Staden himself was able to sustain a cultural performance of some felicity before his Tupi captors, pragmatically expressing his ethnographic understanding through his manipulation of indigenous concepts and categories in a way which saved his life.

This is very evident in the matter of dreaming, which, although Staden himself rejects as a source of prophecy and way of relating to the world, was nonetheless something on which he commented more than once and which, with a better appreciation of its possible role of for the Tupi, was in fact critical to his survival among them. In his recent ethnography of the Parakanǎ (1999, 2001), Carlos Fausto observes that as for the Tupi, a key shamanic ability is that of dreaming, to which all adult men (and some women) have some access and that dreaming itself is intimately linked to warfare and ritual predation, or anthropophagic sacrifice. Also, for the Parakanǎ what is acquired killing another man is not another's subjectivity but a generic capacity to dream, which in turn is associated with two impersonal characteristics of the victims: the smell of their blood (*pyji'oa*) and their "magic-fat" (*kawahiwa*), which impregnate the killer, making him both dangerous and fertile.

In turn dreaming is a mode of relationship with those who are not kin, and everything that appears in dream is designated *akwawa* (enemy). In this way dreams establish the possibility of communication among persons, animals, and spirits. But the nature of the relationship between the dreamer and the dreamed is that of master and pet. The dream enemy is said to be a pet (*te'omawa*) of the dreamer or his magic-prey (*temiahiwa*). In this state of subjection the dreamed becomes ally, not enemy, and such dream pets are also similar to shamans' familiar spirits in other Amazonian groups (Whitehead 2002a: 163–66).

For the Parakanǎ warfare also creates the possibility of interacting with enemies through dreams, where enemies (humans or nonhumans) are familiarized and must be remade as enemies to qualify for ritual killing and to this end are given to a third party, just as was the case for Staden:

> After a short while, the brothers, named Jeppipo Wasu and Alkindar Miri, who had captured me, approached me and told me that they had given me to their father's brother, Ipperu Wasu, out of friendship. He was to keep me and kill me when they wanted to eat me; thus he would acquire another name through me. (*Warhaftige Historia* I, chap. 22)

The specific anthropophagic mode of appropriation practiced by the Tupi required that the victims be different and distinct, that being denoted by their fierceness, which was more evident in the behavior of other Tupi captives, such as the Marckaya (*Warhaftige Historia* I, chap. 36) than in the demeanor of either Staden or the other Portuguese captives, of whom they said, "He is a real Portuguese. Now he screams, he is afraid of death" (*Warhaftige Historia* I, chap. 26). As is evident from the structure of the ceremony of sacrifice (Appendix 69), this is why captives had to be made into enemies once again before being ritually executed.

The relation between dreaming and ritual predation through sacrifice is thus evident a number of times in Staden's account, illustrating the ways in which Staden's Tupi captors were attempting to familiarize him through dreams. Their apparent lack of immediate success in so doing is evident from this passage:

> There were two kings in two other huts, one called Vratinge Wasu, the other Kenrimakui. Vratinge Wasu had dreamt that I had appeared before him and told him that he was going to die. Early in the morning, he came to me and complained to me about it. I told him that, no, there was not going to be any danger, but he also had to stop thinking about killing me, or advising others to do so. He then said, no [he would not hurt me]; since those, who had captured me did not kill me, he would not do me any harm, either. And if they would kill me, he would not eat of me. The second king, Kenrimakui, had also had a dream about me, which greatly terrified him. . . . he had once been at war and had captured a Portuguese, whom he had killed with his

own hands. He had also eaten so much of him that his chest was still aching, and he did not want to eat anything, from anyone, anymore. Now he had dreamt about me, and his dream was so terrible that he thought he was about to die. I also told him that he was not in danger, but that he should not eat human flesh anymore. (*Warhaftige Historia* I, chap. 34)

The preoccupation with dreams and ritual predation is therefore also evident in Staden's account of war expeditions, although his own skepticism at the power of dreaming does not stop his exploitation of his captors' fears in this regard. Staden describes one of their expeditions:

They numbered 38 canoes, and each canoe carried 18 men, more or less. Using their idols, several of them had foretold the outcome of the war by dreams and the other foolery that they use. Thus, they all felt confident about the matter. Their intention was to travel to the area around Brikioka where they had captured me, and to hide in different places in the forest near the settlement. They would then [capture and] bring back those who fell into their hands in this manner. . . . While traveling, they constantly asked me whether I thought that they would capture anyone. To avoid making them angry, I said yes. I also told them that the enemy would engage us. Thus, one night we lay at the place called Uwattibi. . . . That night, the wind blew mightily and they chattered away and wanted to ask me many questions. Then I said: this wind blows over many dead people. Now another party had also set out by water and had entered the lands on a river called Paraibe. Well, they said, they have probably already attacked enemy territory, so that several of them are dead. (I later heard that this had actually happened.) When we were a day's travel from the place they planned to attack, they made camp. . . . Towards evening, the chief called Konyan Bebe walked through the camp. He preached and said that. . . . Each man was to take note of the dreams that he had that night, and they were all to see to it that they were going to dream something fortunate. When his speech was over, they danced with their idols until far into the night; then they slept. As my master lay down to sleep, he told me to dream about something pleasant. I said: I don't take heed of any dreams, they are false. Well, he said, you should nonetheless work out things with your God, so that we capture enemies. At daybreak, the chiefs gathered round a bowl full of boiled fish and while they ate them they recounted their dreams, in so far as they were pleased with them. Several of them danced with their idols. Their decision was to travel closer to enemy territory that day, to a place called Boywassu kange, where they would wait until the evening. (*Warhaftige Historia* I, chap. 41)

Staden also offers a more ethnological account in the second part of the *Warhaftige Historia*:

[T]hey consult the Pagy, their soothsayers, [and ask] whether they are then going to be victorious. They then will probably say yes, but they order them to take heed of those dreams, where they dream about the enemies. If most of them dream and see the flesh of their enemies roasting, that means victory. But if they see their own flesh frying, that does not bode well; it means that they should then stay at home. If their dreams please them, they now arm themselves, prepare much drink in all of the huts, and drink and dance with their idols, the Tammaraka. Each of them beseeches his own idol to assist him in capturing an enemy. Then they set off [to war]. When they then arrive near the enemy territory, their chiefs then, on the evening before they attack the land of their enemies, once more direct the men to remember the dreams that they are going to dream during the night. (*Warhaftige Historia* I, chap. 27)

Just as women were crucially involved in the sacrificial ritual of anthropophagy, so too their capacities to dream and prophesy were noted by Staden:

When they go out to war, the women have to prophesy about the war. One night, the wife of my master (to whom I had been presented to be killed) began to prophesy. She told her husband that a spirit had come to her from a foreign country. It wanted to know when I was to be killed, and had asked where the club was, with which I was to be killed. He answered her that it would not be long and that everything was prepared; only it seemed to him that I was not a Portuguese, but a Frenchman. After the woman had ended her prophecy, I asked her why she was striving for my death, when I was no enemy; and whether she was not afraid that my God would punish her with a plague. She said that I should not bother about it, for it was the foreign spirits [and not her] who wanted to know about me. They have many such ceremonies. *Warhaftige Historia* II, chap. 24)

This suggests that the process of "enemy familiarization" had not unfolded in the way his original captors might have anticipated. Not only were Staden's prophetic utterances, assumed by his captors to have been provoked by dreaming, shown to be true on more than one occasion but also those dreaming of him had not managed to entirely dominate him as a "pet," and were alarmed by a counterpredation implicit in the content of those Tupi dreams that Staden records.

Staden's cultural performance was thus a source of knowing that is both different from and often superior to that of the priestly ethnologies of Jean de Léry and Andre Thevet, as, for example, in Staden's iconic encounter with the war-chief Konyan Bebe (quoted above), which led Viveiros de Castro to note that "Cunhambebe's repartee . . . was certainly a burst of humor: black or Zen, it was unquestionably Tupinamba" (1992: 271). It is precisely this kind of vivid, personal testimony, and the relative absence of an occluding ethnological pretension, which is largely caged within the second part of the work, that makes the record of Staden's encounter so unique and valuable in the annals of Tupinology.

These qualities are also important for the way in which the *Warhaftige Historia*, or at least versions of Staden's experience, were emblematic for the Brazilian modernist movement, the *antropofagistas*, whose intellectual origins and history in the "so-called heroic phase of Brazilian *modernismo* (1920–1930) [which] coincided with the last decade of the Old Republic (1894–1930)" is comprehensively explained by Bellei (1998: 87) as occurring as "the stability of this dominant force . . . was gradually being replaced by the growth of other social groups in formation." Although Bellei indicates that precise definitions of the ideas of the *antropofagistas* are difficult to make, in essence they shared the view that repression and destruction of "primitive," "cannibal" cultures in Brazil amounted to a repression of "a form of primitive wisdom [i.e., cannibalism] that the Brazilian *modernista* revolution should try to recover, redefine, and adapt to the social needs of the industrialised, modern present as a stage in the preparation of the uto-pian future" (93). What those needs were and the kind of utopian futures that might result form the vision of *antropofagia* was a more complex issue since the violent and vengeful imagery of Tupi cannibalism might license a range of political strategies.[63]

A wider analysis of the cultural and literary meaning of such "canni-bal modernities" in the literatures of the Caribbean—that other cannibal zone—as well as Brazil, can be found in the work of Luis Madrueira (1998; 2005). Madrueira takes as his starting point Homi Bhabha's contention that "each repetition of the sign of modernity is different, specific to its historical and cultural conditions of enunciation" (quoted in Madrueira 2005: 2) so that the deployment of the classic texts of colonialism may be subverted by a critical reading from a "subaltern," or at least distinct, point of view sited at the margins, both geographical and intellectual, of the colonial order. This is a different form of critique from that undertaken by nineteenth-century metropolitan intellectuals such as Joseph Conrad or Herman Melville (see note 5). However, the presence of such a metropoli-tan critique is important to recognize in locating the meanings of postcolo-nial thought. They demonstrate that colonial order is not monolithic and indeed is forever struggling against the threat of an exotic transculturation, as in Staden's *Warhaftige Historia*. It was not only the nineteenth-century colonial order that was unstable and fractured by metropolitan conflicts, as again is very evident from the *Warhaftige Historia*, where not only religious but also nationalistic issues drive the literary form and provide the dramatic content to Staden's tale. This entails for Madrueira (2005: 7–13) that the postcolonial alternatives to the grand narratives of imperial destiny con-structed by the colonial orders of Europe also include not just other kinds of writing and thought but, because of the mutual entanglements that colo-nialism initiated and through which it is at the same time rendered vulner-able, through a "tampering" with the "magisterial texts" that the colonial order produced, again, as in the case of the modernist manipulations of the *Warhaftige Historia*.[64]

This process of postcolonial invention and rewriting then entails that "the image of the subaltern, or the 'primitive,' often operates in these texts as both the source of a fundamental cultural 'secret' and the site of an un-transcendable epistemological horizon" (Madrueira 2005: 13). For the *antro-*

pofagia movement a "recovery and resignification" of Tupian ritual sacrifice was critical since it stood in stark opposition to "cannibalism," in the colonial discourse of authority, as giving a license to "civilize" through conquest. If the Tupi were aboriginal Brazilians, then they were also the possible site for the invention or reclamation of a national culture that was distinctly Brazilian. The historical problem was that they had been destroyed as a physical presence for coastal Brazilian culture by the seventeenth century; but this leads to the paradox that the Tupi are then available for the cultural work of nationhood in a way that the politically embarrassing and still often resistant cultures of Amazonia were not. Only in the space of death and erasure can the nostalgia for a premodern and protonationalistic be born, much as has occurred throughout the colonial world,[65] and was arguably part of the way in which the notion of the proud and cannibalistic Tupi was already being deployed by Montaigne in the 1580s and Rousseau 1750s.[66] This underlines not only the distinct nature of the Brazilian *antropofagistas* but also their necessary connection with the wider system of colonialism and capitalism. The Tupi of the *antropofagistas* intellectual desire existed for them only in colonial writings; "*Antropofagia*'s metaphoric return to Brazil's authentic 'cannibalistic' roots, then, cannot but assume the form of a treacherous detour through inauthentic and unstable textual regions" (Madrueira 2003: 13). Despite the fact, then, that *antropofagia* is "indebted to and embedded . . . in the very cultural and philosophical tradition it seeks to displace, *antropofagia* cannot but tacitly (and tactically) acknowledge the extent of its determination by the 'magisterial texts' of the west. By this same token, it also broaches the possibility that those same texts can now be turned in to 'our servants,' as the new magisterium constructs itself in the name of the Other" (Madrueira 2005: 51). This kind of critical approach, which recognizes the necessity of an intellectual engagement with the archives of colonialism lest we deny the possibility of other historicities, is precisely the hermeneutic which is applied to the *Warhaftige Historia* in this work and which informs a wide range of contemporary ethnohistory and historical anthropology.[67]

However, it is therefore also important to recognize, as has been the case for historical anthropologists and ethnohistorians, that the ethnographic encounter, even if initially mediated through the categories of colonial ethnologies, remains a way in which the purely textual impasses of postcolonialism might be averted. It is certainly the case that ethnographic work with South American native peoples has produced a series of experiences of radical alterity that appear no less significant than the "first encounters" with the fifteenth-century Tupi. It is also notable that a refusal to acknowledge the coevalness of persistent alterity has been a way of controlling such experiences through the tropes of colonial encounter, as in the case of Lévi-Strauss's collapse of historical time in *Tristes Tropiques*. Lévi-Strauss avers that "the tropics are less exotic than out of date" (1992: 87), allowing his identification with Jean de Léry and simultaneously a presentation of contemporary native peoples as anachronistic through evidences of their pristine, if evanescent, condition. Other ethnographers, however, suggest that the ritual practices, such as cannibalism or other forms of "savage violence," do indeed persist, not merely as a mimesis of colonial conquest or as a token of historical engagement with colonial regimes but also as a continuing contemporary engagement with the localized forms of modernity throughout the region.[68]

For the *antropofagistas* the reclamation of the Tupi as "Brazilian" was predicated precisely on the twin options of the cannibal as exemplar of premodern freedom and as a figure that could consume and absorb all forms of difference, including that of colonialism itself.[69] Through Oswald de Andrade's *Manifesto Antropófago* (1972 [1928]), *antropofagia* construed "itself as 'vengefully' opposed to the cultural and epistemological legacy of the west," in contrast to "the contemporaneous *modernista* literary production . . . [which] seeks instead to establish a relatively seamless continuity between not just European and Brazilian models of modernization, but between the latter and the colonial project of conquest and territorial expansion" (Madrueira 2005: 14). Both Bellei (1998) and Madrueira (2005) thus together provide a very full account and analysis of the intellectual uses of the idea of anthropophagy in Brazilian modernism. Madrueira (2005: 28) suggests that Léry's *Histoire d'un Voyage* had a specific influence on Andrade and discusses the 1974 film by Nelson Pereira dos Santos, *Como gostoso era meu francés*, which was loosely based on Staden's narrative but which significantly inverts / subverts the role of national identities that is so important in the text of the *Warhaftige Historia* itself. Staden is also quoted directly to introduce both the 1998 and 2005 versions of Madrueira's essay "Lapses in Taste." However, it is notable that neither Bellei (1998) nor Madrueira disaggregate the Tupinological texts to trace specific kinds of readings or borrowings from these materials—nor is it necessarily relevant for them to do so within the terms of their discussions. Nonetheless, and not unlike the case of Frank Lestringant's *Cannibals*, Staden's presence for the *antropofagistas* is implicit rather than overt. Yet the narrative of the *Warhaftige Historia* is quite distinct in character from the rather grandiose ethnological productions of the French texts, while the Portuguese-language materials are scattered across various writing genres (letters, essays, memoirs), are often rather dull and formulaic in their literary character, and cling mostly to a localized evangelical missionary agenda in their choice of topics. It is also notable, then, that Staden's work has the wider popular currency,[70] appearing in adaptations as two films, as children's literature, as a graphic novel, and in the work of the Brazilian modernist painter Candido Portinari. For Brazilians today the Tupi moment is epitomized by Staden, not by Léry, who as the avatar of colonial knowing is instead the European "ethnographer's breviary," as Lévi-Strauss (quoted above) would have it. The alternative modernity of contemporary Brazil is therefore apparently the better expressed through engagement with the *Warhaftige Historia*, indicating its richness as a source of both ancient ethnology of the Tupi and as an early, but clearly modern, novel of self-discovery and knowing through the encounter with difference and distance. The redemptive drive of Lutheranism is certainly a key aspect of the text which itself foregrounds the importance of the individual subject (TenHuisen 2005). But this literary form, in which the miraculous and monstrous is firmly embedded, should not be taken as an anachronistic hangover from medievalism—as perhaps was the case in the more mystical writings of Columbus and his Catholic contemporaries (Greenblatt 1991, 1993; Zamora 1993). Rather, the *Warhaftige Historia* is part of the still current modernist engagement (and later antipathy) with the magical. Johannes Dryander's place in Staden's text demonstrates this since it is not the miraculous and monstrous that he questions so much as the means by which such phenomena, not yet erased by early modern science, might be better known as part of the being and becoming of a civilized and individualized subject. One other aspect of the uniqueness of the *Warhaftige Historia*, which is directly connected to this special position it holds in contemporary Brazil at least, is the visual materials which continue to inspire cinematographers, artists, and cartoonists. The reasons for this may well be numerous, and are particular to the various cases; but in general the close connection between the visual depictions and the events of the narrative in the text, the oral basis of that text—especially the first part, which appears to have been dictated rather than composed as a literary act—as well as the rude vigor of the woodcuts, which are visually even if not aesthetically complex, are all important reasons why the *Warhaftige Historia* has a preeminent importance for the recovery and continuing signification of Hans Staden and his long vanquished and vanished captors, the Tupi. The spectacle of anthropophagy will therefore be further considered below, once the torn and devoured cannibal bodies it displays have themselves become more intimately known.

2. THE CANNIBAL BODY AND THE BODY-POLITIC

[It] will be urged that these shocking unprincipled wretches are cannibals . . . I ask whether the mere eating of human flesh so very far exceeds in barbarity that custom which only a few years since was practised in enlightened England:—a convicted traitor . . . had his head lopped off with a huge axe, his bowels dragged cut and thrown into a fire; while his body, carved into four quarters, was with his head exposed upon pikes, and permitted to rot and fester among the public haunts of men!

—Herman Melville, *Typee*

As a cultural category, cannibalism has always incorporated ethnological judgments of others, albeit usually negative in character. In this way the ethnological record, however, whenever, and by whomever it may have been constructed, has not just an empirical but also a logical connection with cannibalism. As was discussed above, William Arens (1979) was a forceful reminder of this. But the importance of the act of cannibalism, if that is understood as an act of human flesh eating, was less important to Tupian ritual than it was to European witnessing. The *Warhaftige Historia*, and other European accounts, thus give a prominence to that one moment of potential anthropophagy, not simply because of its centrality to the ritual of sacrifice, which was actually somewhat contingent in Tupian ritual terms, but also because of the ideological significance of anthropophagy in the cultural traditions of Europe. Tupian ceremony contained many other key moments of ritual drama and importance, such as the feasting with the captive, the decoration of the executioner's club *iwera pemme*, the politics of the occasion of the sacrifice itself, and so forth, and so it was the relevance of cannibalism to Europeans then (and now) that drove the representational priorities of Staden and other colonial commentators. In this sense critics like Annerose Menniger are obviously right to see the text as keyed to the standard literary tropes and cultural obsessions of the sixteenth century, for it could not be otherwise. This in itself does not constitute a persuasive argument that such representations are invented, since any reported observation is always partly an outcome of cultural expectations. However observations are also the product of experience, and nowhere is the suggestion plausibly made that such an experience among the Tupi was impossible, as is clearly shown by the other contemporary commentaries on the Tupi. Moreover, as mentioned previously, the introduction by Johannes Dryander is not concerned with the issue of cannibalism at all but precisely with that of the epistemology of eyewitnessing and how observation and expectation are to be related through experience.

It also follows, then, that part of the importance of Staden's text is the way it is enmeshed in these broader issues of cross-cultural interpretation and observation, the experience of colonial conquest and the emergence of a postcolonial imagination. Although the *Warhaftige Historia* is but one of many historical texts that reference cannibalism in this way, it nonetheless still represents one of the earliest and most highly ethnographic forms in which the idea of cannibalism was inscribed in the imagining of America and its native peoples. Although it was the writings of Columbus and his contemporaries in the Caribbean which gave us the term "cannibal," Staden's text stands out as the most complete representation of such a practice in all the colonial literature from the Americas. The descriptions of Tupian sacrifice by others may well match the account of Staden in its reporting on details of ritual practice and ceremonial form, but they cannot compete with the first-hand view of someone who himself was intended for sacrifice. This is the irreducible element of Staden's *Warhaftige Historia*, which, despite all its other flaws and biases, makes it a unique and valuable source. The *Warhaftige Historia*'s place within the anthropology of South America, especially its place within a Tupinology, and its iconic status for the culture of contemporary Brazil mean that there is particular relevance to a continuing critical engagement with Staden's account.

There is also a more general relevance to such a critical engagement as recent anthropological publications,[71] no less than media commentary and unfolding global political events, have all thrust into wider cultural debate newly invigorated images of violent, primitive savagery as the all-too-inevitable condition of humanity. One might also reference here related Euro-American cultural obsessions with cannibal serial killers, as well as ethnic violence in the marginalized zones of the modern world-system, particularly where they are expressed through unspeakable forms of mutilation and dismemberment. Recent ethnographic and historical case studies clearly show that more is at play in these violent contexts than merely some collapse back into a premodern savagery. The resurgence of "traditional" or historically inflected forms of violence, such as in the Rwandan genocide, ethnic cleansing in the Balkans, or head-hunting in southeast Asia and cannibalism in China, all suggest that, as with Tupi sacrifice in the sixteenth century, the exotic and sensational representations of such violence becomes a key means by which its internal meanings can be obscured and its external significance manipulated to provide legitimacy to the outrage of the observer and the colonial violence that is simultaneously being enacted.[72] In the case of Tupian sacrifice the connection made in the colonial literature with conflicting religious ideas of eucharistic sacrifice, through the motif of cannibalism, led precisely not to a general condemnation of violence but to more sophisticated notions of how and when violence could be legitimately carried out. As was the case for Jean de Léry, for example, this centered on the public, male, and sacral character of violence in the Tupi and Protestant contexts, contrasted to the physical and secretive cannibalism of children, Christ, and enemies in the Catholic and Ouetaca contexts.

Terror and violence thus occupy central places in the cultural imaginary. This constant imaginative rehearsal of certain forms of death and dying reflects not just some greater awareness of the use of shocking and outrageous forms of violence resulting from the increasing range of colonial reporting through the sixteenth century but also the avowedly conscious construction of violent strategies of local assertion, which has made the idea of cannibalism or anthropophagy such a redolent notion for postcolonial Brazilian culture. As in current contexts of "terrorist" actions, particularly suicide bombings, forms of violence may be overtly designed to achieve an impact on the cultural imagination and subjectivity of others, be they the captive enemies of Tupi war-chiefs or the masters and functionaries of Euro-American colonialism. The physicality of violent assault cannot be limited to its destruction of human bodies but, necessarily, must also be related to the way violence persists as memory, trauma, and in the intimate understanding of one's self-identity. This is precisely the truth that Staden's account seeks to utilize in presenting his captivity account as a vehicle for his personal redemption and, in exemplary fashion, our own as well.

Violent acts thus quite literally as well as figuratively "em-body" complex symbolism that relates to the making and unmaking of the social and cultural order,[73] also thereby giving violence its many potential meanings in the formation of the cultural imaginary, both collective and personal. Ethnographically professional anthropology has proved understandably hesitant in witnessing such acts, since the ethnographer can just as easily be a victim of violence, as an observer of it; and observation itself contributes to the cultural meaning of violent acts, no less than their perpetration. Staden's text thus speaks to such issues in a very relevant way since his situation exactly foreshadowed that of the ethnographic observer as both witness and potential victim of exotic violence, intent on producing cultural meaning from such witnessing (Nordstrom, and Robben 1995, Whitehead 2002). However, Staden's interest in the production of cultural meaning was related to Lutheran redemption and the truth of a Christian God acting in the world, rather than a redemption of Euro-American ways of knowing through ethnographic representation. In both the sixteenth-century and twenty-first-century cases the centrality of redemption through witnessing is important to note, as Johannes Dryander's emphasis on such knowledge in his introduction to Staden's text suggests. Through witnessing acts of violence, and their continuing imagination and anticipation, the meanings of violence are dispersed throughout the social order. The significance of this link between the imagination of violence and its perpetration should not be underestimated. As was the case under early modern European regimes of torture, simply to be shown the instruments of torment was often sufficient to produce the required confession of heresy or apostasy. So today, simply to be shown the aftermath of "terrorism" invites each citizen to rehearse his or her complex political commitments to "freedom" and "democracy," which in turn sustain those regimes of political power that locate and identify the terrorist as a constant threat at the very gates of society, political stability, and economic prosperity. In short, violence is a discursive practice, whose symbols, rituals, and habitual forms are as relevant to its enactment as any immediate pragmatic or instrumental purposes. Why violence is only deemed appropriate or legitimate for certain individuals or groups and how those enabling ideas of cultural appropriateness relate to a given cultural tradition and social organization as a whole are therefore issues that can be addressed directly via Staden's text. For example, at one point shortly after his capture Hans Staden pleads with the French trader, Kawattuware, who is on good terms with his captors, to identify him also as a Frenchman, or at least not a Portuguese, and so save him from sacrifice. However, Staden was abandoned to his fate by Kawattuware, thus directly posing questions for his readers as to how violence is legitimated, and relating the contest for such legitimacy to a wider field of cultural meaning and imagination, in this case that of a religiously and nationalistically conflicted Europe. What is shocking here is not the acts of violence that the Tupi are contemplating against Staden so much as the Frenchman's disavowal of a common humanity with him, thereby exposing Staden to the horrors of a doubly exotic violence, that is, Tupi sacrifice was at one and the same time both culturally strange and a token of his having been socially cast away

In the contemporary "West" the figure of the "suicide bomber," more than the "cannibal," now holds a key place in cultural imaginary, serving as a token of the illegitimacy of political causes that generate such acts. In London, Iraq, New York, and Palestine, the "suicide bomber" evokes the imagination of an irrational and unreasoning violence whose motivations are buried in the obscurity of religious cultism. It is important to note therefore that the "suicide bomber" is, like the colonial cannibal, a Western media formulation, and, as with Staden's early modern cannibals, so modern martyrdom and self-sacrifice, not the murder of innocents, are the ideas that activate perpetrators, just as a savage anthropophagy was for its participants actually a sacral ritual of eucharistic consumption. So too, like the torn and devoured cannibal body, the figure of the suicide bomber also symbolically dramatizes the identification of our bodies with the body-politic itself. Through the social order of power, our bodies are shaped, and defined. They are also joined to locations and landscapes such that destruction of sites of civic or religious identity become felt as bodily invasions, from which the invader must be repelled, purged, and cleansed (Wandel

1994). Even in the absence of specific kinds of bodies—suspects, offenders, terrorists—or in the lack of physically distinguishing features for such categories, the site of a "War on Terror," or against other kinds of "enemies within," must become internalized as an aspect of "mind" and "attitude." In this way we can come to appreciate how acts of violence are necessarily, and sometimes only, acted out in imagination. In turn the enemy within, if not the foreigner-terrorist, is the cannibal serial killer whose very surface normalcy is the deceptive camouflage for the trap of terror and torture into which we fall once they strike.[74]

The subsequent expansion of global media since Staden's day has ensured that many more minds can become imbued with a conviction of the reality of present terror, just as previously an elaborate theater of public punishment and execution, as well as an expanding sixteenth-century print media, imbued minds with a lesson as to how the destruction of the bodies of the marginal and condemned was integral to the reproduction of society, paradoxically achieving the in-corporation of society through the ex-clusion of its victims (Foucault 1977).

It is also significant that early colonial depictions of other rituals of bodily destruction, particularly as encountered in the colonial occupation of America, put great stress on the collective participation of the community in the destructive production of the victim. This was done as a way of illustrating the barbarity of the ritual exercise of "cannibalism," so that both commentators and illustrators repeatedly alluded to the participation of women and children in the cannibal moment. It is striking that it was this community participation in the incorporating cannibal moment that shocked the early modern Europeans, not its cruelties and torments. By contrast, an exclusion, not inclusion, of the victim is envisaged in the European tradition of torture and execution as an adjunct to judicial process. Such has been the fate of the twenty-first-century detainees at Guantánamo USAF base in Cuba whose marked bodies and tortured minds place them in a limbo of nonbeing, excluded from the society of human rights and law. As Edmund Leach also noted in the 1970s,

> We see ourselves as threatened . . . by lawless terrorists of all kinds
> . . . we feel ourselves to be in the position of the European Christians
> after the withdrawal of the Mongol hordes rather than in the position
> of the unfortunate Caribs [or Tupi] . . . at the hands of the Spanish

[or Portuguese] invaders. . . . We now know that the dog-headed cannibals against whom Pope Gregory IX preached his crusade were representatives of a far more sophisticated civilization than anything that existed in Europe at the time. . . . However incomprehensible the acts of terrorism may seem to be, our judges, our policemen, and our politicians must never be allowed to forget that terrorism is an activity of fellow human beings and not of dog-headed cannibals. (1977: 36)

Control over bodies—both live and dead, imaginatively and physically—is a way of engendering political power, and of all the modes of controlling bodies the physical incorporation of body parts most vividly expresses this. Such a ritual and symbolic dynamic then allows us to appreciate the indigenous political significance of the "taste of death" in anthropophagic ritual, and to begin to understand how our own deep traditions of violence still persist as part of a mystical and imaginative search for the final triumph of "progress" over the terror and violence of "barbarity."

In indigenous America this search for a cosmological and social control over violence was not just limited to the ritual of human sacrifice but comprised a worldview in which human violence was a mimesis of the predation of the divine order itself, as in Tupian anthropophagic sacrifice. In his ethnographic account of a Tupian people, the Arawété, Viveiros de Castro (1992) made a direct link between the ritual violence of the sixteenth-century Tupian cultural order and twentieth-century Arawété conceptions of a predatory cosmos. Other recent ethnographic work among other Amazonian peoples likewise suggests that not just the notion of "cannibalism" but also that of predation as features of the cosmological and religious order are a deep historical legacy in the region. This legacy has, as with other traditional religious ideas worldwide, recently become particularly prominent and assertive in the face of postcolonial attempts at economic development and "modernization."[75] Given the historicity of such forms of ritual violence it therefore is also relevant to apply such a framework of interpretation to Staden's text, since colonial intrusion and disruption among the Tupi also changed the meaning of sacrificial rituals. Staden's text is particularly valuable, as already noted, for the way in which it allows us to understand the political significance of such ceremonies in the context of resistance and cooperation with the invading colonial regimes. In the same way that Staden's own plight reflects the unfolding of European religious politics along the Brazil shore, so too the occasion and meanings of ritual sacrifice by the Tupi were intimately connected to their attempts to order the violence of colonialism by cosmological means.

The Torn and Devoured Body

In order to appreciate how and why the Tupi used a measured violence to gain a degree of agency within the unfolding colonial system that came to the shores of Brazil in the sixteenth century it is crucial to consider the meanings of ritual cannibalism, not just for the Tupi but also for Staden and his European contemporaries. The cannibal body, destined to be torn and devoured, was central to European theological and political debates of the time, no less than it was for the Tupi.

As we have seen was the case for Michel de Montaigne, André Thevet, and Jean de Léry, the Tupian theater of ritual cannibalism provided direct and dramatic points of comparison for theological dispute over the nature of the Christian Eucharist. Moreover, this concern for the sacral nature of the human body, at least as exemplified by the incarnation of Jesus Christ, was also in tension with an emergent anatomical and medical science. It is significant in this sense, then, that Johannes Dryander, who wrote the introduction to Staden's work, was also an anatomist. In fact Dryander's works are part of the canonical history of anatomy since he was one of the first to publish anatomical illustrations according to his own dissections.[76] Anatomical dissection and anthropophagic sacrifice can thus appear behaviorally analogous, and the descriptive precision and textual emphasis on the destiny of the dismembered body parts[77] derived from Tupian sacrifice in the *Warhaftige Historia* should be read alongside these avowed interests of Dryander, who must certainly have had some influence on this aspect of the work.

As was evident from the French sources in particular, the cannibal body also serviced theological speculation and debate. In general terms the colonial encounter with indigenous bodies in all forms certainly induced an obsessive speculation about the boundaries of human and nonhuman (or savage) and the notion of the monstrous and abnormal. However, this was not the only source of information that stimulated such speculation and anatomical dissection; enhanced optical observation and mechanical experimentation also clearly contributed to changing ideas of the physical and metaphysical through the sixteenth and seventeenth centuries. In this way Johannes Dryander was very much at the forefront of such changes in understanding, highlighting the way in which Staden's text was important to that process and not just a token of colonial mastery or fantastical projection. Given such a context it is perhaps easier to appreciate the significance of religious debate over the meaning of the Christian Eucharist as Lee Wandel has carefully shown. As Wandel (2006) argues, fundamental categories such as the "body" or "matter" had become unstable and no longer self-evident and thus the Reformation was itself centered on issues of how to understand the words of Christ—"This is my body and blood—Do this in remembrance of me." Christ's injunction to his followers might have implied a mimesis of that moment, involving a specific physical act, or alternatively some form of representation of that act which would inspire believers to recall the moment and so make Christ's presence an emotional and psychological reality.

The mystical form of that blood and body of Christ invited direct comparison with the cannibal moment in a Church that had become global but was no longer universal (Wandel 2006: 12). A Catholic orthodoxy that had prevailed at least up until 1500 held that the bread and wine of the communion changed in substance into the flesh and blood of Christ—hence the doctrinal notion of "transubstantiation." However, as was the case for Tupian ideas of ontological transformation through participation in an anthropophagic ritual that transformed participants into jaguar-like allelophages,[78] so too for Christian theologians the human embodiment of Christ as flesh and blood implied a finite presence, also subject to the same fate as the torn and devoured cannibal body.

Wandel (2006: 71) indicates that in fact doctrines of transubstantiation and a real presence were distinct in Lutheran terms[79] and that this was part of a general destabilization of the intellectual landscape through the sixteenth century, along with challenges to the idea of priests as the only means through which the transformation of the wine and bread was mystically achieved, as well as the idea that this was their essential and exclusive role, not other pastoral activities or forms of prayer. This ever increasing identification of priests with the Eucharist, from as early as A.D. 700 and overtly confirmed in Catholic theocracy by 1215, had the consequence of progressively excluding lay participation in the Christian Mass—in direct counterpoint to the intimacy and community of participation in Tupian sacrifice.[80]

This is not the place to rehearse the theology of Reformation debate but it is important to note that aside from issues as to the meaning of the Eucharist and its transformative potential, the idea of the Mass as sacrifice was also profoundly questioned by Protestant theologians such as Zwingli (Wandel 2006: 80), no less than the radical denial of any spiritual or mystical presence of Christ in the communion. The relevance of American cannibals to such debate was largely polemical in nature, but such was the form of intellectual exchange in the context of the day. Equally, the plethora of new readings of the Bible and the new understandings of the word of God they implied also made reference to the newly encountered exotic as a relevant mode of prosecuting debate and staking out intellectual territories, which the works of Jean de Léry no less than the *Warhaftige Historia* itself perfectly illustrate.

However, there was also an ambivalence toward the cannibalistic in European cultural traditions,[81] especially as a mode of mystical experience, and the writings of Martin Luther (1961) and other theologians were perilously provocative, by our modernist presumptions, in their sensual interest in the "flesh" of Christ. It is also notable that Staden suggests that it was the false basis on which he was to be sacrificed, not the immoral nature of cannibalism itself, that causes sickness among his captors: "this misfortune had befallen him because he had wanted to eat me, [though] I was not his enemy" (*Warhaftige Historia* I, chap. 34). Staden also tries to comfort a fellow captive with the observation that "they would only eat his body. His soul, however, would travel to another place, where the souls of our people also travel and there is much joy. Then he asked whether this was true. I told him: Yes. Well, he said, he had never seen God. I told him that he would see Him in the other life. Having now finished the conversation with him, I left him" (*Warhaftige Historia* I, chap. 36).

In short, the potentially sensual nature of eucharistic cannibalism in sixteenth-century Europe should not be underestimated, just as a medicalized cannibalism persisted in Europe into the early twentieth century, reflecting a continuing fascination with the restorative and life-giving properties of the human corpse as a divine food.[82] In this way the issue of what it is that should be done in remembrance of Christ opened up philosophically a slew of issues concerned with the relation between symbol and act, between ritual and politics, and between performance and imagination—all equally critical in interpreting Tupian ritual. Therefore, as in the case of the Tupi, the incorporation of the body-politic was overtly related to the manner of the incorporation of the sacrificed body of Christ—this is what made religion a political issue. The ferment of ideas and fracturing of dogmas that marked Germany and the rest of Europe during the sixteenth century was resolved in the seventeenth century through the overt identification of political legitimacy with specific ritual forms of the eucharistic cannibalism of Christ.

In this light the community participation in Tupian sacrifice, which Staden ably recorded, was doubly threatening—first as an illustration of the critical role of all members of the community in the sustenance of the ritual and political order,[83] and second for the preeminent role that women played in the ritual production of the victim—captured by men but domesticated by women. The theater of Tupian sacrifice was therefore transgressive of European social and cultural norms, although less for its cannibalistic elements—distasteful or disagreeable though they may have been for some observers (and in particular, of course, Hans Staden as potential victim)—than for the carnivalesque aspects of the sacrificial performance as subversive of political hierarchy and gender roles.[84] The cannibal body here appears as grotesque, in the sense suggested by Mikhail Bakhtin's (1968) discussion of Rabelais, that is, without specific individuality, devoured and devouring.[85] The grotesque in carnival thus devours all order in the world, collapsing the distinctions of flesh and spirit (or discourse and body) which are cannibalized in a never-ending process of consumption and excretion, exemplified through the laugh.[86]

In this vein it is important to compare the public theater, or carnival, of cannibal violence to the European theater of public punishment and execution. Here the destruction of the bodies of the condemned was no less integral to the reproduction of society, the critical difference being that the in-corporation of society took place through the symbolic exclusion of its victims. The stress on collective participation in the destructive production of the victim in European representations was a way of illustrating the barbarity of the ritual exercise, repeatedly alluding to the participation of women and children in the cannibal moment. However, making this comparison also helps to explain why community participation was required among Tupians but not in the punishment of the European criminal—the state, not society, constituted the forms of inclusion and exclusion.[87] The state reserves the right to determine community membership and deploys spectacular violence to that end so that the mutilation and execution of the criminal and heretic becomes a theatrical production which dramatizes the authority of law and ritualizes its enforcement by the agents of the state.[88] These torn bodies are then used to festoon the sites of state power, even as the body and blood of the condemned may be circulated as magically medicinal prophylactics. In this way the state becomes a source of life through violent death, the kind of cannibal divinity implicit in the iconography and theology of the torn and devoured Christ.

The destiny of the bodies and body parts of the Tupian victim was to be distributed among the community as a whole according to the victim's status (see Appendix), thereby signaling that revenge may be made with any member of that community, that any member might be in turn ritually produced as another's victim. At the same time control over this distribution of body parts by powerful leaders was, and is, a potent political power deeply embedded in cosmological ideas as to the significance of the body and sociality. Staden remarks upon, and the illustrations often show, heads impaled on the fortifications of Tupi settlements, in the way that the gates of medieval towns were used for the display of the bodies and body parts of the executed. Just as cannibalism was deployed differently by Europeans and Tupis, so too the meanings of dismemberment and the display of body parts were distinct, but the fact that control over bodies—both live and dead—is a way of displaying and engendering political power means that there are many other important points of analogy between the Tupi and their colonial commentators, not just in matters of sacral cannibalism. Certainly of all the modes of controlling the body-politic, dictating the modes of incorporation of whole bodies (marriage) or torn bodies (sacrifice) most forcefully expresses this.

These ritual and symbolic dynamics, then, allow us to appreciate the indigenous political significance of the Tupian anthropophagic ritual and to begin to understand how it was used to augment the social power of the war-chiefs. Equally, in the same way that the cannibal theater signaled chiefly power within Tupian society, so too the practice of cannibalism also consciously signaled resistance to colonial domination, as Staden's own predicament illustrates. It was a mimetic recognition as to the significance of cannibalism, born of the analogous role of torn bodies in the practice of political power, that gave the anthropophagic ritual its highly charged political connotations in the colonial world.[89]

The cannibal body is not only torn and dismembered; it is also naked and potentially sexual, as in the commentaries quoted in the section above on the Portugese texts. However, such commentary is remarkably absent from the account of Staden himself. The potential sexuality of Tupi nakedness, despite the emphatic depiction in text and illustrations of male and female nakedness, as well as the discursive importance of Staden's own nudity, the physical intimacy of his captivity inside the Tupi long house, the sexual behavior of the Tupi, and his own sexual attitudes, are never overtly discussed or alluded to by Staden.

Rather, the nakedness of Staden himself visually and textually functions to emphasize his helplessness, not the sexually threatening presence of the Tupi, manifestly implicit though such meanings are in his predicament. This must therefore be understood as part of the self-presentation of Staden[90] and the limits of his ethnological ambition, which is certainly secondary to the didactic purposes of his text. Given the close interplay of narrative and visual depiction in the *Warhaftige Historia* this recognition underlines the need to consider its broader discursive properties, in which an emphatic naiveté and powerlessness is crucial to the meaning of God's ultimate redemption. The key motif that buttresses this authenticating naiveté in Staden's text is therefore that of nakedness, read as both a physical and moral condition. Hans is stripped naked on capture:

> They tore the clothes from my body: one the jerkin, another the hat, a third the shirt, and so forth. Then they began to quarrel over me. One said that he had gotten to me first, another protested that it was he who captured me. In the meanwhile, the rest hit me with their bows. Finally, two of them seized me and lifted me up from the ground, naked as I was. (*Warhaftige Historia* I, chap. 18)

On reaching the village where he was to be kept, Uwattibi, Hans was further stripped of his cultural personality:

[A] woman from the crowd approached me. She had a sliver made out of crystal fastened to a thing that looked like a bent branch, and she scraped off my eyebrows with this crystal. She also wanted to scrape off the beard around my mouth, but I would not suffer this and said that she should kill me with my beard. Then they answered that they did not want to kill me yet and left me my beard. (*Warhaftige Historia* I, chap. 22)

But, signaling that the perfidy of other Christians to be as much the cause of Hans's plight as the divine hunger of his captors, it is French steel that signifies Staden's nakedness as both physical and metaphorical, he continues: "But a few days later, they cut it off with a pair of scissors, which the Frenchmen had given to them" (*Warhaftige Historia* I, chap. 22).

One almost feels that he might have added "specifically for this purpose," since they also took him "naked as I was" (*Warhaftige Historia* I, chap. 26) to see the treacherous French trader. Indeed Staden contemptuously strips off even further:

On my shoulders I had a piece of linen cloth, which they had given me (wherever they might have gotten it from) because the sun had burnt me severely. I tore this off and flung it at the Frenchman's feet, saying to myself: if I then have to die, why then should I preserve my flesh any longer for others? (*Warhaftige Historia* I, chap. 26)

As with the scissors, however, it must have been quite evident from where and from whom they obtained the cloth. But when a French trading ship does appear off the village of Uwattibi, Staden's captors will not let him go aboard:

I told them to bring me to the ship themselves; my friends would give them plenty of goods. They said no, these are not your real friends. For those who have arrived with the boat would surely have given you a shirt, since you walk around naked; but they do not care about you at all (which was true). Yet, I told them that they would clothe me when I reached the big ship. (*Warhaftige Historia* I, chap. 40)

Staden appears naked in all the woodcuts illustrating his captivity, except that he retains his beard and long hair. This in turn suggests allusion to the biblical trials of Jeremiah, with whom Staden overtly identifies through direct quotation.[91] Certainly, then, the semeiosis of the hairy nakedness of Staden, the clothed bodies of the French, and the feathered nakedness of the Tupi, highlighted in the title of the *Warhaftige Historia* as well as within the text and illustrations, are important counterpoints. As a result, it is the manner of nakedness that establishes the boundaries between Tupi, German, and Frenchman, just as the manner of cannibalistic incorporation establishes these differences by reference to ritual proclivity. In both Europe and Brazil a spectacular anthropophagy, which is at once semiophagic and semiovestiary, is therefore central to the production of ritual meaning.

3. Spectacular Anthropophagy

A boy with us . . . had a piece of the leg-bone . . . with some flesh on it, which he was eating. I told the boy to throw it away. Then both he and the others grew angry with me, saying that this was their proper food. . . . We traveled for three days . . . it remained just as stormy . . . they decided to . . . come back for the canoe when the weather had improved. As we were about to depart . . . the boy continued gnawing the flesh off the bone. Then he threw it away, and . . . The weather then immediately improved. Well, I said, you did not want to believe me when I told you that my God was angry, because of the boy eating the flesh from the bone. Well, the others said, if he had eaten it out of your sight, then the weather would have stayed fine. . . . Alkindar, asked me whether I had now seen how they treated their enemies.

— *Warhaftige Historia* I, chapter 37

The two brothers furthermore asked me how their cousin Hieronymus was doing. I told them that he lay by the fire roasting, and that I had already seen them eat a piece of Ferrero's son. Then they wept and I comforted them.

— *Warhaftige Historia* I, chapter 42

Hans Staden's *Warhaftige Historia* produces and reflects a spectacle of anthropophagy in both textual and graphic forms and was thereby made redolent with significance for his immediate audience, in a way analogous to how the drama of ritual sacrifice for the Tupi was connected to its qualities as public spectacle. Moreover, in addition to the reasons so far discussed, the anthropophagic spectacle the *Warhaftige Historia* also sustains a modernist significance which has led to various reworkings of Staden's graphic materials, thereby reinscribing the *Warhaftige Historia*, and the cannibal performance it displays, into contemporary cultural consciousness. The *Warhaftige Historia* could be considered an exceptionally important work, just for these reasons alone, as there is no other visual record of this era that is so extensive or so closely interrelated to textual description. There is also a performative aspect to the *Warhaftige Historia*, consisting in the interplay of oral, textual, and image forms, that marks it out as a notable example of early modern print culture itself, for which there was no necessary opposition between, or positivistic superiority of, the literary over the oral (Chartier 2005). Moreover, the relationship between "images" and "facts" in Staden's day was likewise understood as one of an epistemological equity, since some facts, particularly those of the eyewitness, are only present through their imaging and representation.[92] Highly popular single-leaf woodcuts circulated widely in sixteenth-century Germany, and Marburg was a notable center for their production. These broadsheets and their subject matter therefore formed Staden's visual culture in which the *Warhaftige Historia*'s images of bodily dismemberment and ritual anthropophagy would not have been shocking and troublesome in quite the ways we might anticipate. The subject matter of this popular material, which Staden himself must have seen on many occasions, suggests that reactions to depictions of Tupi sacrifice could not have been simply ones of shock and horror at the bodily destruction since this was staple fare of these woodcuts. As Staden himself told Alkindar, one of his captors, "It is terrible that you eat them [your enemies]. Killing them is not so horrible" (*Warhaftige Historia* I, chap. 37). The subject matter of these single-leaf woodcuts was at times far more gruesome and shocking than anything that appears in the *Warhaftige Historia* and also reveals the mentality of the time as unlikely to have found the heavenly portents, signs, and wonders, human cruelty, savagery and violence, and physical difference illustrated in the *Warhaftige Historia* remarkable as such. The subject matter of the popular woodcuts included such scenes as the execution and dismemberment of a werewolf, the appearance of celestial anomalies over various cities, and the presentation of monstrous human births and deformed animals and plants.[93] In which case the possibility of celestial vision and heavenly revelation, or the exercise of Staden's weather magic in compelling the clouds, taken by the Tupi as direct evidence of his shamanic ability if not the existence of a Christian God, would not have appeared improbable to the audience of the day. At the same time the constant representation of the abnormal, deviant, and pathological functioned to delineate the space of the human in this world of proliferating monstrosity and marvel, that proliferation being as much an outcome of the expansion of printing technologies as it was the encounter with exotic cannibals in America. The "truth" of the images circulating in Staden's cultural milieu was, then, as Parshall (1993: 565) writes, "literal, sensory and empirical . . . not the generalized truth . . . meant to reflect a natural and mathematically describable order. On the contrary, these broadsheets of strange and unfamiliar things record a particular instance, a tear in the fabric of that order, a deviation from it." As Parshall suggests, then, the emphasis given to eyewitnessing of preternatural and supernatural events was an important strategy for demystifying the bizarre and extraordinary since both skeptics and believers accepted that sensory apprehension was a final measure of truth. Moreover, as is evident from the *Warhaftige Historia* and Dryander's preamble to Staden's tale, in the Protestant circles of the time both mystical and skeptical impulses were present and the place of personal testimonial had gained a new prominence. This emphasis on testimonies of faith, precisely the literary form of *Warhaftige Historia*, was an important source of propaganda, paralleling a theological emphasis on the direct testimony of the scriptures. For these reasons the eyewitnessing of events was crucial to their "truth," so the supposition must be that if Staden did not himself actually make the wood blocks, he had a direct hand in guiding the process,[94] as indeed the illustrations themselves suggest through his constant eyewitnessing presence in the images and the complexity and detail of events they present.[95] However, the mystical truths of Protestant faith relied ultimately on the spiritual and moral condition of the witness known only to their god, whereas empirical truths of the material world and scientific world were ultimately decided by the very absence and transparency of the eyewitness observer. These tensions between forms of meaning and eyewitnessing are fully present in the *Warhaftige Historia* and to the modernist, rationalist mind are in apparent contradiction. Someone like Staden who credits the moon with a portentous and ominous significance in its appearance, or believes he can cure illness through God's providence, cannot at the same time be expected to report with ethnological objectivity on the ritual practices of the exotic Tupi.

Since complex human actions (i.e. "events") are already theatrical, performed in the sense of both being witnessed and being for witnessing, the strongly visual medium of "theater" in turn functioned to re-create, or "stage" them again, for contemplation, as in a *tableau vivant* or other public spectacles and reenactments. Boorsch (1976: 503) notes that there were probably some seventy such fêtes featuring "America" in theatrical form throughout Europe between 1492 and 1700. The royal entry festival[96] held for Henri II and Catherine de Medici in Rouen in October 1550, for example, featured Tupi from Brazil:

> [B]y all accounts, among the most spectacular ever staged. . . . Of all the sights that the king viewed on his journey through Rouen, none was more remarkable than the one he discovered just outside the city's walls. . . . for there he found constructed an "exact" replica of a Brazilian village. The village had no name, but had 300 inhabitants. Men as well as women, all completely naked. Fifty were Brazilian cannibals. The rest were sailors. . . . The king watched from a viewing stand specially constructed to afford him an unobstructed view. The village's inhabitants seemed to be unaware of his gaze, as they shot arrows at birds, relaxed in the shade, rocked back and forth in their hammocks, and chased after monkeys. Others cut Brazil wood and carried it to a fort built along the Seine where they bartered with sailors. . . . Suddenly, and without warning, a group of savages, who called themselves *Tabagerres*, set upon a rival band called the *Toupinabaulx* who also lived in the unnamed village. The war was fierce, but the *Toupinabaulx* quickly routed their attackers and burned their lodges to the ground. So near did this battle seem to reality that those present who had frequented the land of *Brasil* and the *Canyballes* swore in good faith that its effect was "a certain simulacra of the truth." (Wintroub 1999: 395)

This was exactly how Montaigne actually came to encounter Tupi people in a subsequent royal entry at Noyes in 1574.[97]

In its time the *Warhaftige Historia* therefore did not present itself as problematic for the reasons we might suspect, such as the presence of artifice in the act of representation and its supposed sensationalism in the depiction of violent cannibalism, hardly unique given the contents of other popular publications. However, it was not the first work to offer visual images of the Tupi, and the remote, if unlikely, possibility remains that the images were taken from some other sources.[98] However, comparison of the *Warhaftige Historia*'s illustrative materials with earlier depictions of Brazilian peoples would suggest this was not the case.

The earliest depictions of Brazilian natives appear on maps, such as that known as the "Kunstmann II" map of ca. 1502, notoriously depicting a scene of cannibalism and likely relating to the description of an incident in the voyages of Amerigo Vespucci, whose letters more generally supplied the source for a number of Florentine, Dutch, and German woodcuts depicting the people of the New World. In 1505 a German illustration, which paraphrased lines from Vespucci's letters in the caption, appeared and gained a much wider currency (Sturtevant 1976: 420, fig. 2). It depicts a group of male and female natives, attired in feather-work, with human heads and limbs hung to smoke over a fire in their shelter, while others gnaw on human appendages. Certainly this is a sign that "America" is being proclaimed through the imagery of "cannibalism" and the feathered costumes likewise recall the early observations made in Brazil, but there is little aesthetic connection with the style of the *Warhaftige Historia* and certainly far less useful detail, other than of decontextualized items of dress and weaponry. This is also the case for subsequent renderings, including woodcuts done in 1516–19 by Hans Burgkmair of the tableau vivant for Emperor Maximilian I's Triumph; the drawing in 1515 of a Tupi man by Albrecht Dürer for Maximilian's prayer book; and the "Miller Atlas" of 1519 which shows feathered Tupi with weapons and others collecting wood for trade with the Europeans.[99] Other maps that predate Staden's account do occasionally depict Brazilian natives but these could hardly have been a resource for the fifty-three separate figures that appear in the *Warhaftige Historia*, even in the case of the Jean Rotz map, which has a detailed depiction of a fortified Tupi village and groups of battling warriors. In short, the *Warhaftige Historia* visually explodes onto the sixteenth-century scene, vastly increasing the visual repertoire for depictions of native Brazilians and bringing to that repertoire new elements that are in turn taken up by other illustrators and not at all derived from them. Thevet's *Les Singularitez*, issued at the end of the same year as the *Warhaftige Historia*, certainly contains important illustrations of the Tupi but obviously could not have a source for Staden's own renderings.

There is every reason to think that Hans Staden was, as he claimed, an observing participant to the events he relates and there are other contextual reasons for thinking that he had a direct role in producing the woodcut illustrations, principally the close interconnection of text and graphics, but also the frequent visual presence of Staden himself and the fact that there were no other significant visual catalogues to which the woodblock maker might refer.[100] The accuracy of those depictions in representing what other and later sources also indicate was the appearance and custom of the Tupi likewise suggests that whatever the imaginative elements or "artifice" to these depictions, they nonetheless refract aspects of a real experience. The notion of a refraction rather than the more strict idea of reflection is appropriate here since it allows for the intrusion of imagination in a way that need not entail a supposition of falsehood or systematic deception in the illustrations.[101]

As indicated previously, the textual account appears to have been orally given by Staden and then written down, obviously by someone other than Staden. The oral character of the text itself and the nature of reading in the sixteenth century is also suggested by Staden's opening comments to the book's dedicatee, Count Phillip of Hesse: "[Y]our Highness may, whenever it pleases you, have the story . . . , read aloud, [in order] to hear about the miraculous events that Almighty God granted to me in my distress." There is also a very tight correlation between the narration of the text, the positioning of the woodcuts,[102] and the content of the woodcuts themselves, which suggests that an intimate familiarity with the contents of the narrative would have been required to compose and design the woodcuts. As realistic depictions, in contemporary terms, the images do not make visual sense, not so much for lack of perspectival rigor or aesthetic schooling but because they are part of the text and are narrated by the text even as they depict that narrative. The images therefore do not necessarily stand alone and are not self-explanatory but require the narrative of the text to decode both the nature of an event and the sequence of events that occur in them. Thus some images are spatial frames depicting a single object or event for contemplation; others are temporal, in that they show a sequence of events narrated in the text, similar to the way in which comic book frames work.[103] A good example of the former would be the images illustrating material culture, the *ini* or hammock, male adornments, the feather ruff *enduap*, the flesh-eating rattle *tammarakau*, the executioner's club *iwera pemme* (figures 41–43, 46), the illustrations of the armadillo *dattu* or possum *serwoy* (figure 55), and a palisaded village (figure 35). Except for the portrait of Tuppin Imba warriors (figure 34) and the frontispiece of a reclining cannibal (figure 1), all the other illustrations are of unfolding events: Staden's own capture and transport to the village of Uwattibi, various battles among natives and colonizers, the phases of sacrificial ritual, subsistence activities, and various acts of magic, prophecy, and providence. For example, figure 24 (96), *The Death of the Cario Slave*, perfectly illustrates the dynamic and sequential quality of how the illustrations work visually. Four separate events are shown here, starting at the top right-hand corner, where Staden attempts to heal the sick slave; moving down and to the left, where the slave is nonetheless executed; then down and to the right, where Staden appears again, denouncing the killing and warning against eating the slave; and ending in the bottom right-hand corner with the vignette of the child washing the skull of the slave. The illustrations are therefore very heavily "contextual" and later decontextualizations, as with those widely promulgated by Theodor de Bry (1592) and discussed below, have negatively affected subsequent evaluations of Staden's account itself. As mentioned before, and unsurprisingly in view of the way it is discussed in the text, his long beard[104] marks Staden visually among the crush of Tupi bodies (figures 13–25, 30–31, 44–45), as does a cruciform cross on his chest (figure 26) and his initials "HS" (figure 54). Staden's continuous presence in that intimate mass of Tupi bodies composed of women and children as well as warriors thus visually underlines his authorial presence and eyewitness status.[105]

The woodcuts also function as iconic signs as much as visual representations, since the visual elements of the illustrative "text" of the woodcuts in turn encode cultural references for difference and similarity, natural phenomena, and so forth. These may be summarized into various categories: (1) indications of cosmological and celestial presences shown through stars, suns, moons, winds, clouds, and rain; (2) the cultural-organic, where the presence and positioning of hair, skulls, parrots, cormorants, and ibis birds signal indigenous or colonial cultural affiliations; and (3) the cultural-technical, signaling difference through canoes, long houses, palisades, pots, rattles, labrets, clubs, and bows/arrows, or masted ships, cannon shot, clothing, guns, crosses.[106] In turn various visual conventions govern the deployment of these signs, one of the most striking being the visual convention for illustrating a shock or air wave, as can be seen in the depiction of the firing of cannons or blowing of trumpets.

The vivacity and complexity of the visual depictions in Staden's work are reflected in the fact that they were copied into durable copperplate engravings by Theodor de Bry, thereby "elevating the illustrations into a new technical and artistic dimension,"[107] as did the subsequent manual addition of color to the plates in various editions. De Bry offered twenty-eight copperplate engravings in place of the fifty different woodcut images in the *Warhaftige Historia* and so virtually halved the amount of visual imagery present by the originals. Although elements of the visual organization of the original images were directly transposed into de Bry's versions, particularly the perspectival angles which allowed a maplike depiction of bays, channels, and islands (figures 12–14; compare de Bry 1592: 7 and 122, 10 and 96, 18, 14 and 21, 24 and 26, 34, 37), as well as the massing of Tupi canoes (figures 13, 15, 20, 29; compare de Bry 1592: 37, 41, 66 and 120, 78 and 208) and the stark symmetry of their long houses and palisades (figures 17–22, 35; compare de Bry 1592: 41, 43, 52), also finding expression in an invented depiction of a circle of dancing shamans (de Bry 1592: 228), perhaps inspired by an amalgamation of figures 18, 21–22, 49–50. In general, though, this process also clearly changed the content of those images, and despite the greater aesthetic artistry in de Bry's copper-plates, the sense of movement and action that is so apparent in the less accomplished originals becomes stylized and even wooden in a way the woodcuts are not. In particular de Bry's versions made visual suggestions of uncontrolled and depraved female sexuality, child abuse, and satanic witchcraft.[108] Anthropophagic sacrifice became a scene of monstrous excess and an intense, if mannered, atmosphere of casual and gruesome violence was grafted onto Staden's original tale. As a result, much that was precise and particular in Staden's original renderings was lost or suppressed in the versions by de Bry, which also fractured the close interrelation of text and image that is such a notable feature of the *Warhaftige Historia*. For example, misogynist imagery of cannibalism of the innocent becomes prominent in the representation of female participation in ritual sacrifice, as will be readily apparent in a comparison of figure 53 in the *Warhaftige Historia* with de Bry's reworking of the scene (1592: 66, 128). De Bry's version overtly sexualizes the posture of the woman in the bottom left of the scene by placing one of her hands in her crotch and imparting an unbridled sensuality to the licking of her own erect finger, suggesting both fellatio and masturbation as accompaniment to this cannibal debauchery. In a similar vein, figure 52 shows the dismemberment of the corpse of the sacrificial victim, which, in both text and image, is clearly marked as a male prerogative, but in de Bry (1592: 126 and 213) there is a complete inversion and it is the women who carry out this role. De Bry also gratuitously adds a visual element that was only textually present in the *Warhaftige Historia*, showing the women suggestively plugging the anus of the victim before he is placed on the cooking fire. This scene is then repeated in a slightly different way (1592: 127) with the men this time present to cut up the corpse, and so is in fact closer to the original. However, the overall effect of these changes and redactions is to double the visual register for the sign of cannibalism. By this trompe l'oeil de Bry inflates and changes the role of the women in ways that were no doubt designed to appeal to the more salacious proclivities of his audience,[109] no less than they might fulfill desires to discern a justification for colonial enterprise and conquest of the savages.

Nonetheless, it has been the de Bry illustrations that have perennially attracted editors and publishers and so obscured the valuable content of the original woodcuts to subsequent commentators, who have relied on the presence of illustrations as expressions of the first-hand experience of Staden but have carelessly conflated them with the de Bry's versions.[110] This also has more than a visual consequence since it affects the reading of the text which is so closely intertwined with the woodcuts. De Bry erases all visual references to marvels, wonders, shamanic healing, and prophecy by Staden, and in particular the crucial incident where Staden tells his captors that the moon is angry with them, causing the first of many subsequent hesitations in their dealings with their strange captive. What might have prompted Staden to so refer to the moon is impossible to say but it certainly elided easily with Tupi notions of the presence of celestial bodies in human affairs. Since the incident is indeed followed by epidemic sickness among the Tupi, their circumspection only intensifies further as Staden also then cures them of the very sickness he openly suggests was sent by "his" god. The woodcut illustrating this scene is among the most visually dense and even resorts to a speech bubble to reinforce the significance of the event. In view of the visual erasure of this critical incident, the weight of anticipation and attention, enhanced further by the overall reduction from the original fifty-five figures to twenty-eight figures, given to cannibalistic, even orgiastic, propensities among the Tupi is magnified to the point that it becomes an iconic cipher for historical Tupi identity—the original *antropofagistas* indeed.

One other notable erasure is the depersonalization of the Tupi, who often appear as individual agents in Staden's account, as in the case Konyan Bebe. De Bry's 131 occlusion of the Tupi as heterogeneous agents allows a generalized savage cannibalism to emerge and the cultural gulf between Europeans and Tupis is widened. Equally, interstitial figures that disrupt these emergent categories of civilized and savage are also erased. For example, in de Bry's reworking of the illustration of the French trading ship which visited Uwattibi (1592: 47), the French crew now seem to be trying to haul Staden on board, rather than shove him away and abandon him as they did. In the account given in the *Warhaftige Historia*, figure 25 shows Staden from a distance imploring the crew of the French ship to rescue him:

> [W]hen I saw that they [the Frenchmen] wanted to sail off again with the boat, I thought: O merciful God, if the ship now also sails away without taking me along, I am surely going to die among them [the Tupi]. . . . With these thoughts [in mind], I left the hut, going towards the water, but the savages saw me and came after me. I ran in front of them, and they wanted to catch me. The first man that caught up with me, I struck down. The whole village was running after me, but I escaped them and swam to the boat. When I tried to climb into the boat, the Frenchmen pushed me away. (*Warhaftige Historia* I, chap. 40)

The embroilment of native peoples in intercolonial struggles, and the nature of such conflicts themselves, are thus masked by this generalized and supervening picture of savagery and cannibalism, obscuring the real violence of a colonialism that utterly eradicated the Tupi through warfare and disease.[111] Thus particular events are theatricalized to the point of becoming passive signs not active signifiers,[112] prohibiting the threatening instabilities and uncertainties of Staden's tale from disturbing his induction into the canon of colonial experience, not as a man redeemed but rather as the Cannibal Conqueror par excellence.

One other notable reworking and reinterpretation of Staden's visual record was made in the 1940s by Candido Portinari, the Brazilian modernist, for a projected but never completed American edition of the *Warhaftige Historia*. Here the reworking is entirely overt, being in a throughly modernist style, and seeks the aesthetic and emotive truths conveyed through the *Warhaftige Historia*. The images convey the way in which Portinari was inspired by the story of Staden and also how he saw it as a human tale still relevant to contemporary Brazilians. A collection of those reworked images can be found in *Portinari Devora Hans Staden*.[113]

Portinari sometimes simply redrew a version of an original illustration, as in his composition *Barco e Peixes*, which elegantly and sparingly recalls figure 4 of the *Warhaftige Historia* showing the departure of Staden's ship from Lisbon on his first journey to Brazil. This woodcut also appears as figures 9 and 33, showing respectively *The Passage from Seville to Sao Tome, Guinea* and Staden's final return, *The Catherine de Vatteville's Providential Voyage*. Portinari's *Navio e Peixes* recalls figures 2 and 6 in presenting a lateral view of vessels with four masts. Figure 2 illustrates celestial observations as an aid to navigation with an astrolabe and other navigational instruments being used by navigators who, nonetheless, are no match, as the numerous shipwrecks in the account suggest, for the more certain guidance of God's providence.[114] In general Portinari appears to have borrowed both the overall layout and perspectives and specific figures and motifs from the originals, particularly the impaled skulls, village palisades, and perching parrots, but he was selective in repeating the tableau of events as laid out in the *Warhaftige Historia*. Thus Portinari shows the scene of Staden's first capture by the Tupi, *Hans Preso pelos Índios*, where he is being stripped of his clothing, although the Tupi here conform to the standard visual tropes of Brazilian Indians as wearing feather skirts and coronets,[115] despite the visual information to the contrary in the *Warhaftige Historia*. Portinari also did a series of five scenes entitled *Hans e Indios* which, as well as the drawing titled *Aldeia*, mimic the perspectival angle toward the Tupi village evident from figures 17–22, although somewhat changing and rearranging the events enclosed therein. Most strikingly the figure of Staden himself is now turned to face out of the picture, with his arms raised as if to beseech us to recuse him. Thus, significantly, in view of the kind of erasures made by de Bry, the celestial presence of the sun and an angry moon as well as the figure of Konyan Bebe are reintroduced. This suggests a much greater interest in engaging the subjectivity of Staden himself, which was altogether less relevant to the earlier copyists like de Bry. Portinari's *Índios Atirando* likewise uses this compositional perspective and recreates the frantic activity of figure 20, *The Attack of the Tupiniquins*. The two other village scenes created by Portinari, *Taba con Figuras e Duas Caveiras* and *Índios*, combine various motifs and vignettes from the originals, particularly the association of women with food and drink preparation, as well as a virtually exact copying of the posture of the importuning and imploring figure of Hans, helpless as the Tupi sacrifice the sick Carijó slave (see figures 24, 40, and 53).

The other illustrations reproduced in *Portinari Devora*. are more directly concerned with the individual subjectivity of Staden and the Tupi. There is a stark portrait, *Hans*, showing him naked and enclosed by dark lines, presumably suggesting the bonds of his captivity, while the picture *Dois Homens* hints at a sexualized violence toward the naked and genitally exposed figure of Staden. The illustration *Índio e Canoas* does justice to the aesthetic quality and visual impact of representation in the originals, where the massed and beached canoes of the Tupi are repeatedly shown, as in figures 13–15, 20, and 26–28. *Índios Pescando* mirrors figure 38 and *Índio Esquartejando Um Cadáver* directly focuses on the figure of the man in the much-used scene in figure 52, *The Dismemberment of the Flayed Body by The Men*. *Hans Staden e o Índio* illustrates an incident that was not portrayed in the *Warhaftige Historia*, when Staden protests the gnawing of a human bone in his presence (see above), while the inverse title *Índio e Hans* suggests a transculturation of Staden, who sits patiently, looking now very old with white hair, at the side of a recumbent Tupi resplendent in colored body-paint (all the other illustrations are in monochrome) who seems, through the gesture of an outstretched hand, to be offering Staden instruction if not comfort. *Índio Esquartejando Um Cadáver* is followed in the *Portinari Devora*. volume by two scenes of individual Tupi men. The first, *Índio com Facão*, shows a contemplative figure methodically working a human bone with a knife, indifferent to Hans's imploring figure in the background.

Índio Roenda Osso shows only a dismembered corpse for company as the native hungrily chews at a human bone, perhaps in imitation of the incident in which Konyan Bebe declared how good such fare tasted to one who was a jaguar. The following page shows *Restos de Homem*, the dismembered head, torso, foot, and hand of a man with his eyeball fallen from its socket to stare woefully back at him. The final four illustrations in the Portinari collection[116] reproduced in this volume are of animals—a parrot, a peccary, and an anteater—recalling figure 55, the last of Portinari's illustrations, a Tupi man holding a bird, *Índio com Ave*.[117]

It remains only to consider the cinematic productions that reference the *Warhaftige Historia*, although the spectacle of anthropophagy is notably absent from both the films, Nelson Pereira dos Santos's 1971 *Como era gostoso meu francês* (How Tasty Was My Little Frenchman) and Luiz Alberto Pereira's 1999 *Hans Staden*. As already suggested, the mere existence of these films underlines the continuing relevance of Staden's story to Brazilians, and the lure of cannibalism suggestively present in the title no doubt partly accounts for the wide circulation of the subtitled version of the dos Santos film. The Pereira film is certainly more canonical as far as the account in the *Warhaftige Historia* is concerned, and the dialogue is mostly in Tupi. The perceived strengths of the dos Santos film, made during the period of military dictatorship in Brazil, have precisely to do with its lack of reverence and lack of interest in simply endorsing the authority of Staden's account. The central, and immediately evident, plot inversion through the substitution of a Frenchman for Staden is painfully ironic given the importance of this nationalist dynamic in the *Warhaftige Historia* and to its subsequent commentators The Pereira film, apart from its attempt at didactic fidelity to the original account, is perhaps most notable for the portrayal of the cannibal body in that Pereira's Tupi men are remarkably well muscled and appear to have arrived on set straight from working out at the gym. So too Tupi women are invariably young and somewhat nubile while the rigorous "authenticity" of nakedness (there is no lack of genitalia on display, as is also true of the dos Santos film) certainly masks with a staged naiveté other, more sexual meanings present for the modern gaze. Nakedness in this context actually functions to clothe and cover individual subjectivity and agency in a homogeneous display of Tupi flesh. The fidelity of Pereira's film to Staden's tale seems to inhibit the more subtle truths of the tale from emerging and neither Staden nor any of his captors is particularly engaging, so that, in the words of one reviewer, "Viewers thus never really feel any empathy for either the captors or their captive . . . dos Santos's film . . . on the other hand is saturated with symbolism" (Davis 2001: 695–96). In the dos Santos film the Stadenesque Frenchman does not escape but is eaten at the end of the film. He is also married, or at least given a concubine by his Tupi captors, as was the case for many indigenous prisoners, and appears to actively assimilate himself culturally, even while retaining the urge to escape. His opportunity to do so is lost, however, when he returns to try to persuade his Tupi "wife" to accompany him. As it happens, she is actually among the first of those who will eat him, consistent with the reports and descriptions of the time. For a contemporary audience the elision of sexual and gastronomic consumption, implicit in the figurative meaning of the Portuguese verb *comer*—"to copulate"—is probably the more prevalent perception and is echoed in earlier visual reworkings, such as that by de Bry.

Dos Santos, seen as part of the radical *Cinema Novo* movement despite accepting government finance to make his film (Madrueira 2005: 111–30), is not so much interested in foregrounding Tupi cannibalism as he is to set it in the context of the violence of colonial intrusion more generally and the gap between colonial representations and the historical realities of the conquest. In this sense Madrueira sees the film as "agonistic" in terms of the historical sources rather than "documental" (Madrueira 2005: 126), with the visual action often in contradiction or subverting sequences of narrative voice-over deriving from the colonial records of the day. It is also to be understood as fully participating in the canons of *antropofagia* through the way in which the film thereby cannibalizes the colonial archive. Yet, as Madrueira notes (2005: 129–30), "The film's epilogue is a fragment from Governor Mem de Sá's 1560 letter to the Portuguese Regent describing the amassed bodies of the massacred 'Tupiniquin . . . covering more than five leagues of shoreline.' . . . Whatever cultural and political lesson present-day Brazilians may be enjoined to glean from the vanished Tupi, only in bad faith can the former refuse to recognize that [it] is upon those spectral corpses that the modern nation has been erected." The way in which such cannibal captivities have formed the ideals and practices of modern ethnography must now be considered.

4. Cannibal Captivity and Ethnographic Enchantment

Better sleep with a sober cannibal than a drunken Christian.
—Herman Melville, *Moby-Dick*

Apo Meiren geuppawy wittu wasu Immou—The evil man, the
saint, has made the wind come here now, for during the day he
looked into his hides-of-thunder—by which they meant the book
that I had.
— *Warhaftige Historia* I, chapter 36

Staden as "Captive" and as "Slave"

The form of Staden's captivity needs to be considered more closely since
his experiences, as a prisoner of the Tupinambá, were not unique, even if
his escape from the threat of immediate sacrifice was relatively uncommon.
Indeed, although "escape" should be the logical alternative to "captivity,"
it is obvious from the ambivalent manner of what was to be Staden's final
departure from the village of Abbati Bossange that it was understood by
the Tupi as a conditional absence, even if Staden's intentions were clearly
otherwise. Staden represented himself as striving ceaselessly to escape, as in
no way conforming or accepting of his fate, and so his ruse to get aboard
the French ship on which he finally departs is one which plays on his knowledge of his captors and reaffirms to his readers that he has in no sense been
transculturated by his experiences. As Harbsmeier has argued, the writing
of travel accounts more generally might be seen as part of a voyager's "ritual
of return," a way of reinhabiting a place in the world that is acceptable to
the social context to which the traveler returns,[118] and this certainly should
be understood as applying to Staden's *Warhaftige Historia*. The question
remains open as to whether the *Warhaftige Historia* (Part I), containing
representations to us of his "captivity" and motivations during that period,
is an unvarnished guide to his state of mind or merely a didactic essay on
redemption, the power of a Christian god to salvage the faithful and an
object lesson for the community of believers to whom he wishes to make
a return.[119]

The reasons for the relative prominence of the *Warhaftige Historia* in the
colonial literature are therefore no less related to its success as a particular
form of writing and publication, and here Dryander's advice and involve-

ment must have been important.[120] But the *Warhaftige Historia*'s success, as measured by the reprinting and variety of editions, cannot just be due to the way in which it conforms to important literary genres of the day. Rather its continuing readership has found other messages and meanings in the text, both as part of the imagination of a Protestant America open to the commerce and trade of all, particularly through the various Dutch editions, and also as an intimate account of the subjectivity of the exotic savage and that most beguiling of practices, cannibalism. What Staden's account may have over other captivity narratives is the dramatic claim that he is always about to die and that the certainty of this fate is only ameliorated by providential circumstance. Staden is keen to identify the hand of God in this providence, but other tales of captivity, lacking none of the adventure or high drama of Staden's account, nonetheless tend to refer to providence as luck rather than divine intervention. For example, the account of Anthony Knivet (1625), a Protestant Englishman, shipwrecked and then made prisoner by the Portuguese in Brazil, is no less a tale of high adventure, dire circumstance, cannibal captivity, and repeated misfortune than Staden's.[121] But Knivet, or at least his editor and interlocutor, the colonial propagandist Samuel Purchas, is less interested in inferring religious meaning from his experience than revealing the political, economic, and social basis of the Portuguese occupation of the region, through recounting his tale of the treachery of the Portuguese, the relative nobility of the savage cannibals, and the discomfort of his own physical sufferings.

Whatever the meanings assigned to such captivities by the captive, the fact of captivity itself plays a crucial role in authenticating the veracity of the account. The fact of captivity can therefore be understood as a mode of continuous eyewitnessing, which, for the reasons already outlined, was and remains crucial to observation as a mode of knowledge. For this very reason, of course, the status of eyewitness accounts also remains a matter of debate, and the question as to what forms of knowledge can be built on such ways of knowing is no less problematic today than in Staden's time. However, we can at least say that current ideas about eyewitness knowledge are predicated on the idea that, even if objective knowledge is possible, the statements of eyewitnesses are a component of, not the form of, such knowledge. The ways in which personal proclivities cut across an ideal of "objective" reporting have therefore been at the center of debates on ethnographic writing and representation for the last three decades. With the inception of a professional anthropology at the beginning of the twentieth century, the ability of the observer to report objectively was more favorably conceived, but, following the effect of various forms of literary and epistemological critique since the 1970s, the necessity of positioning the observer in the context of his or her observations as the means through which communicable and valid ethnographic proportions may be made has become an established practice. Therefore, the pro-ethnographic nature of Staden's text is not a question of how objective, enlightened, or rational his intellectual makeup was—and it clearly is not so for the contemporary reader and commentator—but rather whether he was in a position to make the assertions he does (physical presence) and whether what he asserts, given what we can know of his background and cultural proclivities, tells us anything at all about his Tupi captors (intellectual presence).

Comparison with the contemporary writings of André Thevet, as already suggested, indicates that from this point of view, and notwithstanding the ethnological elaboration present in Thevet's writings, Staden was in a much better position to make the observations he claims, and that Thevet, removed from the villages of the Tupi, had little choice but to collate and evaluate the opinions of others who had such an ethnographic advantage. In the case of Léry, his sojourns to Tupi villages and his reporting on his own subjective responses rightly still command the respect of ethnographers, as in the case for Lévi-Strauss. The key question is whether or not Léry's purposes in recalling his experiences of the Tupi are in some sense more valid or more ethnographic than those present in Staden's case.

For Claude Lévi-Strauss they clearly were, even though he does not consider Hans Staden in comparison with Jean de Léry. Lévi-Strauss emphasizes the originality and "freshness" of Léry compared to both Montaigne and Thevet. But he reads Léry almost by accident as, in Lestringant's phrase, "mundane background reading and preparation," but succumbs to Léry's "sorcery" for his ability to communicate over, as Lévi-Strauss terms it, the space of ten thousand kilometers and four centuries from France (Lestringant 1994: 6–7). This self-identification with Léry expands further since the production of, and controversies surrounding, Léry's text are seen by Lévi-Strauss as similar to the problems he himself has struggled with all of his life. As Lévi-Strauss acknowledges, this might appear presumptuous, but he goes on to explicitly document the parallels between himself and Léry.

Léry went to Brazil when he was young, twenty-two or twenty-three years old, and waited eighteen years before publishing his account. Likewise, Lévi-Strauss says he waited fifteen years before publishing *Tristes Tropiques*—the intervals being occupied by the Wars of Religion for Léry and World War II for Lévi-Strauss. More eerily, and perhaps indeed evidencing Léry's sorcery, Lévi-Strauss notes that Léry ended his days as the pastor of Vufflens, where the family of Ferdinand Saussure originated, the linguist who pioneered the form of "structuralism" which Lévi-Strauss famously elaborated as anthropological theory. When Lévi-Strauss and his wife were looking for a country cottage they finally settled on Bourgogne in northern France, not realizing at that time it was near La Margelle, the very parish where Léry was born and where there is still a hamlet bearing his name. For these rather odd reasons, Lévi-Strauss therefore develops a sense of intimacy with Léry or, as Lestringant puts it, "the shadow of Léry falls over all of your being" (Lestringant 1994: 6–8). Avowedly without knowing the circumstances of its production, Lévi-Strauss lauds Jean de Léry's *Histoire d'un voyage* as "modern. Constructed like a contemporary ethnographic monograph—the milieu, the material culture, the subsistence and food processing, kinship marriage, religious beliefs . . . the premier model of an ethnographic monograph" (Lestringant 1994: 8). Lévi-Strauss also sees Léry as proceeding not with a developed ethnographic method but almost by way of self-discovery in Brazil. By contrast André Thevet, who, Lévi-Strauss emphasizes, was only ten weeks in Brazil, produces "une vulgate brésilienne" (*vulgate* is a Latin version of the Bible). The reason for this must then be traced, as Lévi-Strauss suggests, to the "regard" or gaze of Léry, which is that of the interpretive eyewitness, not second-hand like that of Thevet (Lestringant 1994: 9). Lévi-Strauss also candidly confesses that Léry fulfills the ethnographer's dream of being "the first: to see, to encounter the pristine, the 'first White' to penetrate into the indigenous community," as a result of which, "the book is an enchantment," "a great work of literature," and "an extraordinary adventure novel" (Lestringant 1994: 12–13).

However, the second part of the *Warhaftige Historia*, as Neuber (1991) suggests, conforms no less in its own way to a model of ethnographic reporting, which also covers all the topics that Lévi-Strauss indicates, while

Staden's gaze is exceptionally intimate—far more so than Léry's. Although Léry certainly "visited" the villages of the Tupi, we have no evidence that he ever stayed there, or even witnessed ritual sacrifice.[122] So although, as Lévi-Strauss says, Léry's experiences and "regard" were far more close-up than those of Thevet, they were altogether far less intimate than those of Staden. Indeed, Staden's account may be embarrassing to this eulogy for Léry since the *Warhaftige Historia* clearly shows that Léry was not at all the "first White to penetrate into the indigenous community." Moreover, although Léry was in Brazil from March 7, 1557, until May 24, 1558 (fourteen months), Hans Staden's captivity with the Tupi spanned some nine months[123] with his overall time in the milieu of Brazil amounting to over seven years. Indeed, Staden might equally have well written an account of the Carijós since he was shipwrecked in 1550 off Santa Catarina Bay, near the village of Cutia:

> We stayed there in the wilderness for two years, in great peril. We suffered great hunger and had to eat lizards, field-rats, and the other strange food that we could get, as well as mussels clinging to the rocks and similar strange foods. Most of the savages who had at first supplied us with food, left us and went to other places, once they had obtained enough goods from us. (*Warhaftige Historia* I, chap. 11)

He did not, however, because his priorities in writing, whatever may be ours in reading, were precisely to achieve the ends of religious persuasion and justification. Insofar as he also produced a humanist *apodemic*,[124] perhaps with rather more urging on the part of the intellectual Dryander, then this was indeed an ethnological enterprise suggested, as in the case of Léry, by an exceptional experience with regard to the "savage cannibals." It was not that no one else had dealings with the Tupi but rather that the basis of those dealings was not one likely to generate new kinds of insight for a potential readership, whether their interests be theological, economical, or ethnological. Undoubtedly the way in which Léry's account is purposefully and overtly entwined in the wider debates of the time (a role Dryander had to assume for Staden), as well as the obvious literacy and intellectual accomplishment of an educated pastor, together outshine in literary terms the "rude, truthful, and natural" (after Richard Burton, quoted above) appearance of Staden's text. However, the spectacular woodcuts of the *Warhaftige Historia* are a resource and view of the Tupi which even the nice illustrations of Léry's *Histoire* cannot really match in terms of the range of cultural forms and behaviors they illustrate.

Captivity, which might be equally understood as a physical detention or a subjective and intellectual fascination, is a crucial condition of possibility for ethnography, suggesting that as a literary form ethnography is coextensive with the emergence of travel writing more generally.[125] Although the idea of "ethnography" as the professional practice of "participant observation" is conventionally thought to have been inaugurated by the career of Bronislaw Malinowski, there are many reasons to consider a wide variety of cross-cultural contacts and intimate experiences of others that preceded this moment to have been no less productive of the kinds of insight and knowledge which this professionalization at the beginning of the twentieth century sought to standardize and control.[126]

At the same time, the epistemological status of ethnographic propositions, dependent on personal observation, are no longer uniformly considered by anthropologists to be "objective" in the manner of a social science but rather "interpretative" in the manner of humanistic debate and discussion.[127] As a result Staden's appearance of being a neutral observer, which has been the basis on which his ethnographic value has usually been evaluated (Arens 1979, Forsyth 1985, Sturtevant 1976), should rather be understood as an aspect of his own individual predicament and the purposes for which he wrote the account. Staden's uncompromising attitude and belief in divine providence unfold against a backdrop of increasing engagement with Tupi ideas as a strategy to avoid sacrifice. When he realizes he cannot pass himself off as a Frenchman, which actually Anthony Knivet successfully did to avoid a similar fate, Staden exploits the idea of providence in his counternarration to the Tupi of weather events, omens on the eve of battle, celestial appearances, and, most important of all, the occurrence of sickness. For the Tupi an outbreak of sickness would have been evidence of the action of malevolent forces, possibly as directed by human sorcerers. Staden's ideas as to the role of divine providence in directing all manner of natural events meshed with Tupi notions in a way that made him a source of uncertainty and possibly shamanic power since, as with the advent of sickness, so too rain and wind might be sent against them. Staden's notion of divine predestination and providence may have conflicted philosophically with the Tupi view of Staden as expressing and revealing his own desires in weather and epidemic events, but in performative terms there was no difference since Staden assumes the abilities with which the Tupi credit him. Until this point the Tupi had been aware of his ambiguous status and had taken great lengths to ensure that he fulfilled their expectations as to really being an enemy. After Karwattuware, the Frenchman, advises the Tupi that Staden is indeed their enemy,

> Then they led me back to the hut, where they kept me. Then I went to lie down in my net [hammock]. God knows the misery that I was in. Screaming, I began to sing the verse: We now implore the Holy Ghost / For the true faith, first and foremost, / That in our last moments He may protect us / when we journey homeward, away from this misery. / Kyrioleys [Lord, have mercy]. Then they said: He is a real Portuguese. Now he screams, he is afraid of death. This Frenchman was there for two days in the huts. Then on the third day, he went away. They had decided to prepare things and wanted to kill me on the day when they had gotten everything ready. They guarded me very closely, and both the young and the old mocked me a lot. (*Warhaftige Historia* I, chap. 26)

So now that the Tupi are convinced that Staden is a "real Portuguese" for the fear he shows, he has no other recourse left until his encounter with Konyan Bebe at a different village, Arirab [Ariró]. It is clear that Konyan Bebe is not necessarily convinced of his identity as Portuguese, and Staden's prediction of an attack from the Tupiniquins, which indeed occurs, proves the turning point, as subsequent prophecies and curing demonstrate that he cannot simply be assigned the social structural status of "enemy."

In this context Staden's interest is in showing the dynamics of his own faith, which is certainly subject to doubts, as well as the certainties for which his story will eventually be the evidence. His doubts at first are manifold, as when he reveals that "God knows how, if it be His divine will, I sometimes had a heartfelt wish to die, without the savages noticing it, so they could not work their will on me" (*Warhaftige Historia* I, chap. 27), or when he questions the presence of a merciful God: "[T]hey asked me why I was looking at the moon all the time. Then I told them: I can see that it is angry, for the shape that one can see on the moon seemed so terrible to me that I (God forgive me) myself thought that God and all creatures had to be angry at me" (*Warhaftige Historia* I, chap. 30). Until he has evidence that he is in fact righteous, "one of them came to me and said: the brother of one of your masters has come, and says that the others have grown very ill. I was happy and thought that now God is going to do something about it" (*Warhaftige Historia* I, chap. 33). The king Jeppipo Wasu then connects Staden's "angry moon" with their illness: "When I heard him speak like that, I thought to myself that it had to have been Providence, which made me speak of the moon on that evening. I was very happy and thought: God is with me today" (*Warhaftige Historia* I, chap. 34). "Providence" here appears as a more anonymous spiritual force than God, whose interest in Staden is otherwise exceptional. At Jeppipo Wasu's pleading, Staden then "walked around amongst them and laid my hands on their heads, which they beseeched me to do. But God did not want it to be so, and they began to die" (*Warhaftige Historia* I, chap. 34), although this actually leads to a further plea to save them, while other Tupi kings, such as Vratinge Wasu and Kenrimakui, have dreams that Staden controls their fate and so ask that they not be allowed to die. Also at this time the old women begin to call him Scheraeire [Chê-raira = my son], and his status thereby transforms:

> The old women in various huts, who had done great harm to me, by beating and tearing at me, and threatening to eat me, now called me Scheraeire [Chê-raira], which means: my son. [They begged me:] Please do not let me die. We only treated you so, because we thought you were a Portuguese, whom we are very angry with. Besides, we have already captured and eaten many Portuguese, but their God never got as angry as yours. Thus, we now understand that you cannot be a Portuguese. Hence, they then left me in peace for a while. Neither did they quite know what to do with me, nor whether I was a Portuguese or a Frenchman. They said that I had a red beard like the Frenchmen. They had also seen (bearded) Portuguese, but they normally all had black beards. (*Warhaftige Historia* I, chap. 34)

From this point on, Staden has already escaped a certain kind of fate among the Tupi and it only remains to negotiate a form of departure and return, the story of which it is the task of the *Warhaftige Historia* to recount. This is portended by the visit of a Portuguese ship on which a French trader,

Claudio Mirando, poses as his brother, offers trade goods, and tells him that

> I should keep up my spirits; God would make everything all right. But, as I could see, they were not able to help me [now]. Yes, I said, since my sins have deserved to be punished in this way, it is better that God punish me here, rather than in the life after death. Pray to God to help me out of the misery. . . . they [the Tupinambá] said to themselves: He surely has to be a Frenchman, let us treat him better from now on. Thus, for some time I walked around telling them that a ship would soon come to get me, in order to ensure that they treated me well. Now and then, they took me along in the forest and when they had something that needed to be done, I had to help them. (*Warhaftige Historia* I, chap. 38)

In this way Staden's evidencing and witnessing of God, the power of faith, and the certainty of redemption thereby is the source of his objectivity toward the behavior of the Tupi. This allows Staden even to take advantage of, if not pleasure in, the death of his personal enemies and leads him to assign to God the power to influence even Tupi decisions as to who shall be sacrificed:

> I told them how this Cario whom they were roasting and wanted to eat, had always lied about me, saying that I had shot several of their friends while I was among the Portuguese, and that had been a lie, for he had never seen me before. Now, as you well know that he has been several years with you and never grew sick. But now my God has become angry with him because of the lies he fabricated about me, and *He made him sick and made you decide to kill and eat him*. My God will do the same to all evil persons, who have done or will do me evil. Many of them were terrified at my words. (*Warhaftige Historia* I, chap 36; emphasis added)

In exactly these ways, then, the notion of "captivity" validates observation as "participant" rather than "passing," for it implies a substantive engagement with the lives of others since it cannot simply be terminated at the whim of the observer. Just as Malinowski is rightly lauded for having come down off the colonial verandah to take part in the everyday life of the Trobriand islanders among whom he worked,[128] so more generally the ability to observe without consequence, to survey from the colonial verandah, or other kinds of privileged position, is the essence of the traveler and tourist. The intimacy implied by Staden's physical captivity and the lurking potential for anthropophagic sacrifice are far more convincing grounds on which to base an ethnographic representation of the Tupi than the eco-tourism of Jean de Léry. Moreover, Staden's descriptions continually emphasize the ritual and obligatory nature of the cannibal rite—not its savagery—in order to underline the certainty of his fate, without God's deliverance. This in turn imparts an ethnographic quality to the text because he needs to demonstrate in detail the cultural and historical inevitability of his fate, and that it is not merely hanging on the whim of an individual, such as Konyan Bebe, since this makes the threat of death all the more convincing and so his redemption all the more miraculous and providential.

The meaning and therefore ethnographic potential of captivity itself is also partly dependent on the attitude of the captive, and it is this which links Staden's involuntary detention with the voluntary "rapture" of contemporary ethnography.[129] In the religious context of Staden's attitudes such captivity was part of a destiny designed by God, but in contemporary ethnography the iconic experience has become one of surrender rather than resistance to the condition of capture and the form of transculturation it implies.

Transculturation of enemies through anthropophagic sacrifice was key to the logic of Tupian warfare and meaning of "revenge," for the Tupian perspective "from-the-enemy's-point-of-view," like the iconic "from-the-native's-point-of-view" in contemporary anthropology, implies other-becoming, either through the intimacy of eating or that of cultural knowing and translation. The question is not, then, whether Staden was transculturated, and therefore perforce committed to objectifying the Tupi as savages in order to recover a European individuality and subjectivity, but rather to what extent the Tupi were successful in transculturating Staden without eating him. He was given to Abbati Bossange, who "called me his son, and I went hunting with his sons" (*Warhaftige Historia* I, chap. 49), and removed from the supervision of Alkindar, who "was very cruel towards me and would have liked the man, whom he offered me to, to kill me.... Although it would not be fitting for him to kill me, he would gladly have done so all the same. However, his brother always prevented him, because he was afraid of the subsequent plagues that might then befall him" (*War-

haftige Historia I, chap. 37). This suggests that transliteration of Staden did occur to some degree, in Tupi terms. Moreover, as Staden tells us that as he is about to finally depart on a French ship, Abbati Bossange was most upset and ran about the ship shouting that he "looked upon me as his son and was very angry with those from Uwattibi, who had wanted to eat me" (*Warhaftige Historia* I, chap. 51). This also strongly suggests that his role in curing the sick, prophesying the attacks of enemies, and staying the hand of storms was already evidence enough for his captors that he was acting to their advantage, making his looming sacrifice redundant.

Viveiros de Castro (1992) had the insight, on the basis of his ethnography of the Tupian Arawété, that the incorporation of others, literally and figuratively through the notion of anthropophagy, was fundamental to Amazonian social systems. This powerful mechanism for both collective conquest and individual eminence was present in Tupian cosmologies as a mimesis of the divine, a mimesis not unlike the eucharistic cannibalism of the Christian Europeans, as already noted. However, the gods of the Tupi world were not thought to be loving but predatory, as Staden records:

> [T]he soothsayers tell them to make war and capture enemies, for the spirits who are in the Tammaraka [shamanic rattles and idols] crave the flesh of slaves. Then they set off to war. After the soothsayer, the Paygi, has made gods out of all the rattles, each person takes his rattle away. He calls it his beloved son and builds a separate, little hut where it is kept. He places food before it and asks it to provide him with everything that he needs, just as we pray to the true God. Such are their gods. (*Warhaftige Historia* II, chap. 23)

In this way Tupi cosmology and shamanism encouraged an expansive and therefore transculturating social system that broke down the rectitude of social and cultural individuation which was so important to the emerging system of European national colonialisms. Tupi society was therefore capable of ingesting Portuguese, French, Spanish, English, Dutch, German in a way diametrically opposed to the growing importance of religious and national differentiation of sixteenth-century Europe, although such differentiation was also referenced by modes of sacral cannibalism. If Staden appears at all points to resist any kind of compromise or seduction by Tupi culture, this must in part be understood as a resistance to an irresistible form of transculturation—anthropophagic sacrifice. One could not become more Tupi than by being bodily dispersed among their communities and absorbed into individual bodies. This also helps us understand why Tupi themselves did not necessarily resist such a fate, as is strongly evidenced by many other accounts than Staden's, such as that by Cardim (1625: 432): "[S]ome are as contented though they are to bee eaten, that in no wise they will consent to be ransomed for to serve; for they say that it is a wretched thing to die, and lie stinking, and eaten with Wormes."

While Staden tells us of a Marckaya (Maracaiás) prisoner he tries to comfort on the eve of his sacrifice:

> Now when this moment came, I went up to the captive. It was on the eve of the day on which they were going to drink in preparation for his death, and I said to him: So, you are ready for your death. He laughed and said: . . . Yes, he thought that he was all well prepared, only the Mussurana [rope to bind the prisoner] was not long enough (for it lacked some six fathoms in length). Well, he said, his people had better ropes. And he spoke and acted as if he were going to the parish fair.(*Warhaftige Historia* I, chap 56)

Even a Tupi could not become more Tupi or properly Tupi without the possibility of this outcome. "Brave people who are fit to fight die in enemy territory" (*Warhaftige Historia* I, chap. 43), Staden tells us. The souls of the dead not so consumed were doomed after death to a complete ontological erasure through the divine cannibalism of the gods unless they were first themselves transformed and inducted into the rank of the protodivine through their prior acts of human cannibalism of the enemy. This in turn makes the enemy all important as a category of social reproduction and individual destiny so that nothing could be gained through eating others who did not evince this status. The status of Staden as enemy was therefore sufficiently ambiguous for him to evade that fate, as was palpably not the case for those Portuguese captured after him, or the Carijó slave whose sickness threatened to rob his captors of their opportunity to augment their divine becoming through the addition of beautiful names earned in the process of ritual sacrifice. If Staden was not good to eat, he was good to think with.

It is evident from Staden's descriptions that a captive might be considered a slave as much as a potential sacrificial victim, and this was the situation of the Carijó, who had been captive, like Staden, for quite some time;

> Now there was a slave among them who belonged to a nation called Carios, a people who were also enemies of those savages who were the friends of the Portuguese. This man had belonged to the Portuguese, and had then escaped from them. They do not kill those [slaves] who escape to them, unless they commit some particular crime. Instead, they keep them as their own slaves who have to serve them. This Carios had been among these Tuppin Inba for three years. (*Warhaftige Historia* I, chap. 39)

Once Staden's abilities as a healer and prophet were realized, and he was passed to Abbati Bossange, it was no longer evident to Staden that he was going to be sacrificed, and his situation becomes quite different from that of those more recently captured from Brikioka. The turning point comes in the war-camp of Meyen Bipe:

> That night, after they [the savages] had now camped, I went into the huts where they kept the two brothers. I wanted to talk with them, for they were good friends of mine from Brikioka, where I was captured. They asked me whether they were also going to be eaten . . . they wept and I comforted them. . . . Then I continued to say that, properly speaking, this ought to affect me more than them: I come from foreign lands and am not accustomed to the dreadful acts of these people. You have always been here, in these lands; you have been born and raised here. Well, they said, I had been so hardened by misery that I did not take notice of it anymore. . . . With this, I left their hut and passed through the whole camp, visiting the captives. Thus, I walked around alone and no one took notice of me, and I could probably have escaped on this occasion. . . . However, I refrained on account of the Christian captives, of whom four were still alive. For I thought: if I escape, the savages will get angry and will kill them very soon.[130] Maybe God will meanwhile preserve us all. I decided to remain with them and comfort them, which I did. All the same, the savages were very favorably disposed towards me, since I had predicted that they have luck when the enemy would encounter

us. Since it had now turned out to be true, they said that I was a better prophet than their Maraka. (*Warhaftige Historia* I, chap 42)

Staden appears to have changed his status among the Tupi and to have been, like the Carijó slave who was only to be killed when death through sickness was imminent, a slave with every possibility of living on for a number of years. Those badly wounded in battle were summarily sacrificed and not even hauled back to the village, as was Staden on his capture. Staden also records that for some captives, "They give him a woman who attends to him and is also doing things [sex] with him. If she becomes pregnant, they raise the child until it is grown. If it then enters their minds [to do so], they kill and eat the child" (*Warhaftige Historia* II, chap. 29). This was not the case for Staden by his account, and although this may well have been an aspect of his enforced intimacy with the Tupi that he wished to repress or suppress, it was not uniformly the case that this custom was followed, as is evident from the fate of various captives that Staden describes. Such a practice may well have been desirable in some cases and not others, particularly as Tupi warfare more widely became increasingly entangled with the colonial regimes of the region and the character and number of war captives changed and even increased. Without being able to reconstruct the way in which such decisions were made and the kinds of considerations that underlay them we can only note that Staden's wish to present himself as a paragon of sexual rectitude may not have been the only reason that he himself did not benefit from the custom which he openly records.

The words of his captors that Staden records when they first seize him are highly illuminating for understanding Tupian cultural practice:

They tied the cord around my neck high up in a tree, and they lay around me all night and mocked me calling me: *Schere inbau ende* [Chê reimbaba indé], which in their language means: You are my bound animal [pet]. (*Warhaftige Historia* I, chap. 20)

Captives and abducted children are often conceptualized as pets by contemporary native peoples, as thus appears to have been the case for the sixteenth-century Tupi. Similar observations have been made in recent ethnography for the capture of children among the Txiçao and also among the Arawété, for whom a killer is thought to capture the spirit of the dead enemy, learning to control it during a period of seclusion and abstinence and then putting it to the service of the community as a source of new songs and names, as with the new names given to Tupi executioners.[131] A captive taken in war was "adopted" by the family of his future executioner, who fed and protected him. His condition was that of a wife-receiver and so he was understood to be under the strict control of his father-in-law and brothers-in-law. This situation may be directly compared to that of a pet. The social position of the captive altered on the eve of sacrifice (see Appendix). He was separated from his adoptive family and assumed the position of an enemy again by being subjected to rituals recalling the original capture. Thus Tupi ritual anthropophagy was not predicated on ideas of the fertility or the person-producing capacity of sacrifice but was instead related closely to the growth of the personal capacities and social power of warriors, which may be why the children of captives were also sacrificed, since the resource they represented was not new beings but the means to the enhancement of the life potentials of those already living.

Certainly, then, for the Tupi, at all points, captivity and the status of enemy implies a necessary form of intimacy. Even though he was initially destined for sacrifice, daily relationships were more relaxed between Staden and his captors than we might at first presume, dark though Tupi humor was. At one point we can directly sense the consequences of this enforced intimacy as storms threaten the harvesting of crops:

> For, they said, as I could see, we had nothing to eat in the hut. These words moved me and I prayed to the Lord from the bottom of my heart, to use me to demonstrate His power, since the savages desired this from me. (*Warhaftige Historia* I, chap. 47)

Staden's text does not perfectly mask this aspect of his life with the Tupi, but as a text through which he made an emotional and psychological return, no less than a public and cultural one, the *Warhaftige Historia* more often narrates his distancing.[132]

The *Warhaftige Historia* is in fact one of the earliest captivity narratives to emerge, and its themes and obsessions prove to be perennial for the genre as a whole. Strictly speaking, however, it is preceded by Álvar Núñez Cabeza de Vaca's famous account of his journeys through the southern parts of the United States and into Mexico, which has often been taken as the first example of a captivity narrative. The account was written between 1537 and 1540 and first published in 1542, although that edition is very rare and it is the second edition of 1555 that is more widely known. In fact, as Cabeza de Vaca's account itself makes clear, while there are incidents of captivity and forced residence, this is but one kind of relationship that Cabeza de Vaca and his small band of companions had with the native peoples on their journeying. As such, then, Cabeza de Vaca's account is not strictly a captivity narrative, not least because this was not the condition in which his group spent the major portion of their time. His story begins with a shipwreck off the Florida coast; unlike Staden's situation, the local population is more bemused by the Spaniards than intent on their capture. Indeed, one of the key aspects of the account is the way in which the potential shamanic powers of these strange castaways is successively exploited by the native groups they encounter in their enforced residence on the Louisiana coast and their journey toward Mexico through Texas.[133] The account of Cabeza de Vaca is certainly, in its original published form, much better known and studied than the *Warhaftige Historia*, and its literary characteristics offer important points of contrast that allow us to better appreciate the qualities of the *Warhaftige Historia* itself. In particular, Cabeza de Vaca's account foregrounds the drama of repeated shipwreck. In narrative terms this is a means of explaining to his audience, including the royal authorities in Spain, both the legitimate nature of his actions and the detailed accuracy of the account, owing to his status as an eyewitness participant in the events narrated. The account also presents itself in the tradition of travel writing as an account of travail, which, being successfully overcome, can inform and instruct a readership. At the end of his wanderings Cabeza de Vaca was appointed to the governorship of Rio de la Plata, where he was a controversial figure and was ultimately returned to Spain in chains. He then published a second work, reflecting on and justifying his action in Rio de la Plata, which was the occasion for him to also reissue his account of 1542. The replay of his shipwreck and heroic journeying thus was also important in recuperating his station following the disgrace of his governorship.

As Voigt (2001: 38–44) perceptively indicates, Cabeza de Vaca's self-fashioning in the eyes of the Spanish political hierarchy is also linked to another transformation that he undergoes during his seven years' wandering, from shipwreck to enslavement and then independence as a trader and shamanic healer. Had Staden not left Brazil on the French ship when he did, it is conceivable that he too might have gone on to become a prophet and healer in the longer term. It is also relevant to note that Cabeza de Vaca did not enter a context in which native groups were already substantively engaged in the politics of colonial rivalry, as was the case for the Tupinikin and Tupinambá in Brazil. Unlike Cabeza de Vaca, Staden was by no means the first European to have been encountered, and the stimulus given to the Tupi war and sacrifice complex by their entanglement in the colonial world meant that there was considerably less room for negotiation in his status. The drama of Staden's tale is thus partly connected to the way in which the inevitability of his fate as a sacrificial victim makes his evasion of that destiny all the more remarkable and providential. The very longevity of Cabeza de Vaca's wanderings would have in itself required a more complex and subtle transculturation than that envisaged by anthropophagic sacrifice, and so, without such an apparent threat, the possibility emerges for Cabeza de Vaca to not only be transculturated but to actively avow and practice categories of thought and action encountered in native culture.[134] Cabeza de Vaca thus uses his account to underwrite his authority and identity as Spanish, both of which are based on contact and familiarity with an "other" culture, and like Staden, he ultimately seeks to return to his own cultural origins. But, as with the deployment of the cannibal ritual in the writing of Staden, what authenticates his text is a paradoxical fascination and repulsion with regard to the native.

The account of Cabeza de Vaca thus points more to the figure of the castaway than that of the captive, in the sense of the kind of captivity endured by Staden. But clearly the trope of captivity is closely related to that of the castaway since such captivities, as in the case of Cabeza de Vaca, may ensue from being cast away from one's cultural circumstance. This means such accounts as those of Staden and Cabeza de Vaca anticipate and even inspire important literary and more widely read workings of these themes. This is the case for the genre of Puritan captivity narratives, relating to the colonial occupation of North America, as well as some notable fictional accounts, such as Daniel Defoe's *Robinson Crusoe*, or, in Spanish literature, the captivity of Miguel Cervantes[135] as recounted in *Don Quixote*. Surprisingly, the secondary scholarship on the captivity narrative genre completely overlooks Staden's account, despite its being one of the earliest examples from the Americas.[136] Nonetheless, the careful analyses of some of the key North American texts that these authors provide is always suggestive for a reading of Staden since they demonstrate the same kinds of attempts at mediating both the condition and course of captivity itself as well as the critical matter of enabling a cultural return. As Ebersole (1995: 240) indicates, in some cases of course there was a complete transculturation, as in the story of John Tanner mentioned above. The literary and cultural popularity of this kind of account was far less than that of those that redeemed not just the captive but the cultural context of civilization as well, and accounts like Tanner's which conclude with a reject of Euro-American culture have never the object of serious scholarship. However, as Ebersole (2000: 6) also notes, the fact that abduction and captivity was a "fairly common occurrence" of frontier life, also reflected in the popularity of various compendia of such stories, underlines the relevance of this literature for a better understanding of culture and cultural exchange more generally. Pauline Strong therefore makes the cogent and important suggestion that both the politics and poetics, the history and literary features of such narratives need to be considered in tandem. Literary form, as in the case of Staden or Cabeza de Vaca, obviously relates to the purposes and reception of such accounts, while, as ethnographic description, the coding of eyewitness observation in these ways makes a comprehension of their characteristics vital if such materials are to be used as ethnohistorical or anthropological sources.

Both Cabeza de Vaca and Staden also allude to a variant form of captivity, that of the castaway, no less redolent of the perils of exotic adventure than the "savage" captivities they experienced. Both Staden and Cabeza de Vaca experience shipwreck as a prelude to their captivities, and the captivity itself is but one outcome that might have emerged from their being cast away by the sea. Central to the Euro-American imagination of such an experience is the literary classic *Robinson Crusoe* by Daniel Defoe. Notably, the firmly bourgeois sensibilities of Defoe's character utterly erase the sociality of the cannibal savage by supplanting the need for other people with technological fixes and instrumental ingenuity. But the social impossibility of such a situation is firmly represented by the intrusion of the cannibal (and nearly cannibalized) Man-Friday. As Lestringant (1997: 137–43) nicely expresses it, Robinson Crusoe has become the "exterminating angel" of civilization, slaughtering without question Friday's captors and promptly retraining Friday to a more acceptable diet. Defoe's work, inspired in part by the real-life tale of the "voluntary" castaway John Selkirk, marooned on an island off the coast of Chile, also reinscribed the imaginative creation of that isolated but persistent node of savagery, the cannibal island. Thus in later literary weavings of the cannibal tapestry we find Herman Melville's account of cannibal captivity, *Typee*, set in the Marquesas Islands, whose insularity is frequently invoked to explain the cultural geography of anthropophagy in the region.

In these ways, then, it is not just cannibalism but also captivity that underlies continuing fascination with Staden's account. The importance of captivity to the way in which colonial relationships were mediated is evident from the wider genre of captivity literature. But the enduring tragedy of colonialism's victims is that their captivity can never be ended, for the relationship is the product of, and historical possibility for, the condition of colonialism to exist at all, giving rise to the postcolonial dilemma of trying to construct nationality with the categories of the colonial conqueror.

Equally, to have been castaway[137] is a useful fiction for claiming territory since it does not require intent or evidence of colonial achievement in order to establish a physical priority and so a moral claim to possession. In turn the performance of such territoriality is an important ritual of colonial conquest—providing its moral and cultural grounding. In this way the elaborate "ceremonies of possession" in the New World (Seed 1995), as performed in differing ways by the various colonial powers, were very much in the spirit of those simple acts of possession, implicit through a mere physical presence, by a wide range of colonial actors who may have not known where they were, but knew they were there to take something, as with the archetype, Christopher Columbus.

Nonetheless, such ceremonies often rebound upon themselves for, as in the presentation of mirrors and hawk bells to the natives of Hispaniola by Columbus, these acts simultaneously imply a prior, native occupation. In this light gifts and exchanges of this kind are intended to nullify the other's status as indigenous. Brazilian cultural identification and preoccupation with Staden's *Warhaftige Historia* could be viewed in this way, as with other postcolonial nostalgic reinventions of the primitive. The uninhabited island, shorn of the complicating native presence, can become an imaginative zone of physical, and therefore moral, rectitude and is thus the perfect site for the erasure of possibly threatening social experimentation and cultural mutation. In Staden's case the nature of his captivity depends on how he has become a castaway—is he, as a German, to be identified with his Portuguese employers, or is he simply nonindigenous and so to be assimilated to the French, the allies of his captors? Captives, like castaways, can thus become the basis for territorial claims, but unlike castaways they are not mute, for through mere presence the castaway establishes a form of priority, while the actions of the captive can unravel putative claims based only on physical presence, precisely as evident in the ambiguities of "ceremonies of possession" mentioned before. A couple of examples from the Americas help illustrate this—during the conquest of Yucatan the Spanish encountered Maya armies led by a Spaniard, castaway on those shores some ten years previously, but in the Orinoco region the crew from the "lost ship of Ordaz" are reencountered a decade later when one of them appears in a Spanish coastal town to offer alliance with native groups.

In other colonial contexts the castaway as cultural captive might either be turned to advantage or could become the basis of a damaging challenge to colonial authority in a region. Being castaway can also be a source of social significance through a dangerous potential to remake the cultural order through the presentation and living instantiation of the exotic—and this is amply attested to through the literatures of travel and ethnography more generally. This is further borne out by the most dangerous possibility of all—that the castaway could never return—that he had, in the parlance of British colonialism, "gone bush" and become, in subjective identity as well as social status, forever castaway and foreign. Those in power might control the cultural meaning of exotic captivity as both a moral and physical condition but they could not control its meanings to those individuals who underwent such experiences. In the North American genre of captivity literatures the early colonial years are marked by redemptive texts similar to that of Staden, but as the complexity of colonial conquest and control increases so the focus is less on the moral condition of the captive and more on the moral dissolution of the captors. This transition reflects the dynamic nature of social and cultural boundaries as constantly in flux and effectively porous. As a result we begin to hear more frequently of the transculturation of the captives, a reluctance to return, a disenchantment with one's cultural home and so also a countersuspicion of those too long away. Fascination with the condition of the captive and castaway from Robinson Crusoe to the Robert Zemeckis film starring Tom Hanks, and so vividly in the case of the *Warhaftige Historia* itself, thus signals the uncertainty of existing categories of identity and territory, and in this way such figures become an always potent social site for the remaking of cultural worlds.

HANS STADEN'S—

The True History

and Description of

a Country Populated

by a Wild, Naked, and

Savage Man-munching

People, situated in the

New World, America . . .

Warhaftig

Historia vnd beschreibung eyner Landt=
schafft der Wilden/ Nacketen/ Grimmigen Menschfressen
Leuthen/ in der Newenwelt America gelegen/ vor vnd nach
Christi geburt im Land zü Hessen vnbekant/ biß vff dise ij.
nechst vergangene jar/ Da sie Hans Staden von Hom=
berg auß Hessen durch sein eygne erfarung erkant/
vnd yetzo durch den truck an tag gibt.

Dedicirt dem Durchleuchtigen Hochgebornen herrn/
H. Philipsen Landtgraff zü Hessen/ Graff zü Catzen=
elnbogen/ Dietz/ Ziegenhain vnd Nidda/ seinem G. H.

Mit eyner vorrede D. Joh. Dryandri/ genant Eychman/
Ordinarij Professoris Medici zü Marpurgk.

Inhalt des Büchlins volget nach den Vorreden.

Getruckt zü Marpurg/ im jar M. D. LVII.

The true history and description of a country populated by a wild, naked, and savage man-munching people, situated in the New World, America; unknown in Hesse, both before and after the birth of Christ, until two years ago when Hans Staden from Homberg in Hesse came to know of it through his own experiences, and now makes it known in print.

Dedicated to the Serene and Highborn Prince and Lord, Lord Philip, Landgrave of Hesse, Count of Catzenelnbogen, Dietz, Ziegenhain and Nidda, his Gracious Lord.

With a preface by D. Joh.[annes] Dryander, known as Eychmann [Eichmann], *Ordinarii Professoris Medici* [Full Professor of Medicine] at Marburg.

The table of contents for this little book follows after the prefaces.

Printed at Marburg in the year M.D.LVII. [1557]

Inhalt des Büchlins volget nach den Vorreden.

Getrudt zu Marpurg/ im jar M. D. LVII.

1 *Sete Katu*[1]

1. The words read "Sete Katu," which can be translated as "It is good"—see also the comments by Fouquet (1963: 190).

TO THE SERENE AND HIGHBORN PRINCE AND LORD,
LORD PHILIP, LANDGRAVE OF HESSE, COUNT OF
CATZENELNBOGEN, DIETZ, ZIEGENHAIN AND NIDDA ETC.,
MY GRACIOUS PRINCE AND MASTER.

Mercy and peace in Jesus Christ, our Savior.

Gracious Prince and Lord! In the hundred and seventh Psalm [107: 23–32] the holy King and Prophet David speaks:

Some went down to the sea in ships, doing business on the mighty waters; they saw the deeds of the LORD, his wondrous works in the deep. For he commanded and raised the stormy wind, which lifted up the waves of the sea. They mounted up to heaven, they went down to the depths; their courage melted away in their calamity; they reeled and staggered like drunkards, and were at their wits' end. Then they cried to the LORD in their trouble, and he brought them out from their distress; he made the storm be still, and the waves of the sea were hushed. Then they were glad because they had quiet, and he brought them to their desired haven. Let them thank the LORD for his steadfast love, for his wonderful works to humankind! Let them extol him in the congregation of the people, and praise him in the assembly of the elders.

Therefore I thank the Almighty Creator of the Heavens, the Earth, and the Sea, his Son Jesus Christ, and the Holy Ghost, for the great mercy and pity, wholly unexpectedly and marvelously shown to me by the Holy Trinity when I was captured in the land of Brazil by the savage people called Tuppin Imba [Tupinambás], who eat human flesh and kept me captive for nine months amidst many dangers. [I also thank God] that I now, after long, miserable risk to life and limb, and after several years, have once more returned to your Highness' principality, my most beloved fatherland. I should humbly relate to your Highness my travels and voyages, which I have described as briefly as possible. Thus, your Highness may, whenever it pleases you, have the story of how I with the help of God have traveled across land and sea, read aloud, [in order] to hear about the miraculous events that Almighty God granted to me in my distress. And, lest your Highness were to think that I tell tall tales, I personally offer your Highness a passport to support this report.[2] To God alone be the Glory. I commend myself to your Highness in all humility.

Dated at Wolfhagen, the twentieth of June, Anno Domini
[in the year of our Lord] Fifteen Hundred and Fifty-Six.
Your Highness's subject by birth,
Hans Staden of Homberg in Hesse,
presently citizen of Wolfhagen.

2. See chapter 52 and the concluding address at the end of Staden's account.

Hans Staden, who now commits this book and story to print, asked me whether I would first take a look at his work and written stories, correct them, and wherever necessary, improve them [before publication]. I have complied with his request for a number of reasons. Firstly, I have known the author's father (who was born and raised in the same town as I, namely, Wetter) for about fifty years, and I have always known him — both in his hometown, and in Homberg, in Hesse, where he now lives — as an upright, pious, and brave man, who is also versed in the liberal arts.[3] And since the proverb says that the apple always tastes of the tree, one can expect Hans Staden, the son of this honorable man, to resemble his father in virtue and piety.

Furthermore, I approach the labor of revising this book with all the more joy and satisfaction, because I gladly deal with matters that have to do with mathematics, such as cosmography — that is the description and measuring of countries, towns, and routes of travel — of which much will be presented in this book, in various ways. I happily delve into such matters when I sense that the events are related and disclosed in truth and honesty. I have no doubt that the aforementioned Hans Staden has thoroughly and conscientiously written and reported his story and travels from his own

3. Basic education of the seven liberal arts was the precondition for further studies at the university, *guten künsten*, although it was also used to describe the education immediately prior to studies at the university.

experience, and not from the accounts of others. He has no false cause and he is led neither by ambition nor worldly renown; on the contrary, he seeks only to praise the glory of God and express thankfulness for his salvation. His chief purpose in bringing this story to light of day is to enable everyone to see how mercifully God, our Lord, against all hope delivered this man, Hans Staden, from so many dangers, when he faithfully called upon Him, and restored him from the ferocity of the savage people to his beloved fatherland in Hesse. Every day and hour, for nine months, he expected to be killed without mercy and eaten.

He says that he very much wants to be thankful to the Lord for this unspeakable mercy, and make the blessings shown to him known to everyone, as far as his humble capabilities allow him, in order to praise God. Carrying out this good deed, the course of events caused him to relate all things that happened during his travels, in his 9 years abroad.

And since he relates this in a simple manner, without decorative or fancy words and arguments, this makes me believe that his intent is genuine and sincere. Also, he could never gain any advantage from lying instead of telling the truth.

In addition, he comes from this country, as do his parents, and he does not wander around from place to place like the gypsies, vagabonds, or liars. Hence, he would have to reckon with the possible arrival of other travelers who have been on the islands and could give him the lie [expose him as a liar].

A particularly strong piece of evidence that his intent and the descriptions in this story are sincere is that he states the time and place of his encounter in the country of the savages with Heliodorus, son of the learned and well-known Eoban of Hesse, who went abroad long ago to seek his fortune, and was thought by us to be dead.[4] According to Hans Staden, Heliodorus saw how he was pitifully captured and led away.

This same Heliodorus, I say, may return sooner or later—and everyone hopes that this will happen. If Hans Staden's story is false and fabricated, he will be able to put him to shame and denounce him as a worthless good-for-nothing.

4. Helius Eobanus Hessus (1488–1540), famous author of Latin poems, was professor of poetry and history at the university of Marburg from 1536 to his death. His son Heliodorus Hessus probably was born in 1527 and went to Sâo Vicente sometime before 1553, where he was responsible for a sugar plantation and sugar mill until his death in a battle against the French in 1568.

I will for now leave these weighty arguments and conjectures, which bolster and support Hans Staden's integrity, and briefly mention why it is that accounts of this type generally receive so little credit and applause.

First of all, vagabonds with their ludicrous lies and reports of false and imagined things have brought matters to such a pass that honest and upright people returning from foreign countries are now hardly ever believed and the saying goes: he who wants to lie should lie about things afar. For no one wants to go there, but prefers to believe what he hears rather than making the effort to experience it for himself.

Yet nothing is gained by mutilating the truth for the sake of lies. One has to note that many matters appear incredible to the ordinary man,[5] yet when they are presented to knowledgeable persons who assess them, they are found to be the known and proved facts that they really are.

This can be illustrated by one or 2 examples from astronomy. We who live in Germany or neighboring countries know by long-established experience the duration of winter and summer, as well as [the length] of the two other seasons, autumn and spring. Likewise, we know how long the longest and shortest days and nights in summer and winter last.

When it is then reported that there are places in this world where the sun does not set for half a year, and that among these people the longest day and the longest night each last six months or half a year; furthermore, that in certain places the quatuor tempora, that is, the four seasons, are duplicated, and two winters and two summers succeed each other in the course of the same year.

And likewise, that the sun and the stars, even the smallest star in the heavens, regardless how small they appear to us, are greater than the entire Earth, and are innumerable.

Now when the ordinary man hears such things, he utterly scorns them and considers them incredible and impossible. Yet these natural phenomena have been presented by astronomers in such a manner that the experts do not doubt them.

So, just because the crowd considers these things to be false, it does not follow that this is then the way it has to be. The science of astronomy would stand low indeed, if it could not demonstrate and show how the heavenly

5. The phrase *der gemeyne man* is repeatedly used by Dryander in the preface and also might be translated as "the man in the street" or "the common people."

bodies work, and on a firm basis foretell the solar and lunar eclipses to the very day and hour. These eclipses have, indeed, been foretold hundreds of years in advance, and experience has found these [predictions] to be correct. Well, some will say: Who has been in the sky and has observed and measured these things? The answer is: Because the day-to-day experiences concur with the demonstrations, one has to consider them just as certain as the fact that 2 and 3 make 5. Proceeding from the established facts and scientific demonstrations, one can measure and calculate how far it is to the moon up in the sky, and onwards to all planets, all the way to the stars in the sky;[6] yes, [one can] also [calculate] the diameter and size of the sun, the moon, and other heavenly bodies. With the aid of geometry and astronomy, that is the observation of the sky, one can even calculate the distance, circumference, breadth, and length of the Earth itself. Yet all these matters are hidden to the ordinary man and are considered to be impossible. The ignorance of the ordinary man is excusable, for he has not studied much *Philosophia*.[7] But it is both a shame and also dangerous that highly respected and very learned persons should doubt matters that have been established as being true, since the ordinary man looks up to them and thus has his delusions confirmed and says: If these things were true, so and so would not have disputed them. That means . . . and so forth.

The same applies to St. Augustine and Lactantius Firmianus,[8] the two holy scholars well versed in both theology and in the liberal arts. They doubt and refute the existence of the antipodes, that is humans, who stand at the other side of the earth, down below us, walking with their feet directed towards us, and their heads and bodies hanging down towards the skies, without falling off.

Though this sounds strange, the ruling opinion among the scholars is nonetheless that it is true and it cannot be otherwise, regardless of how vehemently the said holy and learned authors have denied it. For it has to be certain and true that those who live *ex diametro per centrum terræ* [at diametrical points from the center of earth] are Antipodes. It is *vera propositio*

6. Contemporaries, who propounded the theory of separate, celestial layers encapsulating the Earth, would probably have read the expressions "Mons hymel" and "die gestirnten hymel" as "the lunar sky" and "the stellar sky."
7. The sixteenth-century concept of "philosophy: was much broader than today and is comparable to the level and range of knowledge that is implied by the modern Bachelor of Arts degree.
8. Lucius Caelius Firminianus Lactantius (d. after 317), another of the Latin Church Fathers.

[a true proposition]. *Omne versus coelum vergens, ubicunque locorum, sursum est.* [Everything which points towards the sky is upright, wherever it may be located.]

Nor is it necessary to travel downwards unto the New World to seek the antipodes, for they are also here in the upper half of the globe. For if one calculates and compares the uttermost country of the West, namely, Cape Finisterre in Spain, with the East where India lies, these most distant peoples and inhabitants of earth are almost a kind of antipodes.

Certain pious theologians want to infer from this that the plea of the mother of the sons of Zebedee has been fulfilled. She entreated the Lord Jesus that one of her sons might sit at his right hand, and the other at his left. This, they say, has been fulfilled since S. Jacob [St. James] supposedly lies buried at Compostel [Santiago de Compostela], where he is held in honor, not far *a fine terræ* [from the end of the Earth], the place which is called the Dark Star [Finisterre]. The other apostle [St. John] rests in India towards the rising sun. The antipodes have, therefore, long been present, and although the New World of America had not been discovered on the lower hemisphere in the days of St. Augustine, the antipodes were nevertheless present in this manner. Other theologians, in particular Nicholas Lyra (who is otherwise regarded as an excellent man), have insisted that the globe swims half immersed in water. The one half that we inhabit projects above the waters, but the lower half beneath us is totally immersed in the water of the sea and is therefore uninhabitable.

But all of this is contrary to the science of *Cosmographia* and the many voyages of the Spaniards and the Portuguese have now shown it to be otherwise. The Earth is inhabited everywhere, even the Torrid Zone, for which our forefathers and all writers of old would not allow. Our daily spices, sugar, pearls, and similar commodities are brought to us from these countries. I have taken pains to explain this paradox of the antipodes and the measurement of the heavens in order to support my argument. There are many other matters that could be brought forward, if I wanted to bore you with my long writings.

Yet many similar arguments may be read in the book written by the worthy and learned Magister Casparus Goldtworm, your Highness's diligent superintendent and chaplain at Weilburg. The book is divided into six parts and treats miracles, wonders, and paradoxes of former and present times, and it is due to be printed shortly. I hereby refer the benevolent reader who desires further instruction and understanding to this work[9] and to many others dealing with such matters, such as his [book] *Libri Galeotti, de rebus vulgo incredibilibus* etc.[10]

This should suffice to prove the point that matters, which seem strange and unusual to the ordinary man, do not necessarily immediately have to be all lies. In this account, for instance, the people on the island all walk around naked; they have no domestic beasts for food, and none of the things, which are common to us for the sustenance of the body, such as clothes, beds, horses, pigs, or cows; not even wine or beer, etc. They have to maintain and help themselves in their own manner.

To bring this preface to an end, I will also briefly state the reasons that led Hans Staden to put [the account of] his two voyages and travels into print. Many might take affront of this [publication], thinking that the writer desired fame or wanted to make a great name for himself. I have heard otherwise from him and I am certain that his intent is very different, which can also here and there be inferred from the account.

For he has experienced such misery and suffered such adversity, which constantly placed his life in peril, and he had no hope that he would be freed and would return to his home. Yet God, in whom he always trusted and called upon, did not only release him from the hands of his enemies but was also moved by his faithful prayers to show the godless people that the righteous and true God was still ever-present, mighty, and powerful. It is well known that the faithful through their prayers should not set limitations on God concerning the goal, the bounds, or the time; but since it pleased God to work his wonders before the godless savages through Hans Staden, I would not be able to make any objection to it.

Everybody knows that in distress, grief, misfortune, and illness etc. people normally turn to God and that they in their distress more often call upon God. Some people have previously, in the papist manner, pledged to some saints to make a pilgrimage or sacrifice to attain help in their misery. Such vows were also held sternly, except for those who thought of deceiving

9. Caspar Goltwurm, *Wunderwerck und Wunderzeichen Buch . . .* [The Book of Wondrous Works and Signs . . .] (Franckfurt am Main: David Zephelius, 1557). Caspar Goltwurm (1524–59) was the author of a number of books for priests of the early protestant church (see Deneke 1974).

10. I.e., *The Books of Galeottus, of things that are normally said to be incredible, etc.*, probably by the astronomer Martius Galeottus from Narni in Umbria, is no longer extant.

the saints with their vows. In his *colloquiis* on the *Naufragio* [colloquy on shipwrecks], *Erasmus Roterodamus* [Erasmus of Rotterdam] writes of one person who cried out to S. Christophorum [St. Christopher], whose image is to be seen in Paris, standing some ten ells high like a great Polyphemus. He vowed that if this saint delivered him from distress, he would offer him a wax candle as tall as the saint himself.[11] Knowing of his poverty, his closest neighbor who sat next to him scolded him for this vow: even if he sold all his worldly goods, he still would not procure sufficient wax to make so great a candle. The other answered him, whispering lest the saint should hear him: Once he has delivered me from this distress, I will give him a tallow candle[12] worth a farthing at the most.

And the other story about the shipwreck of a knight is quite similar. When he saw that the ship was about to founder, this knight called upon S. Niclaus [St. Nicholas] and vowed that if he was saved from distress, he would offer him his horse or his page. His lad then reproached him and told him not to do this, and asked him how he would then ride. The knight then spoke to the lad in a low voice, so that the saint would not hear it: Keep quiet. If he helps me, I won't even give him the tail of my horse. Thus, both of these two men planned to deceive their saints and readily forget the favor given them.

Lest the said Hans Staden should also be taken for a man who, now that God has rescued him, is about to forget this boon, he has set upon himself to honor and praise God by way of this publication and description of his experiences. In Christian disposition, he makes the aid and mercy shown to him known wherever he can. His intention is both honorable and fitting—if this were not so, he would surely have spared himself this time-consuming effort and labor, and the considerable expense of printing this work and cutting the blocks [for the woodcuts].

This account has been humbly dedicated by the author to the Serene and Noble Prince and Lord, the Lord Philip, Landgrave of Hesse, Count of Catzenelnbogen, Dietz, Ziegenhain, and Nidda, his Prince and Gracious Master, in whose name it has been published. Furthermore, Hans Staden was questioned closely a long time ago, in my presence and in the presence of many others, by His Highness, our Gracious Lord, in all matters regard-

---

11. According to popular legend, St. Christopher was a giant.
12. Corrected in the *Errata* at the end of the book. Instead, it should read: "a simple candle."

ing his voyage and captivity, of which I have many times dutifully made report and account to Your Highness and other Lords. Taking this into consideration and having long known Your Highness to be a great lover of such and related matters of astronomy and cosmography, I have therefore dedicated my preface to Your Highness, begging that it may suffice until such time as I am able to publish something more worthy in Your Highness's name.

I subscribe myself to your Highness in all humility.

Dated at Marburg on St. Thomas' Day in the year M.D.LVI. [1556]

THE CONTENTS OF THE BOOK

1

Of the two sea voyages, which Hans Staden
undertook in nine and a half years.[13]
The first expedition to the New World, America,
left from Portugal; the second left from Spain.

2

How Hans Staden served as an arquebusier[14] in the country
of the savage people called the Toppinikin, who are subject
to the King of Portugal, fighting against the enemy.
How he was finally captured and carried off by the enemy, and
was under constant threat of being killed and devoured by them,
for nine and a half months.

3

Furthermore, how God after this year [among the savages]
delivered this captive in merciful and wonderful manner,
and how he returned home to his beloved fatherland.
All submitted to the print for the glory of God,
in gratitude for His gentle mercy.

13. Fouquet (1963, 1964) suggests this is a misprint and corrects it to "eight and a half years." However,
Hans Staden's original dating, even where apparently inaccurate, is preserved in this edition, and the
length of his journeys actually did span over nine years;- see CC note 6.
14. German "Büchsenschütze"; the arquebus was gradually being replaced by the more compact mus-
ket at this time.

What's the use of the night watchman in the town,
and the mighty ship navigating the seas,
if God does not protect them?

2 *Navigators and God's Providence*

In this landscape [map], I have reported the said harbors that I have partially seen in America; the degrees [in latitude] where the harbors lie; the names of the inhabitants; and the extent of their lands—all in a manner easily understood by the experts, and according to the best of my memory.

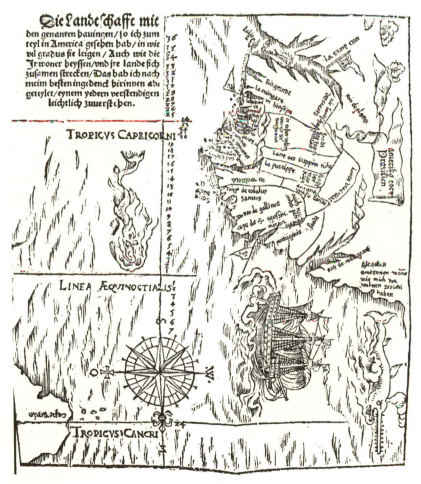

3 Map of Brazil

[I]

I, Hans Staden of Homberg in Hesse decided to go and see India, if God so pleased. With this intent, I traveled from Bremen to Holland. At Campen [Kampen], I found ships that wanted to load salt in Portugal. I then embarked, and on the 29th of April in the year 1547 we arrived at a town called Saint Tuval [Setúbal]. It took us four weeks at sea to get there. From there, I reached Lissabon [Lisbon], which lies five miles from St. Tuval. At Lissabon, I lodged at an inn owned by a man, who was called the young Leuhr and was a German. I stayed with him for some time. I told my host that I had left my fatherland and asked when I could sail for India. He said that I had stayed on too long. The King's ships bound for India had departed. As I had missed this travel, I asked him to help me to find another, since he knew the language. In return [for this], I said, I would owe him a favor.

He got me a position on a ship as an arquebusier. The captain of the ship was named Pintiado [Penteado] and wanted to travel to Brazil to trade. He also had permission to attack the ships that were trading with the White Moors in Barbary.[15] If he met French ships in Brazil trading with the savages, he could also seize them as prize. He also had to transport several pris-

---

15. Staden distinguishes between the "Black Moors" (as in the English racist term "blackamoor"), and the "White Moors" (often just "Moors") indicating people of Berber / Arab descent in northwest Africa and the Iberian peninsula, the former often being called "the Barbary Coast."

4 *Departure from Lisbon*

oners to this land [Brazil], who deserved punishment but had been spared
with the object of using them to settle the new lands.

Our ship was well-equipped with all armaments needed at sea. We were
three Germans on board, one called Hans von Bruchhausen, another named
Heinrich Brant of Bremen, and I.

CHAPTER 2

THE DEPARTURE FOR MY FIRST VOYAGE FROM
LISSABON IN PORTUGAL. CAPUT II.

We sailed from Lissabon with another small, little ship, which also belonged to our captain. We first arrived at the island called Eilga de Madera
[Madeira], which belongs to the King of Portugal and is inhabited by Portuguese. It is fruitful and produces wine and sugar. At a town there called
Funtschal [Funchal], we took in more provisions on our ship.

Then we sailed from the island towards Barbary, to a town called Cape de Gel [Cape Ghir in present-day Morocco], which belongs to a king of the White Moors, called Schiriffi.[16] This town formerly belonged to the King of Portugal, but this Schiriffi took it from him again. At this town we expected to find the above-mentioned ships that were trading with the infidel.

We arrived there and found many Castilian fishermen close to the shore. They informed us that there were ships near the town. As we were sailing in that direction, a vessel that was very well laden comes [sic] out of the harbor. We pursued this ship and captured it, but the crew escaped in the boat. We then spotted an empty boat lying on the shore, which would serve the captured ship well; [then] we sailed there and took it.

The White Moors rode down strong in numbers and wanted to defend it, but were not able to do so because of our guns. We took the boat, and sailed to the Eilga de Madera with our booty, which was sugar, almonds, dates, goat-skins, and Arabic gum. The ship was well laden with these goods. Since this [booty] partly belonged to Valencian and Castilian merchants, we dispatched our small ship to Lissabon to get orders from the King, regarding how we were to proceed with such booty.

The King replied that we should leave the booty on the islands and continue our voyage. In the meanwhile, His Altesa [Portuguese: Highness] would thoroughly examine the details of the matter.

We did as commanded, and returned to Cape de Gel to see if we could capture more booty. But our undertaking was in vain. A land wind turned against us and hindered us.

On the night before All Saints Day,[17] we sailed from Barbary for Brazil in a great storm. When we were about 400 miles from the coast of Barbary, many fish surrounded the ship. We caught them with fish hooks. Some of these, which the sailors called "albakore," were large; others, called "bonitte," were smaller, and others were called "durado."[18] There were also fish about as large as herrings, which had wings on either side, like a bat. They were closely pursued by the larger fish. When they sensed the others behind them, they lifted themselves out of the sea in vast numbers and flew

16. Though it formally refers to a descendant of the prophet Muhammad through his daughter Fatima, the term *sharif* is used as title of any of various Arab rulers, magistrates, or religious leaders.
17. All Hallows Eve on the 31st of October, the present-day Halloween.
18. Albacora (*Thunnus alalunga*); Bonito (*Sarda sarda*); Dourado: Dolphinfish (*Coryphaena hippurus*).

Within the illustration: *Capode celi*

Schariffi in Barbaria.

5 *The Battle with the White Moors*

some two fathoms above the water; several flew very far, almost as far as one could see. Then they dropped into the water. We often found them in the morning lying on the deck, where they had fallen at night while flying. In Portuguese, they are called "pisce bolador" [peixes voadores, literally, flying fishes]. Then we came level with the equinox. There it was very hot, for the sun stood right over our heads at noon. For days there was no wind. Great thunderstorms arrived at night with rain and wind and departed as quickly as they came. We had to keep a vigilant watch, lest they surprise us while we were under sail.

A wind now came which grew to a storm and lasted for several days, blowing against us. We began to fear starvation if it were to continue, and cried out to God for a favorable wind. Then it came to pass one night that we were in the midst of a great storm and in great danger. Blue lights began to appear before us in the ship, such as I had never seen before.

6 *A Storm with St. Elmo's Fire*

The waves struck in front of the ships, and then the lights disappeared. The Portuguese said that the lights were a sign of coming good weather and were sent by God Himself to comfort us in our distress. And as they thanked God with a collective prayer, the lights vanished again. These lights are called Santelmo, or Corpus santon.[19]

When day broke, the weather improved and a favorable wind arose. We now saw with our own eyes that these lights must have been a wonder worked by God.

We sailed through the sea with a good wind. On the 28th day of January, a hill came into view, near la Cape de Sanct Augustin [Santo Agostinho]. Eight miles farther on, we reached the harbor called Prannenbucke

19. The natural phenomenon known as *corpo santo* or St. Elmo's Fire, which many seamen viewed as a sign of the protection of St. Elmo (St. Erasmus, died c. 300 A.D.), an early Christian martyr and a patron saint of sailors.

[Pernambuco]. We were 84 days at sea before we sighted land. In this place the Portuguese had founded a settlement called Marin [Olinda]. The commander of the hamlet was named Artokoslio [Duarte Coelho]. We delivered our prisoners to him and unloaded some of our cargo, which they kept. We settled our business in the harbor and wanted to sail on, to take in cargo [elsewhere].

CHAPTER 3

HOW THE SAVAGES OF THE PLACE NAMED PRANNENBUCKE HAD BECOME REBELLIOUS AND STROVE TO EXTERMINATE THE PORTUGUESE IN THE SETTLEMENT. CAPUT III.

It so happened that the savages, who inhabit this place, had become rebellious against the Portuguese, which they had not done before. This happened because of the Portuguese. The commander of this region begged us, for the love of God, to occupy the settlement called Garasu [Igaraçu], five miles from the harbor of Marin where we lay. The savages wanted to capture the settlement, and the people from the settlement of Marin were unable to help the other settlers, for they also feared that the savages would fall upon them.

We came to help those in Garasu with forty men from our ship, traveling there in a small boat. The settlement was situated on the banks of an arm of the sea, which extends two miles inland. The defending force was made up by some ninety of us Christians, aided by thirty Moors, and Brazilian slaves belonging to the settlers. The savages besieging us were estimated to number about eight thousand. We, the besieged, only had a palisade of stakes surrounding us.

CHAPTER 4

THE LAYOUT OF THEIR FORTS, AND HOW THEY FOUGHT AGAINST US. CAPUT IIII.

The settlement in which we were besieged was surrounded by woods, where the savages had made two forts out of thick trees. There they sought refuge during the night, and when we attacked them, they took cover there. In addition, they had dug pits in the ground around the settlement; they stayed there during the day and only left them to skirmish with us. When we fired at them, they dropped into the pits and thought they could escape the shot. Indeed, they had laid such close siege to us that we could neither leave nor be relieved. They closed in on the settlement and fired many arrows into the air, wanting them to hit us in the settlement. They also used arrows bound with cotton and wax which they lit, hoping to set fire to the roofs of our houses, and they threatened to eat us, if and when they got hold of us.

We only had a few morsels left to eat, and these supplies soon ran out. For it was the custom of the land to fetch fresh [manioc] roots every day or every other day, to make flour or cakes out of them. We could not get to such roots.

Seeing that we were growing short on provisions, we traveled to a settlement called Tammaraka [Itamaracá] with two barques[20] to get more provisions there. But the savages had placed great trees across the narrow stream, and crowded both shores to prevent us from traveling. By use of force, we were able to break through these obstructions, but then the low tide came and we were stuck on dry land. The savages could not reach us in our ships, but from their rampart they threw down dry wood between the boats and the shore. They intended to set fire to this and to burn the pepper that grows in this country and thus chase us from our boats with the fumes. However, they did not succeed, and in the meantime the tide turned. We sailed to Tammaraka. The inhabitants there gave us fresh provisions. With these, we then sailed back to the besieged settlement.

Once again, they had blocked our path, at the very same spot. They had placed trees cleverly across the narrow stream, and were lying nearby along the shore. They had also cut through two trees at the trunk, almost felling them; at the tops, they had tied some things called Sippo, which grows like hops but is thicker.[21] They held the ends of the Sippo in their rampart, intending to pull them when we arrived and again tried to break through their barricade. The trees would then immediately break and fall down on our ship.

We sailed by and broke through: the first tree fell towards their camp and the other fell short behind our little ship, into the water.

Before we began to break through their barricade, we called to our com-

20. A barque is a sailing ship with three or more masts.
21. *Cipó*, Portuguese for liana, a plant with a creeping, more or less, woody stalk.

7 *The Defense of Iguaraçu*

panions in the settlement to come and help us. Once we began to shout, the savages also shouted, so that our companions in the settlement could not hear us. Even though we were close to them, they could not see us, due to a thicket between us. If the savages had not shouted, they would have heard us. We brought the provisions to the settlement, and when the savages saw that there was nothing they could do about it, they sought peace and withdrew. The siege lasted almost for a month. Several of the savages were dead, but we Christians had lost no one.

When we saw that the savages had departed in peace, we returned to our main ship at Marin and took in fresh water and manioc flour for provisions. The commander of the settlement of Marin thanked us.

8 *The Battle with the French at Buttugaris*

CHAPTER 5

HOW WE SAILED AWAY FROM PRANNENBUCKE TO A COUNTRY
CALLED BUTTUGARIS, AND ENCOUNTERED A FRENCH VESSEL
WITH WHICH WE BATTLED. CAPUT V.

We sailed for forty miles from there to a harbor called Buttugaris [Poti-guaras in Paraíba], where we meant to load a cargo of brazil wood and to raid the natives for more provisions. As we arrived there, we found a ship from France that was loading wood, and we attacked it, hoping to capture it. However, they destroyed our mainmast with one shot and sailed away; several on our ship were killed or wounded.

We then decided to set out once more for Portugal, for due to contrary winds we could not return to the harbor, where we had intended to get provisions. With unfavorable winds and very sparse supplies, we sailed to Portugal, suffering greatly from hunger; some ate the goat-skins that we had on board. Each day, they gave each of us a small scoop of water and a little [amount of] Brazilian roots-flour [manioc flour]. We were 108 days at sea. On the 12th of August, we arrived at the islands called Losa Sores [The Azores], that belong to the King of Portugal. There we anchored, rested, and fished. Here we saw a ship at sea, and sailed towards it to see what manner of ship it was. It was a pirate who defended himself, but we gained the upper hand and captured the ship. They [the pirates] escaped in the boats, sailing towards the islands. The ship contained lots of wine and bread, which refreshed us.

After this, we encountered five ships belonging to the King of Portugal. They were awaiting the ships from India, to escort them to Portugal. We remained with them, and helped to escort a ship arriving from India to the island of Tercera [Terceira], where we remained. A lot of ships, all of which had come from the New World, had assembled at the island, some bound for Spain, some for Portugal. We left Tercera in the company of almost a hundred ships, and arrived at Lissabon about the 8th of October, in the year 1548. We had been voyaging for sixteen months.

After this, I stayed in Lissabon for some time and decided to travel with the Spaniards to the new lands belonging to them. I therefore left Lissabon in an English ship bound for Castile and landed in a town called Porta Santa Maria [Puerta de Santa Maria], where they wanted to load the ship with wine. From there, I traveled to a town called Civilien [Seville] where I found three ships being refitted. They were bound for a country called Rio de Platta,[22] in America. Together with the land called Pirau [Peru], which is rich in gold and was discovered some years ago, and Brazil, this land forms one mainland.

Ships were sent there several years ago to conquer this country. One of them returned for further assistance. Many talked about the abundance of gold that is supposedly found there. The captain of these three ships was called Don Diego de Senabrie [Don Diege de Sanabria]. He was meant to be the King's commander in the country. I took hire on one of the ships, which were being very well equipped. We sailed from Civilien to

22. Rio de la Plata: The estuary formed by the convergence of the Paraná and Uruguay rivers, situated at the border between Argentina and Uruguay.

9 *The Passage from Seville to São Tomé, Guinea*

Saint Lucas, where the river from Civilien enters the sea [San Lucar at the mouth of the river Guadalquivir], and here we stayed, waiting for favorable winds.

CHAPTER 6

THE DEPARTURE FOR MY SECOND VOYAGE, FROM CIVILIEN IN SPAIN TO AMERICA. CA. 6.

On the 4th day after Easter in the year of our Lord 1549, we set sail from Saint Lucas. The wind blew against us and we entered the harbor at Lissabon. When the wind improved, we sailed for the islands Camarias [Canary Islands] and anchored close to an island called Pallama [Palma]. Here we took on some wine for the voyage. The navigators also agreed where to meet on the coast, in case the ships were separated at sea: twenty-eight degrees south of the equinoctial line. From Palma we sailed towards Cape Virde

[Cape Verde], that is the Green Head, which lies in the country of the Black Moors. There, we were nearly shipwrecked. From there, we traveled along our course. The wind blew against us and repeatedly blew us off course, carrying us to the land of Gene [Guinea], which is likewise inhabited by the Black Moors. Thereafter we arrived at an island called Saint Thome [São Tomé] which belongs to the King of Portugal. This island is rich in sugar, but unhealthy. Portuguese live there and have many Black Moors, who belong to them [who are their slaves]. We took in fresh water on the island and sailed straight away. During a storm in the night, we had lost sight of the two ships that accompanied us and therefore sailed on alone. The winds were very much against us, for in these seas they tend to blow from the south, whenever the sun is north of the equinoctial line. In the same way, when the sun is south of the line, the winds blow from the north. They tend to blow continuously from one direction for five months, and thus hindered our journey for four months, preventing us from following the right course. When the month of September came, the winds began to blow from the north, and we set our course south-south-west for America.

CHAPTER 7

HOW WE REACHED AMERICA AT XXVIII.
[28] DEGREES [SOUTH] WITHOUT FINDING THE
HARBOR TO WHICH WE HAD BEEN DIRECTED, AND HOW
A GREAT STORM AROSE OFF THE COAST. CAP. 7.

Then one day, on the 18th of November, when the navigator took measure of the sun's height and found that we were at twenty-eight degrees [south], we began to seek land towards the west. Later, on 24th of that same month, we sighted land.

We had been six months at sea and had often been in great danger. As we drew closer to land, we could neither discern the markings, nor the harbor to which the chief navigator had directed us. Since we could not risk entering an unknown harbor, we tacked along the coast. A great wind began to blow, and at every moment we expected to be dashed to pieces on the rocks. We bound empty casks together, filled them with powder, and stopped up the bung-holes, tying our weapons to them so that if we were shipwrecked, and any of the people onboard survived, they would find their weapons on

10 *Arrival in Brazil, near Shipwreck in Supraway*

land, for the waves would carry the barrels ashore. We tacked and tried to
draw away from the land, but in vain. The wind pushes [*sic*] us on to the
rocks, which lay hidden some 4 fathoms beneath the water. We had to sail
towards the shore because of the great waves, and we were certain that we
were all going to die. But God wills it otherwise, so that when we were
right next to the rocks, one of our men spotted a harbor. There, we entered.
In this place, we saw a small ship. It fled before us and sailed behind an
island, so that we could not see it and find out what manner of ship it was.
However, we did not follow it. Instead, we cast anchor, and praised God for
having saved us from this misery. We rested and dried our clothes.

When we cast anchor, it was probably about two hours after noon.
Towards evening, a big canoe filled with savages arrived by the ship. They
wanted to talk with us, but none of us could understand their language
properly. We gave them several knives and fishing hooks, and they then
departed. At night, a second big canoe full of savages came out, bringing

33

with them two Portuguese, who asked us where we came from. We then told them that we were from Spain. They then thought that we must have had a skilled navigator on board in order to make it to the harbor. For although they knew the harbor well, they would not have known how to enter it in a storm such as the one during which we had arrived. Then we told them everything: how the wind and the waves had wanted to bring us to shipwreck; how, being convinced that we were all going to die, we had suddenly spotted the harbor; and that against all hope, God had directed us to it, and had rescued us from shipwreck; and that we did not know where we were.

When they heard this, they marveled and praised God. They told us that the harbor we were in, was called Supraway [Superaguí], and that we were some eighteen miles from the island called Saint Vincente [São Vincente], which belongs to the King of Portugal. They lived there. The people in the small ship, which we had seen, had fled because they had thought that we were Frenchmen.

We also asked them how far it was to the island of Saint Catharina [Santa Catarina], for we wanted to go there. They told us, that it was some thirty miles away, to the south, and that there was a nation of savages called Carios [Carijós], of whom we should beware. They said that the savages of this present harbor were called Tuppin Ikins [Tupiniquins] and were their good friends, from whom we had nothing to fear.

We asked them at which latitude this land [the island Santa Catarina] lay? They said twenty-eight degrees, which is correct. They also gave us information on how we could recognize the country.

CHAPTER 8

HOW WE THEN SAILED OUT OF THE HARBOR AGAIN, TO SEEK
THE COUNTRY WHERE WE WANTED TO GO. CAPUT VIII.

When the east-south-east wind had dropped, the weather improved, and the wind blew from the northeast. We set sail and traveled back to the aforementioned place [Santa Catarina]. We sailed for two days seeking the harbor, but could not find it. But we could see by the lie of the land, that we must have sailed past the harbor. Since the sun had not been visible, we had not been able to take measure of it. However, we could not return due to the wind that was against us.

But God is an able helper in times of need. When we held the evening prayers, we had prayed to God for mercy. It so happened that before night-fall, clouds arose in the south, where the wind was driving us, and before the prayers had been completed, the north-east wind dropped and blew so softly that it could not be felt. Then the south wind arose, which generally does not prevail at this time of year, and brought with it such thunder and lightning, that we were struck with terror. The seas grew very rough, for the south wind met the waves of the northern winds. It also became so dark that one could not see anything. The crew grew fearful of the great thunder and lightning, and no one knew where he should give a hand in order to turn the sails. We were also convinced that we were all going to drown that night. Yet God let it so happen that the weather changed for the better. We sailed [back] to the place we had come from during the day, and looked for the harbor again. However, we could not find it, for there were many islands near the mainland.

As we now again arrived at 28 degrees [south], the captain then told the pilot to steer in among the islands and drop anchor, so that we could take a look and see what kind of land this was. We sailed in between two islands. There we found a beautiful harbor, where we anchored. We decided to send out a boat to explore the harbor more closely.

CHAPTER 9

HOW SEVERAL AMONG US SET OFF IN A BOAT TO INSPECT THE HARBOR, AND FOUND A CROSS STANDING ON A ROCK. CAP. IX.

It was on Saint Catherine's day in the year 1549 [should be: 1550] that we dropped anchor. On the same day, some of us departed in a boat, well armed, to explore the harbor. It seemed to us that it had to be [the mouth of] the river called Rio de Sancto Francisco [Rio São Fransisco], which is in this province. The farther we went, the longer the river seemed to be.

Every so often, we looked about us, to see if we could spot smoke, but we saw nothing. Then we thought we could see some huts in front of the wilderness in a valley, and we passed close by. They were old huts, and we

Acutia

Insulæ sanctæ Katrhia

11 *A Providential Arrival at Santa Catarina*

could not find any people in them. We went on. Then evening came, and a small island lay in the river in front of us. We sailed there to spend the night in this place, since we hoped to be best able to guard ourselves there. When we reached the island, night had already fallen, and we would normally not have dared to land and rest there for the night. However, several among us circuited the island to see if anybody was there, but we saw no one. Then we lit a fire and felled a palm-tree. We ate the pulp and spent the night there. Early in the morning, we sailed further into the land, for we were determined to know whether the country was inhabited. Having seen the old huts, we thought that there had to be people in the country. Now, as we were sailing on, we saw from afar a piece of wood standing on a rock. It looked like a cross. Several of us wondered who might have placed it there. We sailed by, and found it to be a great wooden cross fastened to the rock with stones. A piece from the bottom of a cask had been fastened to it, upon which letters had been cut, but we could not read the writing. We wondered what kinds of ships might have been here and set up such a thing. We did not know whether this was the harbor, where we were supposed to meet [the other two ships, cf. chapter 6].

After this, we again sailed forth to further explore the land, leaving the cross behind but taking the bottom of the cask with us. While we were thus traveling, one man sat down and studied the writing on the cask and began to understand it. The writing was cut in the Spanish language: *Si vehu por ventura ecky la armada de su Maiestet, Tiren vhn Tireaj Aueran Recado.*[23] In German this means: If any of his Majesty's ships should by chance come to this place, they should fire a cannon, and would then be further notified.

Then we quickly sailed back to the cross, fired a small falconet,[24] and began to sail further inland.

As we were thus sailing, we saw five canoes full of savages, who rowed straight towards us. We made our guns ready. As they now drew closer to us, we saw a person who wore clothes and had a beard, in one of the boats. He stood up in front of the canoe, and we saw that he was a Christian. We then shouted to him to make halt and come closer to us in one of the canoes, so that we could talk.

As he now came close, we asked of him in what country we were? He said: You are in the harbor called Schirmirein [Jurumirim] in the tongue of the savage people. And he said: To make you better understand, it is also named St. Catharin's harbor [Santa Catarina]. The one who found it first, named it so.

Then we rejoiced, for this was the harbor that we were seeking. We were there and did not know it, and we had even arrived on Saint Catherine's Day.[25] Here you hear how God helps and saves those that sincerely call upon Him in their distress.

He then asked us where we came from. We then told him that we were the King's ships from Spain, and that we wanted to go on to Rio de Platta

23. Si viene por ventura aquí la armada de su Majestad, tiren un tiro, ahí habrán recado.
24. The falconet was a light type of cannon.
25. St. Catherine of Alexandria, celebrated November 25. The timing of their arrival, and the near-shipwreck, are as much evidence of God's providence as his later delivery from the Tupinamba will be—but it is the singularity of that latter experience which makes it worth the telling in print.

[Rio de Plata]. Additional ships were on the way, and we hoped that, God willing, they would arrive shortly, for we had wanted to meet with them at this place. He then said that he was very pleased, and that he gave thanks to God, for he had been sent by sea three years ago from a place called La Soncion [Asunción], which belongs to Spain and lies 300 miles away in the province of Rio de Plata. He was to persuade the people called Carios [Cari-jós] (who are friendly to Spain) to plant manioc roots, so that ships arriving there could obtain provisions from the savages, if they needed any. These had been the orders given to him by the captain, who had returned to Spain with the latest news. This captain was called Captain Salaser [Salazar], and he returned again with the other ship [see chapters 11 and 12].

We now returned with him to the huts, where he lived among the savages. They were kind to us in their manners.

CHAPTER 10

HOW I WAS SENT WITH A BOAT FULL OF SAVAGES TO OUR GREAT SHIP. CAPUT X.

Our captain then asked the man whom we had found with the savages, to ask for a manned canoe that would carry one of us to our big ship, so that it could also come to this place.

Then the captain sent me with the savages to the ship. We had been away for three nights, and the people in the ship did not know what had happened to us.

As I, along with the canoe, now entered within crossbow distance of the ship, they set up a great cry and prepared to defend themselves. They would not allow me to approach with the canoe, but called out to me, asking what was happening? Where were the others? And how had it come to be that I was alone in a canoe full of savages? I was silent and did not reply, for the captain had ordered me to look sad, in order to see what the ship's crew would do.

As I did not reply, they shouted out to each other that something was wrong. The others must be dead, and they arrive with this one person and are perhaps planning to take the ship in an ambush. They wanted to shoot, but called to me once again. I then began to laugh and said: Don't worry. Good news. Let me approach, then I will tell you. Then I told them what the situation was, which made them very happy. The savages sailed back home with their canoe. We sailed with the big ship to the settlement of the savages and dropped anchor. There, we lay waiting for the other ships that we had lost in the storm, and which were supposed to arrive.

The village in which the savages live is called Acuttia [Cutia], and the man whom we found there was called Juan Ferdinando [Fernando], a Biscayan from the town Bilba [Bilbao]. The savages were called Carios [Cariós], and they brought us much game and fish. In return we gave them fishhooks.

CHAPTER II

HOW THE SECOND OF OUR SHIPS, WHICH WE HAD LOST AT SEA, ARRIVED, CARRYING THE CHIEF NAVIGATOR. CAP. XI.

After we had been there [at harbor of Santa Catarina] for about three weeks, the ship carrying the chief navigator arrived.

However, the third ship had been lost; we heard nothing more of it.

We immediately prepared to leave. For six months, we collected provisions, for we had a voyage of some 300 miles before us. Then one day, when everything was ready, the big ship sank in the harbor, so that the voyage could not be made.

We stayed there in the wilderness for two years, in great peril. We suffered great hunger and had to eat lizards, field-rats, and the other strange food that we could get, as well as mussels clinging to the rocks and similar strange foods. Most of the savages who had at first supplied us with food, left us and went to other places, once they had obtained enough goods from us. We could not wholly trust them. Hence, we did not want to stay there and die.

Therefore we agreed that most of us should travel overland to the place called Sumption [Asunción], some 300 miles away. The rest should sail there with the one remaining ship. The captain selected several of us to travel with him by water. Those who were to travel by land took along provisions for the journey through the wilderness and took several savages with them. But many of these [crew members] died of starvation. The rest arrived at the destination, as we learned afterwards. And as for the rest of us [remaining at St. Catarina], the ship was too small to carry us across the sea.

CHAPTER 12

HOW WE TOOK COUNSEL AND SAILED FOR SANCTE
VINCENTE, WHERE THE PORTUGUESE OWN THE LAND,
INTENDING TO HIRE ANOTHER SHIP FROM THEM TO
COMPLETE OUR VOYAGE; HOW WE SUFFERED SHIPWRECK
AT SEA IN A GREAT STORM, NOT KNOWING HOW FAR WE
WERE FROM SANCTE VINCENTE. CAP. XII.

Now the Portuguese have taken possession of an island close to the mainland called Sancto Vincente (in the savage tongue: Urbioneme) [São Vicente; Upaû-nema]. This province lies some seventy miles from the place, where we were. Thus, our intention was to sail there and find out if we could hire a ship from the Portuguese to Rio de Plata, for the ship we had was too small to carry all of us. Several among us sailed for the island of Sancte Vincente with Captain Salaser to inquire about this. None of us had ever been there before, except a man called Roman, who thought that he could find the place again.

We left from the harbor called Inbiassape [Imbeaçá-pe], 28,5 degrees south of the equinoctial line, and sailed about two days. Forty miles later, we arrived at an island called Insula de Alkatrases [Ilha dos Alcatrazes], where we had to anchor, because the wind was contrary. This island abounded with the sea-birds called Alkatrases [Albatrosses], which are easy to catch, since it was their nesting time. We landed there in search of fresh water and found some remains of old huts and fragments of pottery made by the savages, who had lived on the island a long time ago. We found a small source of water on top of a rock. There we killed many of the aforementioned birds and also brought their eggs to the ship, where we cooked these birds and eggs. Now having eaten, a great storm arose from the south, so that our anchors almost gave way, and we became very afraid that the wind would smash us against the rocks. By this time, it was already close to the evening. We thought that we could still reach the harbor of Caninee [Cananéia], but before we arrived there night fell, and we could not enter there. Instead we were sailing away from the coast in great peril. We were certain that the waves would beat back the ship, for we were close to the mainland where the waves are more furious than out in the middle of the deep sea, far away from land.

12 *Shipwreck off São Vicente (Upaunema)*

During the night, we had been driven so far from land that by morning we had lost sight of it. However, after a long time, we sighted land again. The storm was so great that we could scarcely keep afloat any longer. Seeing the coast, the man [named Roman] who had been in these lands more often, then said he thought it was Sancte Vincente. We sailed towards it, but then fog and clouds covered the land, so that it was difficult to keep it in sight. Because of the great waves, we had to throw all heavy things we had overboard into the sea, in order to lighten the ship. We were thus very afraid and sailed on, hoping to reach the harbor where the Portuguese live. But we were wrong.

When the clouds lifted a little, so that one could again see land, Roman said he thought that the harbor was now before us. If we steered towards a certain rock, the harbor would be behind it. We sailed closer to it, but as we arrived, we saw nothing but death before our eyes, for there was no harbor. Because of the wind, we had to head straight for the shore and suffer shipwreck. The waves beat so strongly upon the rocks that it was a horror to see. Then we prayed to God to have mercy on our souls, and did what is fitting for sailors about to be shipwrecked.

As we drew closer to the place where the waves beat against the shore, we sailed so high up on the waves that we looked directly down, as from a wall. The ship broke apart at the first impact with the land. Some jumped off and swam towards land; several of us came to shore hanging on to fragments of the ship. And so God helped all of us to reach land alive. It was raining and the wind was so strong, that we were completely stiff from the cold.

CHAPTER 13

HOW WE LEARNT WHAT COUNTRY OF THE SAVAGE PEOPLE WE HAD BEEN SHIPWRECKED IN. CAPUT XIII.

Having now safely landed, we thanked God that he had let us reach land alive, but we were nonetheless very depressed, because we did not know where we were. Roman did not recognize this country, and could tell us neither whether or not we were close to the island of Sancte Vincente, nor whether the place [that we were now in] was inhabited by savages, who might seek to hurt us. Then one of our companions, a Frenchman named Claudio who was running along the shore to warm himself, saw a village behind a thicket. The houses there were built in a Christian manner. He went there and found that it was a settlement called Itenge Ehm [Itanhaem], inhabited by Portuguese. It is two miles from Sancte Vincente. He then told them how we had been shipwrecked, and that the people were almost frozen stiff, and did not know what to do. They then came running and carried us to their houses, where they clothed us. We remained there some days until we had recovered.

From there, we traveled overland towards Sancte Vincente, where the Portuguese received us respectfully and for a while provided us with food and drink. Then each of us began working, in order to provide for himself. Seeing that we had lost all our ships, the captain sent out a Portuguese ship to fetch our companions, who had remained behind at Byasape [Imbea-pe]. They did actually manage to do that.

13 *Tupiniquin and Portuguese try to rescue Staden*

CHAPTER 14

WHERE SANCTE VINCENTE LIES. CAPUT XIIII.

Sancte Vincente is an island and lies close to the mainland. There are two settlements on the island: one is named Sancte Vincente in Portuguese but Orbioneme in the savage tongue [São Vicente; Upaû-nema]; the second settlement lies some two miles away and is called Ywawa supe [Enguaguaçú]. There are also several houses, called Ingenio [Engenhos], where sugar is made, on the island.

The Portuguese who live on the island are on friendly terms with a Brazilian nation called Tuppin Ikin [Tupiniquins]. Their country extends 80 miles inland and for about 40 miles along the coast.

This tribe is surrounded by enemies to the north and south. Those to the

43

south are called Carios [Carijós]; those to the north are named Tuppin Inba [Tupinambás]. They are also known by their enemies as Tawanar [Tabaiaras], which means enemy. The Portuguese have suffered much injury from these [enemy] peoples, and they still fear them, even today.

CHAPTER 15

THE NAME OF THE PLACE FROM WHERE THE ENEMY MOST STRONGLY PERSECUTED THEM, AND WHERE IT LIES. CAP. XV.

A place named Brikioka lies five miles from Sancte Vincente. The enemy savages gather here to sail between the mainland and an island called Sancto Maro [Santo Amaro].

Several Mameluke brothers were stationed at this point to prevent the savages from passing through. Their father was a Portuguese, and their mother a Brazilian woman, and they were Christian. They were skilled and experienced in both the Christian and the savage languages and manners of fighting. The eldest among them was named Johan de Praga [Braga]; the second, Diego de Praga; the third, Domingus de Praga; the fourth, Francisco de Praga; the fifth, Andreas de Praga; and the father was named Diego de Praga.

About two years before I arrived, these five brothers had begun working with the friendly savages to build a fort constructed in the savage manner, as protection against the enemy. They had also completed this work.

Several Portuguese had moved there to live with them, for there was fine land there. Their enemies, the Tuppin Imba, had noticed this and had prepared themselves for war in their own country, which is some 25 miles away. They had arrived there one night with 70 canoes and had attacked the settlement an hour before dawn, as they customarily do. The Mamelukes and the Portuguese had run into a house, which they had built of earth, where they defended themselves. The other [friendly] savages had crowded together in their huts and defended themselves as best they could. Hence many enemies were killed. In the end, however, the enemy prevailed and burnt the settlement of Brikioka [Bertioga]. They captured all the savages, but had not been able to do any harm to the Christians, numbering about 8, and the Mamelukes, for God decided to protect them. As for the friendly savages, which they [the enemy savages] had captured there, they immediately cut them to pieces and divided them up. Then they returned to their own lands.

CHAPTER 16

HOW THE PORTUGUESE REBUILT BRIKIOKA AND THEN CONSTRUCTED A BULWARK ON THE ISLAND OF SANCT MARO. CAPUT XVI.

It did not seem wise to the commanders and the community to abandon this place. They instead decided to rebuild it and make it much stronger, since the whole country could be defended from here. And they did so.

Now once the enemies observed that the small settlement of Brikioka was too strong to be attacked, they nonetheless sailed to the settlement during the night. They then captured whoever they could get hold of in the area surrounding Sancte Vincente, for those who lived inland thought that they were free of danger, now that this settlement had been founded and fortified, so close by. Therefore they suffered damages.

Then the inhabitants decided to build a house by the waterfront on the Island of Sancte Maro [Santo Amaro], which lies immediately opposite Brikioka, and furnish it with men and guns, to prevent the savages from passing by. They had then begun to set up a bulwark on the island, but had not completed it, because—as they told me—no Portuguese arquebusier dared to stay there.

I was there to inspect the area. When the inhabitants heard that I was a German with some knowledge of guns, they wanted me to stay in the house and help to look out for the enemy. They said they would provide me with some assistants and would pay me a good wage. They also said that if I would do this, I would receive favors from the King [of Portugal], who was particularly inclined to show himself as a merciful lord towards those who offered help and counsel in these new lands.

I then made an agreement with them to serve in the house for four months. After this time, a commander sent by the King was due to arrive with ships and build a stone blockhouse, which would then be stronger. This [construction of the blockhouse] was also done. I spent most of the time in the blockhouse with two others and some guns. We were in great danger because of the savages. The house was not strong, and we had to keep a vigilant watch lest the savages should slip past in the darkness. They tried to do so on several occasions, but God helped us to discover them during watch.

Several months later, the King's commander arrived. The people had written and told the King about the insolent attacks by the enemy that came from this direction, and had also told how fine a country it was, and that it would not be useful to abandon it. The commander named Tome de Susse [Tomé de Souza], arrived to improve matters, survey the country, and inspect those places which the community wanted to be fortified.

Then the community made a report to the officer concerning my services. They told him how I had taken up service in the [block] house, where no Portuguese would go, since it was so badly defended.

The officer was very pleased with this and promised to report my case before the King, if God brought him safely home to Portugal, and he told me that I would be rewarded. My period of service, namely, four months, was now over, and I handed in my resignation, but the commander and the people wanted me to remain in their service for some time longer. I consented and agreed to serve for another two years, on condition that when this time was over, they would then, without making any trouble, place me on the first ship heading for Portugal, in order to obtain the reward for my services. Then the commander gave me the privileges that are customarily bestowed on those among the King's arquebusiers, who demand it.[26] They constructed the bulwark of stone and placed several cannons in it. I was ordered to take charge of the bulwark and the cannons, and maintain a careful watch and supervision there.

CHAPTER 17

HOW, AND FOR WHAT REASONS, WE HAD TO EXPECT THE
ARRIVAL OF THE ENEMY MORE DURING ONE PARTICULAR
SEASON OF THE YEAR THAN DURING OTHERS. CAP. XVII.

We had to guard ourselves against them during two seasons of the year, when they plan to assault the enemy territory. The first of these two seasons

26. Such "privileges" were due to the pivotal role of arquebusiers in defeating armored knights. on European battlefields and the relative novelty of guns and their handling.

occurs in the month of November, when a certain fruit ripens, which they call Abbati in their language [Abatí]. They make a drink out of it called Kaa. wy. [Cauim]. They also have the root called Mandioka [manioc], which they add when the Abati is ripe, in order to make the drink. The Abati is ripe when they return from war. Then they have Abatis to produce their drink. If they have captured some of their enemies, they eat them together with this [Cauim] drink. All year long, they look forward to the beginning of the Abati-season.

We also had to be on guard in August when they follow a species of fish, which leaves the sea and enters the freshwater that flows into the sea, in order to spawn. This fish is called Bratti [Piratís] in their language, but the Spaniards call them Lysses [Liesses].[27] During this period, they [the enemy savages] also usually set out and fight, so that they can increase their food supplies. They catch a lot of these fish with very small nets and also shoot them with arrows. Then they bring many of them roasted back to their homes and make a flour out of them, which they call Pira Kui [Piracuí].

CHAPTER 18

HOW I WAS CAPTURED BY THE SAVAGES, AND THE
MANNER IN WHICH IT OCCURRED. CAP. XVIII.

I had a savage man from a group called Carios [Carijós]. He was my slave. He caught game for me, and I sometimes went along with him, into the forest.

However, after some time it so happened that a Spaniard from Sancte Vincente came to me in the bulwark where I lived, on the island of Sancte Maro that lies 5 miles away [from Bertioga]. A German called *Heliodorus Hessus*, son of the late *Eobanus Hessus*, also came along with him. He had been stationed on the island of Sancte Vincente in an Ingenio [Engenho] where they make sugar. This Ingenio belonged to a Genoese named Josepe Ornio [Giuseppe Adorno]. He was the clerk and manager of the merchants who belonged to the Ingenio. (The houses where sugar is made are called Ingenio.)

I had had dealings with this Heliodorus before. When I was shipwrecked

27. The "bratti" is the mullet or dogfish (*Mugilidae*).

14 *Staden is Captured*

with the Spaniards, I met him on the Island of Sancte Vincente, and he had
been friendly to me. He came to see how I was doing, for he had probably
heard that I was rumored to be ill. The day before, I had sent my slave into
the forest to hunt for game. I wanted to follow the next day to fetch the
catch, so we might have something to eat, for in that country there is little
to be had, except what comes out of the wilderness.

As I was walking through the forest, loud screaming—such as that made
by savages—sounded both sides of the path. People came running towards
me. Then I recognized them. They had surrounded me on all sides and were
pointing their bows and arrows at me and shot at me. Then I cried out: May
God now have mercy on my soul. I had scarcely uttered these words, when
they beat me to the ground, and shot and stabbed at me. God be praised
that they only wounded me in the leg. They tore the clothes from my body:

one the jerkin, another the hat, a third the shirt, and so forth. Then they began to quarrel over me. One said that he had gotten to me first, another protested that it was he who captured me. In the meanwhile, the rest hit me with their bows. Finally, two of them seized me and lifted me up from the ground, naked as I was. One of them grabbed one of my arms, another took the other one; several stayed behind me, while others were in front. Thus they carried me swiftly through the forest towards the sea, where they had their canoes. As they brought me to the sea, I saw the canoes about a stone's throw away. They had dragged them out of the water and hidden them behind the bushes. A great crowd was gathered next to them. As soon as they saw how I was being led there, they all rushed towards me. They were all decorated with feathers according to their custom, and they bit their arms, threatening me that they wanted to eat me in this way. A king walked in front of me, carrying the club with which they kill their captives. He preached and told them how they had captured me, their slave, the Perot (that is how they name the Portuguese). They would now avenge the deaths of their friends on me. And as they brought me to the canoes, several among them beat me with their fists. Then they hastily launched the canoes, for they feared that an alarm might be raised at Brikioka, as indeed happened.

Before launching the canoes into the water, they bound my hands together. They were not all from the same place, and since every *aldea* [settlement] disliked going home empty-handed, they began a dispute with those two holding me. Several said that they had all been just as near me when I was captured, and each of them demanded a piece of me and wanted to have me killed on the spot.

I stood there and prayed, looking around, awaiting the blow. But at last the king, who wanted to keep me, gave orders to carry me back alive, so that their women might see me alive and celebrate their feast with me. For they intended to kill me Kawewi Pepicke [cauim pepica]: that is, they wanted to make drinks and gather together for a feast where all of them would then eat me. With these words, they let it be and bound four ropes round my neck. I had to climb into a canoe while they were still standing on the ground, fastening the ends of the ropes to the canoes. Then they pushed them into the sea, to sail home.

CHAPTER 19

HOW THE SAVAGES WANTED TO BRING ME BACK;
HOW OUR PEOPLE ARRIVED, INTENDING TO RECAPTURE ME
FROM THEM; AND HOW THEY [THE SAVAGES] TURNED AROUND
TO SKIRMISH WITH THEM [OUR PEOPLE]. CAP. XIX.

There is another island close to the island where I was captured, where the water-birds with red feathers, named Uwara,[28] nest. The savages asked me whether their enemies, the Tuppin Ikins, had already been there that year to catch the birds and their young. I told them yes, but they nonetheless wanted to see for themselves, for they greatly value the feathers of these birds, since their adornment is mostly made from these feathers. When the Uwara birds are young, their first feathers are a whitish-gray. When they take flight, they turn a darker gray, and thus they are for about a year. Then the feathers turn red, as red as paint. The savages sailed to the island, hoping to find the birds there. When they were some two gun-shots away from the place, where they had left their canoes, they looked back and saw that it was full of Tuppin Ikin savages, along with several of the Portuguese. For a slave who had followed me, had escaped them when I was captured and had raised alarm, telling how they had taken me captive. Therefore, they wanted to rescue me and cried out to my captors that unless they were cowards, they should come back and fight with them.[29]

They turned their canoes about to face those on land, and the ones on land shot at us with guns and arrows. Those in the canoes shot back at them. They untied my hands, but the cord was still fastened to my neck.

Now the king of the canoe where I was placed, had a gun and a little powder, which a Frenchman had given him in exchange for some brazil wood. I had to shoot at those on land with it.

After they had skirmished for a while, my captors made off, fearing that

28. Guará, Scarlet Ibis. The family *Ibidae* inhabit both the New World and the Old. Numerous species are known. They are large, wading birds, having a long, curved beak, and feed largely on reptiles. The sacred Ibis of the ancient Egyptians (*Ibis aethiopica*) has the head and neck black, without feathers. The Scarlet Ibis (Guará rubra) and the White Ibis (Guará alba) inhabit the West Indies and South America, and are rarely found in the United States.

29. A comment printed in the margin to this passage in the German original [see Plate E (56)] states: "The content of this chapter is contained in the illustration of Chapter 14, above." The illustration is actually found in chapter 18.

those on shore might also get hold of canoes and pursue them. Three of them were shot. They passed the bulwarks at Brikioka at a distance about as far as a small falconet can shoot [the falconet is a light type of cannon]. I had been stationed there, and as we passed, I had to stand up in the canoe, so that my companions would see me. They fired two large guns from the bulwarks, but their shots fell short.

In the meantime, some canoes from Brikioka had set out in pursuit, hoping to catch up with us, but they [the captors] rowed too fast. When the friends saw that they would not make it, they headed back to Brikioka.

CHAPTER 20

WHAT HAPPENED DURING THE RETURN VOYAGE TO THEIR COUNTRY. CAP. 20.

When they had traveled about 7 miles from Brikioka towards their country, it was, judging by the sun, about 4 p.m., on the same day that they had captured me.

They passed by an island and ran the canoes ashore. They wanted to spend the night there, and carried me from the canoe to the land. When I came ashore, I could scarcely see, for I had been beaten in the face, and I could not walk properly either, because of the wounds in my leg. I had to lie down on the sand. Then they stood around me and threatened me, saying that they would eat me.

Being so full of fear and despair, I considered matters to which I had never given a thought before, namely, the vale of tears in which we lead our lives. Then I began to sing, with tearful eyes and from the bottom of my heart, the Psalm [130]: Out of the depths I cry to you, O LORD. Then the savages said: Look how he cries, now he is moaning.

Then it occurred to them that the island was probably not a suitable place to spend the night, and they returned to the mainland where there were huts, which they had built previously. When we arrived, it was night. The savages beached the canoes and lit a fire. Afterwards they brought me there. There I had to sleep in a net, which they call Inni [Ini] in their language. These nets are their beds. They fasten the net to two posts above the ground, or if they are in the forest, they tie them to two trees. They tied the cord around my neck high up in a tree, and they lay around me all night

15 *The Bound Animal*

and mocked me calling me: Schere inbau ende [Chê reimbaba indé], which in their language means: You are my bound animal [pet].

They left again before daybreak and paddled all day. By vespers [evening], we were two miles away from the place, where they intended to spend the night. Then great, black, terrible clouds arose and pursued us, and they rowed fast to reach land and escape the wind and clouds. Seeing that they could not escape them, they said to me: *Ne mungitta dee. Tuppan do Quabe, amanasu y an dee Imme Ranni me sis se*, [E mongetá nde Tupã ťokuabé amanasú jandé momaran eyma resé] which is to say:

Speak with your God so that we may escape the wind and rain. I kept silent and prayed to God, because they had asked me to do it, and said:

O Almighty God, You Lord of Heaven and Earth, who from the beginning has helped those that call upon You among the heathen. Demonstrate Your mercy to me so that I may know that You are still with me, and show

Ocarasu

16 *The Weather Shaman*

the savage heathens, who do not know You, that You, my God, have heard my prayer.

I lay bound in the canoe and could not observe the weather, but they constantly looked back and began to say: *Oqua moa amanasu* [Okuá amõ amanasú], which means: The great storm is moving away. Then I raised myself a little and saw that the great clouds were passing. Then I thanked God.

As we now came ashore, they did with me as before: they bound me to a tree, and lay around me in the night. They said that we were close to their country; we would arrive there in the evening of the following day. I was not very happy hearing about this.

53

CHAPTER 21

HOW THEY TREATED ME ON THE DAY WHEN THEY
BROUGHT ME TO THEIR DWELLINGS. CA. 21.

We caught sight of their dwellings on the same day. Judging by the sun, it was about vespers [the evening]. Thus, the journey home had taken us three days. The place to which I had been led was thirty miles away from Brikioka, where I had been captured.

When we came close to their dwellings, it turned out to be a small village with seven huts, called Uwattibi [Ubatuba]. We landed on a beach by the sea. Close by, their women had a field with the root vegetables, which they call Mandioka [manioc]. Many of their women were walking in the field, tearing up roots. I had to shout to them in their language: *A Junesche been ermi vramme* [*Aju ne xé peeÞ remiurama*], which means: I, your food, am coming.

As we now landed, all of them, both young and old, came running out of the huts, which were built on a hill, to look at me. The men went to their huts with their bows and arrows, and left me to their women. They led me along, some in front and some behind, dancing and singing a song—the song which they usually sing to their own people, when they want to eat them.

Then they brought me in front of the huts to the Ywara [Caiçara], which means to say, in front of their fortifications. They build their fortifications out of great, long sticks placed around their huts, just like a fence around a garden.

They build this for protection against their enemies. As I now entered, the females ran up to me and beat me with their fists, tearing my beard and saying in their speech: Sehe innamme pepike a e [Xe anama poepika aé], which is to say: With this blow, I take revenge on you for my friend, the one who was killed by those, among whom you have been.

Afterwards they took me into the huts, where I was forced to lie down in an Inni [hammock]. Then the women approached me and beat me and pulled at me, and threatened me by showing how they wanted to eat me.

The men were assembled in a hut by themselves, drinking a drink which they call Kawi [Caium]. They had their gods, called Tammerka [Maracá], among them. They sang in their honor, since they had accurately predicted to them that they were going to capture me.

I heard this singing. For half an hour, none of the men came to me, solely women and children.

CHAPTER 22

HOW MY TWO LORDS CAME TO ME AND TOLD ME THAT THEY HAD GIVEN ME TO ONE OF THEIR FRIENDS, WHO WAS FIRST TO KEEP ME AND THEN SLAY ME, WHEN THEY WANTED TO EAT ME. CAPUT XXII.

[Back then] I did not know their customs as well as I later on got to know them. I thought to myself: now they are preparing to kill you. After a short while, the brothers, named Jeppipo Wasu and Alkindar Miri [Nhaêpepô-oaçú and Alkindar-Miri], who had captured me, approached me and told me that they had given me to their father's brother, Ipperu Wasu [Ipirú-guaçú], out of friendship. He was to keep me and [then] kill me when they wanted to eat me; thus he would acquire another name through me.

The reason was that the said Ipperu Wasu had captured a slave a year before and had, out of friendship, presented him to Alkindar Miri, who had slain him and gained another name. Alkindar Miri had therefore promised to give Ipperu Wasu the first captive he caught. And I was that captive.

Both the aforementioned captors furthermore told me: the women are now going to lead you out to Aprasse [Poracé]. Back then, I did not understand this word but it means, to dance. Thus they again dragged me by the rope, which was still round my neck, out of the huts to the square [of the settlement]. All the women in the seven huts came and took hold of me, and the males went away. The women led me away, some by the arms, some by the rope round my neck, pulling it so tight that I could hardly breathe. While they were dragging me with them, I was unsure about what they wanted to do with me. I began to think about the suffering which our Savior Jesus Christ suffered innocently at the hands of the mean Jews. In this way, I comforted myself and was all the more patient. They then brought me to the hut of their king who was called Vratinge Wasu [Guaratinga-açú]; in German this means the Great White Bird. There was a small heap of fresh

17 *The Arrival at Uwattibi—Aprasse Dance*

earth in front of this hut. They brought me to it and placed me there, and several held me fast. I was certain that they would slay me there at once, and I began to look about for the Iwera Pemme [Ibera-pema], the club which they use to kill their captives. I asked whether they were going to kill me at once. They then answered: not yet. Then a woman from the crowd approached me. She had a sliver made out of crystal fastened to a thing that looked like a bent branch, and she scraped off my eyebrows with this crystal. She also wanted to scrape off the beard around my mouth, but I would not suffer this and said that she should kill me with my beard. Then they answered that they did not want to kill me yet and left me my beard. But a few days later, they cut it off with a pair of scissors, which the Frenchmen had given to them.

18 *The Dance with the Arasoya*

CHAPTER 23

HOW THEY DANCED WITH ME IN FRONT OF THE HUTS WHERE THEY KEPT THEIR IDOLS, THE TAMERKA. CA. 24.[30]

After this they carried me from the place where they had cut off my eye-brows, in front of the huts where their idols, the Tammerka, were kept. They formed a ring around me. I was in the center with two women next to me. They tied several things that rattled on a string, around my leg. They also bound a disk made out of bird tails arranged in a square, behind my neck, so that the bird tails stood up above my head. This ornament is called

30. Most of the chapters in the remainder of the first book are numbered incorrectly.

57

Arasoya [Araçoiá] in their language. Then the females all begin [*sic*] to sing together, and at the moment when they sang, I had to make a step with the leg to which they had tied the rattles, so that it rattled and was in tune with their song. My wounded leg was so painful that I nearly could not stand up, for they had not yet bandaged me.

CHAPTER 24

HOW THEY BROUGHT ME HOME TO IPPERU WASU AFTER THE DANCE, WHO WAS TO KILL ME. CAPUT XXIIII.

After the dance had now ended, I was handed over to Ipperu Wasu. There they kept me well guarded. He then told me that I still had some time to live. They brought all the idols they kept in their huts and set them up around me, saying that they [the idols] had prophesied that they [the savages] would capture a Portuguese. Then I said: These things have no power and cannot speak. They lie about me being a Portuguese. Rather, I belong to the friends of the French, and my native land is called Allemanien.[31] Then they said that it was I who lied, for if I was truly the Frenchmen's friend, what was I then doing among the Portuguese. They well knew that the French were as much the enemies of the Portuguese as they were, since the French came every year in their ships, and brought them knives, axes, mirrors, combs, and scissors. In exchange, they [the savages] gave them brazil wood, cotton, and other goods, such as feathers and pepper.

Therefore, they were their good friends. The Portuguese had not done so. For in past years, the Portuguese had come to this country, and in the area where they [the Portuguese] were still living, they had made friends with their [my captors'] enemies. Then they [the Portuguese] had come to their country and wanted to trade with them. They [my captors] had sailed to their [Portuguese] ships in good faith and gone aboard them, as they do today with the French ships. Then they told me that when the Portuguese had gathered enough of them on board, they had attacked and bound them, and carried them away to give them to their enemies, who had then killed and eaten them. They had shot several of them with their cannons. They also told of many other preposterous acts that the Portuguese had

31. I.e., the French word for Germany.

committed against them; they had also frequently arrived with their enemies and waged war to capture them.

CHAPTER 25

HOW THOSE WHO HAD CAPTURED ME MADE ANGRY COMPLAINTS THAT THE PORTUGUESE HAD SLAIN THEIR FATHER, WHICH THEY WANTED TO AVENGE ON ME. CAP. XXVI.

Furthermore, they said that the father of the two brothers, who had captured me, had had his arm shot off by the Portuguese, so that he had died.
They wanted to take revenge on me for their father's death. Then I asked
why they wanted to take revenge on me. I was no Portuguese, but had arrived a short while ago with the Castilians. We had suffered shipwreck and
had remained with them [the Portugese] for this reason.

Now there was a young lad from their people who had been a slave
among the Portuguese. The savages among whom the Portuguese live [the
Tupiniquins] had traveled to the land of the Tuppin Imba to wage war on
them and had captured a whole village and eaten the old people. They had
bartered off several of the young people in exchange for goods. Thus, this
young lad had also been bartered off to the Portuguese, and stayed in the
vicinity of Brikioka with his master, a Galician named Antonio Agudin.

Those who had captured me had captured this slave some three months
before me. Now since he belonged to their lineage, they had not killed him.
This slave knew me well, and they asked him what kind of man I was. He
said that it was true that a ship had run ashore, and that they had called
those who had got away [from the shipwreck alive], Castilians. They were
friends of the Portuguese. I had been among them, but he knew nothing
more about me.

As I now heard that there were Frenchmen among them who used to
arrive there in ships, and since I had also been told so earlier, I stuck to my
story and said that I belonged to the friends of the French, and that they
should keep me alive until the Frenchmen arrived and recognized me. And
they kept me in close confinement. Then several Frenchmen, who had been
dispatched from ships to collect pepper, arrived.

CHAPTER 26

HOW A FRENCHMAN DISPATCHED BY THE SHIPS TO
STAY AMONG THE SAVAGES, CAME TO SEE ME THERE AND
TOLD THEM THAT THEY SHOULD EAT ME, SAYING THAT
I WAS A PORTUGUESE. CAPUT XXVI.

Four miles away from the huts where I was, there was a Frenchman. As he now heard the news, he came and entered one of the huts opposite to the one in which I was kept. Then the savages came running to me and said: A Frenchman has now arrived here. Now we want to see whether you are a Frenchman or not. This made me very happy, and I thought: he is a Christian; he is probably going to put in a good word for me.

Then they took me to him, naked as I was. It was a young lad, and the savages called him Karwattuware [Caruatá-uára]. He addressed me in French, and I could not understand him well. The savages stood around and listened to us. Then, as I could not answer him, he spoke to the savages in their own language: Kill and eat him, the good-for-nothing. He is a real Portuguese, your enemy and mine. This I understood well. Therefore I begged him for God's sake, to tell them not to eat me. Then he said: They want to eat you. Then I remembered the saying in Jeremiah Chapter XVII [17:5] where he says: Cursed are those who trust in mere mortals. And with this I left them again, with a heavy heart. On my shoulders I had a piece of linen cloth, which they had given me (wherever they might have gotten it from) because the sun had burnt me severely. I tore this off and flung it at the Frenchman's feet, saying to myself: if I then have to die, why then should I preserve my flesh any longer for others? Then they led me back to the hut, where they kept me. Then I went to lie down in my net [hammock]. God knows the misery that I was in. Screaming, I began to sing the verse: We now implore the Holy Ghost / For the true faith, first and foremost, / That in our last moments He may protect us / when we journey homeward, away from this misery./ Kyrioleys [Lord, have mercy].[32]

---

32. The extended version of the hymn "We now implore God the Holy Ghost," *Nun bitten wir den Heiligen Geist*, composed by Martin Luther and published in 1524, is still among the more popular in the Lutheran liturgy. This version of the first stanza modifies the English interpretations from the nineteenth and twentieth centuries that are currently in liturgical use, in order to give a more accurate translation of the German original.

Then they said: He is a real Portuguese. Now he screams, he is afraid of death.

This Frenchman was there for two days in the huts. Then on the third day, he went away. They had decided to prepare things and wanted to kill me on the day when they had gotten everything ready. They guarded me very closely, and both the young and the old mocked me a lot.

CHAPTER 27

HOW I SUFFERED FROM A GREAT TOOTHACHE. CAPUT XXVII.

As the saying goes, troubles never come alone. It so happened during my misery that one of my teeth began to ache so badly that I was felled by the pain. Then my master asked me how it came to pass that I ate so little. I said: my tooth aches. Then he came with a thing made of wood and wanted to pull it out. I told him that it did not hurt me that much. He wanted to pull it out by force, but I resisted so much that he gave up. Well, he said, if I did not eat and gain weight, they would kill me before [the set] time. God knows how, if it be His divine will, I sometimes had a heartfelt wish to die, without the savages noticing it, so they could not work their will on me.

CHAPTER 28

HOW THEY LED ME TO THEIR HIGHEST KING CALLED KONYAN BEBE, AND HOW THEY DEALT WITH ME THERE. CAP. XXVIII.

Several days later, they took me to another village, which they call Arirab [Ariró], to their highest king who was called Konyan Bebe [Cunhambebe]. He was the most prominent king among them. Several others had assembled with him and they had made a great feast in their manner. He had ordered that I should be brought there on that day, for they also wanted to see me.

As I now arrived close to the huts, I heard a great noise from singing and the blowing of trumpets. In front of the huts, some fifteen heads had been set up on posts. These were the heads of the people, whom they had eaten. These are also their enemies, and are called the Markayas [Maracaiás]. As they were leading me past them, they also told me that the heads were from their enemies, who were called Markayas. Then I became afraid. I thought that they were also going to treat me the same way. As we were now entering the huts, one of those who guarded me went ahead and spoke in a loud voice, so that all the others would hear it: Here I bring the slave, the Portuguese. He thought it a fine thing to behold someone having his enemy in his power. He spoke of many other things, following their custom. He took me to the place, where the king sat and drank with the others. Together they became drunk on the drink that they make called Kawawy [Caium], and they all sent me grim looks, saying: Have you, our enemy, arrived?[33] And I replied: I have come to you, but I am not your enemy. Then they also gave me something to drink. Now I had heard a lot about this king called Konyan Bebe. He was supposed to be a great man, and also a great tyrant, who ate human flesh. There was one man among them, whom I took to be him. I went over to him and spoke to him, picking the words that they use in their language, saying: Are you Konyan Bebe? Are you still alive? Yes, he said, I am still alive. Now then, I said, I have heard much about you, that you are such a fierce man. Then he rose up and began to walk around me with great arrogance. He had a round, green stone thrust through his lips (as is their custom). They also make white paternoster [rosaries] from a kind of sea-shell, which they use for ornaments. This king wore about six cords of them around his neck. On the basis of this ornament, I understood that this had to be one of the most prominent persons.

The king then sat down again and began to question me as to what his enemies, the Tuppin Ikins and the Portuguese, were up to. He continued and asked why I had tried to shoot them near Brikioka, for he had learnt that I had been an arquebusier [firing] against them there. Then I said that the Portuguese had placed me there, and that I had had to do it. Then he said that I was also a Portuguese. He called the Frenchman who had seen me, his son, and said that this [French]man who had seen me, said that I had not been able to speak with him, and claimed that I was a real Portuguese. Then I said: Yes, it is true. I have been away from the land for a long time and have forgotten the language. Then he said that he had already helped to capture and eat five Portuguese who had all said they were Frenchmen, and had lied about this. This was so bad that I abandoned all hopes of life and commended myself to God, for everyone told me that I

33. An alternative translation would read the original as *Bistu [ge]kommen [als] unser feindt ?*, Have you come as our enemy?

19   *The Speech of Konyan Bebe to his Hopping Food*

was going to die. Then he began to question me again as to what the Portuguese said of him, for surely he must terrify them. Then I said: Yes, they
have a lot to say about you, about the big war you wage against them, but
now they have strengthened Brickioka. Yes, he said, then he would occasionally capture some of them in the forest, as he had caught me.

I then furthermore told him: Well, your true enemies the Tuppin Ikins,
they were preparing twenty-five canoes and will soon arrive and attack your
country. This did happen. While the king was questioning me in this manner, the others stood and listened. In short, he asked me a lot and told me
much. He bragged to me about how he had already slain a good number of
Portuguese, and many more of the other savages, who had been his enemies.
While he was speaking to me like that, all drink in the hut had in the meantime been drunk. They went on to another hut to continue drinking. Thus
he also ended his speeches. Afterwards they began to mock me in the other

hut. The son of the said king [Cunhambebe] tied my legs in three places, and I was then forced to hop through the hut with my feet pressed together. They laughed about it and said: here comes our food hopping along. Then I asked my master who had led me there, whether he had brought me there to kill me. He said no; it was customary to treat enemy slaves like this. They untied my legs again and then began to walk round me, grabbing at my flesh. One of them said that the skin on my head was his; another claimed that the thigh was his. After this I had to sing for them, and I sang spiritual songs [psalms]. Then I had to explain them in their language. Then I said: I have sung about my God. They said that my God was a piece of dirt, in their language this is called Teuire [teõuira]. These words hurt me and I thought: O Good God, sometimes You must suffer a lot. On the following day—when those from the village had now seen me and subjected me to all kinds of mockery—the king, Konyan Bebe, gave orders to those who guarded me, telling them that I was to be kept under close watch.

As they were leading me out of the hut and bringing me towards Uwattibi where they were to kill me, the people mocked me, yelling after me that they would soon come to my master's hut to drink upon my death and eat me. My master constantly comforted me, saying that I was not yet to be killed.

CHAPTER 29

HOW THE TUPPIN IKIN ARRIVED, AS I HAD TOLD
THE KING, WITH 25 CANOES, PLANNING TO ATTACK
THE HUTS WHERE I WAS KEPT. CA. 17.

In the meantime it so happened that one morning 25 canoes from the group of savages who are the allies of the Portuguese, attacked the village. Above, I have already told that they had decided to make war on this area, before I was captured.

Now when the Tuppin Ikins [Tupiniquins] decided to attack these huts and all began to shoot at us, those in the huts became very afraid and the females wanted to take flight. Then I said to them: You take me for a Portuguese, your enemy. Now, give me a bow and arrows and free me; then I will help you to defend the huts. They gave me a bow and arrows, and I shouted and shot my arrows and did things their way, as well as I could. I

64

20 *The Attack of the Tupiniquins*

spoke to them and told them that if only they were courageous, there would
be no trouble. My plan was to break through the stockade surrounding the
huts and run to the others, for they knew me well and also knew that I was
in the village. However, they guarded me far too well. As the Tuppin Ikins
now saw that they could not achieve anything, they returned to their canoes
and departed. As soon as they had departed, I was placed under surveillance
again.

CHAPTER 30

HOW THE CHIEFS ASSEMBLED DURING THE EVENING IN THE MOONLIGHT. CAP. 30.

On the same day when the others [the Tupiniquins] had departed, they [the
chiefs] assembled in the area between the huts. It was towards evening, and

21 *The Angry Moon*

the moon was shining. They deliberated amongst themselves and decided when they wanted to kill me. They placed me in their midst, and mocked and threatened me. I was depressed, and as I looked at the moon, I thought to myself: O my Lord and my God, help me out of this misery and bring it to a blessed end. Then they asked me why I was looking at the moon all the time. Then I told them: I can see that it is angry, for the shape that one can see on the moon seemed so terrible to me that I (God forgive me) myself thought that God and all creatures had to be angry at me.

(The prayer seen in this picture reads: *O mein Herr und Gott/ hilf mir dieses ellende/ zum helligen endt*, O my Lord and God, help me out of this misery to a bright [happy] end.)

Then the king called Jeppipo Wasu—one of the kings of the huts, the one who wanted to have me killed—asked me who the moon was angry at.

Then I said: It is looking towards your hut. He began to speak angrily with me because of these words. To change the meaning of what I had said, I told him: It will not be your hut. It is angry with the Carios slaves. (There is also a group of savages thus named.) Yes, he said, may all misfortune fall upon them. With this, he let it be; I did not think about it again.

CHAPTER 31

HOW THE TUPPIN IKINS HAD BURNT DOWN ANOTHER
VILLAGE CALLED MAMBUKABE. CAPUT XXXI.

The next day, news came from a village called Mambukabe [Mambucabe] that after the Tuppin Ikins [Tupiniquins] had departed from [the settlement] where I was a captive, they attacked the village of Mambukabe. The inhabitants had all escaped, except for a small boy, whom they had captured. Then they had burnt down the huts. Then this Jeppipo Wasu (who could do what he wanted to me and injured me a lot) went there, since they were the relatives of his friends. He wanted to help them rebuild their huts, so he brought along all the friends from his hut. He also wanted to bring back clay and root-flour to finish preparations for the feast and eat me. As he departed, he gave orders to Ipperu Wasu, to whom he had given me, that he should guard me closely. So they were away for more than fourteen days, [helping them with] rebuilding [the huts] there.

CHAPTER 32

HOW A SHIP ARRIVED FROM BRIKIOKA AND ASKED FOR ME, BUT
WAS ONLY GIVEN A BRIEF REPORT BY THEM. CAPUT XXXII.

In the meantime, a Portuguese ship arrived from Brikioka. It anchored not far from where I was and fired a cannon, so that savages would hear it and come to parley with them.

As soon as they heard this, they said to me: Here are your friends, the Portuguese. Perhaps they want to hear whether you are still alive; they might want to buy you. Then I said: This is going to be my brother, for I expected that the Portuguese ships, which passed by this part of the land, would ask them about me. In order not to make the savages think that I was a Portuguese, I told them that I had a brother among the Portuguese, who was also a Frenchman. Now as the ship arrived, I told them, that this was going to be my brother, but they were convinced that I was a Portuguese. They approached the ship close enough to parley with them. Then the Portuguese had asked [them] what had happened to me. Then they had replied that they should not ask for me any more. Then the ship sailed on, probably thinking that I was dead. God alone knows what I felt when I saw the ship depart. Amongst themselves, they said: We have the right man. They are already sending out ships to get him.

CHAPTER 33

HOW THE BROTHER OF KING JEPPIPO WASU RETURNED FROM MAMBUKABE AND TOLD ME ABOUT HIS TROUBLES: HOW HIS BROTHER, AND MOTHER, AND ALL THE OTHERS HAD FALLEN SICK; HE ENTREATED ME TO WORK OUT THINGS WITH MY GOD, SO THAT THEY WOULD BE CURED. CAP. XXXIIII.

Every day, I was expecting the return of the others, who, as stated above, were away and preparing for my death. Then one day, I heard screaming in the hut of the king who was away. I became afraid and thought they had returned (for it is the custom amongst the savages, for the friends of a person, who has not been away for more than four days, to scream with joy when he returns). Soon after the screaming, one of them came to me and said: the brother of one of your masters has come, and says that the others have grown very ill. I was happy and thought that now God is going to do something about it. Then after a short while, the brother of one of my masters came to the hut where I was kept, and sat down by me. He began to wail, saying that his brother, his mother, and his brother's children had all fallen sick. His brother had sent him to me, he said, to tell me that I should work out things with my God, so that they would be cured. He said: My brother is certain that your God must be angry. I told him: Yes, my God is angry with him for wanting to eat me, and for having gone to Mambukabe to prepare the feast. And I told him: You say I am a Portuguese, though I am not. And I told him: Go to your brother and tell him to come back to the huts. Then I would speak to my God and he would be restored to health. Then he said that his brother was too ill to come; he well knew and had observed that if I merely wished it to be so, his brother would also recover in that place. Then I told him that his brother would certainly recover enough to come home to his hut, where he would then be restored to full health. With this answer, he returned again to Mambukabe, which lies four miles from Uwattibi, where I was.

CHAPTER 34

IN WHAT MANNER THE AILING KING JEPPIPO WASU RETURNED HOME. CAPUT XXXV.

After several days, all of the sick persons came back together. Then was I taken to his [the king's] hut, and he told me how all of them had fallen ill. I had certainly known about it [in advance], he told me, for he well remembered that I had said that the moon was angry at his hut. When I heard him speak like that, I thought to myself that it had to have been Providence, which made me speak of the moon on that evening. I was very happy and thought: God is with me today.

I then furthermore told the king that it was true: this misfortune had befallen him because he had wanted to eat me, [though] I was not his enemy. He then said that if he recovered, no one would do me harm. I did not know how I should pray to God. I thought: If they recover, they would kill me, nonetheless; if they die, the others will say: Let us kill him, before greater misfortunes befall us because of him — [something] which they were indeed beginning to say. I left the matter to God. The king again pleaded with me to effect a cure for them. I walked around amongst them and laid my hands on their heads, which they beseeched me to do. But God did not want it to be so, and they began to die. First, one of their children died. Then his mother died, an old woman who [had] wanted to prepare the pots for the drink, for when I was to be eaten.

Some days later, one of his brothers died, and then again a child, and then another brother, the one who had first brought me the aforementioned news that they had fallen ill. When the king saw that his children, his mother, and his brothers were dead, he began to very much fear that he and his wives would also die. Then he told me to tell my God to end His wrath, so that he would stay alive. I gave him great comfort, telling him that he was not going to be in danger; however, once he recovered, he had to give up all thoughts of killing me. He then said he would not do so [eat

22 *Death and Curing*

me], and also ordered those in his hut to stop mocking me, and threatening to eat me.

Nonetheless, he remained sick for some time, but recovered; as did one of his wives who had [also] been sick. However, about eight of his friends died, along with others who had also badly mistreated me.

There were two kings in two other huts, one called Vratinge Wasu, the other Kenrimakui [Guaratinga-açú and Carimã-cuí]. Vratinge Wasu had dreamt that I had appeared before him and told him that he was going to die. Early in the morning, he came to me and complained to me about it. I told him that, no, there was not going to be any danger, but he also had to stop thinking about killing me, or advising others to do so. He then said, no [he would not hurt me]; since those, who had captured me did not kill me, he would not do me any harm, either. And if they would kill me, he would not eat of me.

The second king, Kenrimakui, had also had a dream about me, which greatly terrified him. He called me into his hut, gave me something to eat, and then complained to me about this [dream]. He said that he had once been at war and had captured a Portuguese, whom he had killed with his own hands. He had also eaten so much of him that his chest was still aching, and he did not want to eat anything, from anyone, anymore. Now he had dreamt about me, and his dream was so terrible that he thought he was about to die. I also told him that he was not in danger, but that he should not eat human flesh anymore.

The old women in various huts, who had done great harm to me, by beating and tearing at me, and threatening to eat me, now called me Scheraeire [Chê-raira], which means: my son. [They begged me:] Please do not let me die. We only treated you so, because we thought you were a Portuguese, whom we are very angry with. Besides, we have already captured and eaten many Portuguese, but their God never got as angry as yours. Thus, we now understand that you cannot be a Portuguese.

Hence, they then left me in peace for a while. Neither did they quite know what to do with me, nor whether I was a Portuguese or a Frenchman. They said that I had a red beard like the Frenchmen. They had also seen [bearded] Portuguese, but they normally all had black beards. After the terror [of the plague] and once one of my masters recovered, they did not talk to me about [possibly: using me as] food anymore. But they nevertheless guarded me closely and would not let me go about alone.

CHAPTER 35

HOW THE FRENCHMAN, WHO HAD TOLD THE
SAVAGES THAT THEY SHOULD EAT ME, RETURNED;
I ASKED HIM TO TAKE ME WITH HIM. BUT MY MASTERS
WOULD NOT LET ME LEAVE. CAP. 36.

I have already told about the Frenchman Karwattuware [Caruatá-uára], who left me and went together with the savages, who guided him and were the friends of the French, to collect pepper and a kind of feathers, which are the goods that the savages possess.

As he was now travelling to those parts of the land called Mungu Wappe and Iterroenne [Monguape and Niterói] where the ships arrive, he had to pass by the place where I was held captive. Now when he left me, he was certain that the savages would eat me, and he had also ordered them to do so. He had been away for some time and expected me to be dead.

As he now came into the hut to me, he spoke to me in the savage language. This time, I walked around freely. Then he asked me whether I was still alive, and I answered yes, [and said that] I thanked God that He had protected me for so long. He [the Frenchman, Caruatá-uára] might have been told what had happened by the savages. I drew him aside to a place where the savages could not hear what I said, and told him that God had spared my life for so long. I was no Portuguese; I was a German, who had suffered shipwreck with the Spaniards, and had therefore found myself amongst the Portuguese. He should now also tell the savages, as I had told him, that I belonged to his friends, and that he would take me along to the place where the ships arrived. For I feared that if he did not do so, the savages would think that all I had told them were lies, and when they sooner or later got angry, they would kill me.

And I rebuked him in the language of the savages. I asked whether he [in the moment] when he had advised the savages to kill me, had also had a Christian heart beating in his body, and whether he had considered that another life was to come after this one. Then he began to regret [his past actions] and said that he had been certain that I was a Portuguese, who were such nasty scoundrels that if they [the French] could only catch them anywhere in the province of Brazil, they would hang them at once. This is indeed so. He also said that they [the French] had to adapt to the [ways of the] savages and be content with their treatment of their enemies, since they were the traditional enemies of the Portuguese.

In accordance with my plea, he told the savages that at the first meeting he had not recognized me properly; but I was from Allemanien and was one of their friends. He wanted to take me to the place where the ships usually arrive. Then my masters said no, they would not hand me over to anyone, unless my own father or brothers came there and brought them a shipload of goods, and gave them these goods; namely, axes, mirrors, knives, combs, and scissors. They had captured me in enemy territory, and I belonged to them.

When the Frenchman heard this, he told me that, as I myself could understand, the savages would not let me go. Then I begged him, for the love of God, to send for me and take me back to France with the first ship that arrived. He promised me to do so, and told the savages to take care of me and not kill me, for my friends would soon come to collect me. And with this he departed.

Now after the Frenchman had left, one of my masters, named Alkindar Miri (not the one who was ill), asked me what Karwattuware (the name of the Frenchman in the language of the savages) had given me, and whether he was one of my countrymen. I said yes [he was a countryman]. Then he got angry and said: why did he not give you a knife, which you could have given to me? Later, when they had all recovered again [from the illness], they began to grumble, saying that the Frenchman were just as worthless as the Portuguese. This began to make me afraid again.

CHAPTER 36

HOW THEY ATE A CAPTIVE AND TOOK ME ALONG TO [THE FEAST] THERE. CAP. 37.

However, some days later, they wanted to eat a captive in a village called Tickquarippe [Ticoaripe] about six miles away from where I was kept captive. Thus, several [persons] from the huts where I was, set out, taking me along with them. The slave whom they wanted to eat, belonged to a nation called Marckaya [Maracaiás], and we traveled there in a canoe.

(When they are about to eat a human, it is their custom to make a drink from roots called Kawi [Caium], and after they have drunk this, they kill him.) Now when this moment came, I went up to the captive. It was on the eve of the day on which they were going to drink in preparation for his death, and I said to him: So, you are ready for your death. He laughed and said: Yes. (Now the rope with which they bind the captive is called Mussurana, and it is made of cotton, being thicker than a man's finger.) Yes, he thought that he was all well prepared, only the Mussurana was not long enough (for it lacked some six fathoms in length). Well, he said, his people had better ropes. And he spoke and acted as if he were going to the parish fair.

Now I had a book in the Portuguese language with me, which the savages had taken from a ship they had captured with the help of the French. They gave this book to me.

I left the captive, read in the book, and was consumed with pity for him.

Then I returned to him and talked with him (for the Portuguese are also friends with the group of Markaya) and said to him: I am also a captive just like you, and I have not come to eat you; on the contrary, my masters have brought me along. Then he said that he well knew that our people did not eat human flesh.

I further told him to be comforted, for they would only eat his body. His soul, however, would travel to another place, where the souls of our people also travel and there is much joy. Then he asked whether this was true. I told him: Yes. Well, he said, he had never seen God. I told him that he would see Him in the other life. Having now finished the conversation with him, I left him.

On the night of the day that I had talked with him, a high wind arrived and blew so terribly that it blew off parts of the roofs on the huts. Then the savages began to grow angry with me and said in their language: Apo Meiren geuppawy wittu wasu Immou. [Aipó mair angaipaba ybytu guasa omou.] The evil man, the saint, has made the wind come here now, for during the day he looked into his hides-of-thunder—by which they meant the book that I had. They said that I was doing this because the slave was a friend of the Portuguese, and perhaps I wanted to prevent the feast through bad weather. I prayed to God, the Lord, for they were very angry with me. I said: Lord, you have protected me until now, keep protecting me.

When day broke, it was fine weather, and they drank and were very content. Then I went to the slave and told him that the great wind had been God, who had wanted to take him. Then he was eaten on the following day. How this takes place, you will find described in the last chapters.[34]

CHAPTER 37

WHAT HAPPENED ON THE JOURNEY BACK,
AFTER THEY HAD EATEN HIM. CAP. 38.

After the feast had now been celebrated, we returned to our dwellings, and my masters brought some of the roast meat back with them. Normally, one could easily make the journey back in one day, but it took us three days because of strong winds and rainstorms. In the evening of the first day, as

34. See chapter 24 of the second book.

we were setting up huts in the woods to camp there, they told me to make the rain stop. Now there was a boy with us who still had a piece of the leg-bone of the slave with some flesh on it, which he was eating. I told the boy to throw it away. Then both he and the others grew angry with me, saying that this was their proper food. So I let it be. We traveled for three days.

When we got within a quarter of a mile from our dwellings, we could not proceed because of the big waves. We beached the canoe and decided that if the weather turned better on the next day, we would bring the canoe back home. But it remained just as stormy. Then they decided to walk across the land and come back for the canoe when the weather had improved. As we were about to depart, they were eating, and the boy continued gnawing the flesh off the bone. Then he threw it away, and we set out across the land. The weather then immediately improved. Well, I said, you did not want to believe me when I told you that my God was angry, because of the boy eating the flesh from the bone. Well, the others said, if he had eaten it out of your sight, then the weather would have stayed fine. The matter was left at that. As I returned to the hut, one of the men who owned a part of me, Alkindar, asked me whether I had now seen how they treated their enemies. Then I said: Yes, I think it is terrible that you eat them. Killing them is not so horrible. Well, he said, this is our custom, and we also do so with the Portuguese.

This Alkindar was very cruel towards me and would have liked the man, whom he offered me to, to kill me. For as you will have read above, Ipperu Wasu had given him a slave to kill, in order for him to gain another name.[35] In return, Alkindar had vowed to present him with the first enemy he caught. Although it would not be fitting for him to kill me, he would gladly have done so all the same. However, his brother always prevented him, because he was afraid of the subsequent plagues that might then befall him.

Before the others had taken me to the place where they ate the man, this Alkindar had renewed his threats to kill me. As I now returned, he had in the meanwhile, during my absence, suffered from eye trouble, and was [still] forced to lay still. For a time he could not see, and he continually told me to speak with my God so that his eyes would be all right again. Then

35. See chapter 22 of the second book.

I said yes, as long as he would stop harboring evil designs on me. He said no [he promised not to do so]. Then several days later, he was restored to health.

CHAPTER 38

HOW A SHIP WAS ONCE AGAIN SENT BY THE PORTUGUESE TO GET ME. CAP. 39.

It was my fifth month among the savages when another ship now arrives [sic] from the island of Sancto Vincente. Thus, it is the custom of the Portuguese from time to time to send well-armed ships into the country of their enemies, to trade with them. They give them knives and sickles in exchange for manioc flour, which the savages in several of these regions, have in great amounts. The Portuguese have many slaves to tend the sugarcane and they need the flour to feed these slaves. When the ships come to bargain in this manner, one or two savages row out in a canoe and hand over their goods as fast as they can. Then they demand what they want in return, which the Portuguese then give them. While those two savages are close to the ship, several canoes filled with them [with other savages] observe [the barter] at a distance. When the bargaining is over, the savages often draw closer and skirmish with the Portuguese, and shoot their arrows at them. Then they sail back.

The crew of the aforementioned ship fired a cannon, so that the savages could hear that a ship was there. The savages went there. Then they asked about me, whether I was still alive. They [the savages] answered: Yes. Then the Portuguese had wanted to see me, saying that they had a box full of goods brought by my brother, who was also a Frenchman and was on the ship with them.

Now there was a Frenchman along with the Portuguese in the ship, who was named Claudio Mirando and had been my mate. I declared this man to be my brother and said that he might be on the ship, asking for me, for he had already once made the voyage there.

The savages returned ashore from the ship. They told me that my brother had returned once more, bringing me a box of goods, and [said] that he would like to see me. Then I said: Bring me closer so that I can speak with my brother. The Portuguese will not understand what we say, and I will

23 *The Tupiniquin Trading with the Portuguese*

tell him that when he returns home, he should notify my father [and tell him] to come with a ship full of goods and take me away. They agreed to this, but were concerned that the Portuguese would understand us, for they planned to wage war during the month of August on the area around Brikioka, where I was captured. I knew all their plans well, and they were afraid that I would talk with them about this. But I said no, the Portuguese would not understand the language of me and my brother. Then they took me to within a stone's throw of the ship. I was always walking around with them without clothes. I spoke to those in the ship as naked as I was, and said: God, our Lord be with you, my dear brothers. Let one person speak to me alone and do not allow it to be heard that I am not a Frenchman. Then a man named Johann Senches, came forward, a Boschkeyer [Biscayan] whom I knew well. He said: My dear brother, we come with this ship for your sake and we did not know whether you were dead or alive, for the first ship did not bring any news of you. Now Captain Brascupas at Sanctus [Captain Braz Cubas at Santos] has ordered us to find out whether you were still alive, and if so—if we found you alive—then first of all to hear whether they want to sell you. If not, we are supposed to try and capture some of them, and exchange them for you.

Then I said: Now may God reward you in eternity, for I am in great fear and peril here, and I do know not what they might plan to do. They would already have eaten me, if not God Himself had prevented it. I furthermore told them: They will not sell me to you, so don't even think of this [bargain], and don't do anything which suggests that I am not a Frenchman. Give me, for the love of God, knives and fishhooks. They did this. One of them went to the ship and fetched them.

As I now saw that the savages would not allow me to speak any more with them, I told the Portuguese: Be aware, they are going to wage war on Brikioka again. Then they told me that their savages were also strongly preparing for war and would attack the very village where they kept me. I should keep up my spirits; God would make everything all right. But, as I could see, they were not able to help me [now]. Yes, I said, since my sins have deserved to be punished in this way, it is better that God punish me here, rather than in the life after death. Pray to God to help me out of the misery.

Then I commended them to God, our Lord. They wanted to speak further with me, but the savages would not permit me to speak with them any longer and took me back to the huts again.

Then I took the knives and fishhooks and gave these to them [my captors], saying: My brother, the Frenchman, gave me all of this. Then they asked me what it was that my brother had spoken to me about all this time. Then I said that I had told my brother to escape from the Portuguese, return to our fatherland, and bring a ship well stocked with goods [to give to them] and [then] collect me. For you are devout and treat me well, and I want to reward you when the ship comes. Thus, at all times I had to pretend that everything was fine, and they liked that very much.

Afterwards they said to themselves: He surely has to be a Frenchman, let us treat him better from now on. Thus, for some time I walked around telling them that a ship would soon come to get me, in order to ensure that

78

they treated me well. Now and then, they took me along in the forest and when they had something that needed to be done, I had to help them.

CHAPTER 39

HOW THEY KEPT A SLAVE, WHO ALWAYS LIED ABOUT ME, AND WHO WOULD HAVE LIKED TO SEE THEM KILL ME. THIS PERSON WAS KILLED AND EATEN IN MY PRESENCE. CAP. XL.

Now there was a slave among them who belonged to a nation called Carios [Carijós], a people who [like my captors] were also enemies of those savages who were the friends of the Portuguese. This man had belonged to the Portuguese, and had then escaped from them. They [my captors' tribe] do not kill those [slaves] who escape to them, unless they commit some particular crime. Instead, they keep them as their own slaves who have to serve them.

This Carios had been among these Tuppin Inba [Tupinambás] for three years. He said that he had seen me among the Portuguese, shooting at the Tuppin Inba on several occasions when they had come to wage war there.

Now some years ago, the Portuguese had shot one of their kings. This Carios said that I had shot this king. He constantly urged them to kill me, saying that, as he himself had seen, I was their true enemy. But these were all lies, for he had already been among them for three years, and only a year had passed since I had reached Sancto Vincente, the place that he had escaped from. And I constantly prayed God to protect me from these lies.

Then it came to pass that in the sixth month of my captivity, sometime during the year 1554, this Cario falls ill [sic]. The master who owned him asked me to help him, so that he would get well again and would [be able to] catch game and we could get something to eat. For I knew well, he said, that whenever he [the slave] brought him something, he also gave me a part of it. But if it seemed to me that he would not recover, then he would give him to a good friend of his, so that he could slay him and gain a name for himself.

Now he had already been ill for about nine or ten days. They [the Tupinambás] have teeth from an animal that they call Backe.[36] They sharpen

36. Tupi—*paca*, a game animal of the rodent family (*Coelogenus paca*).

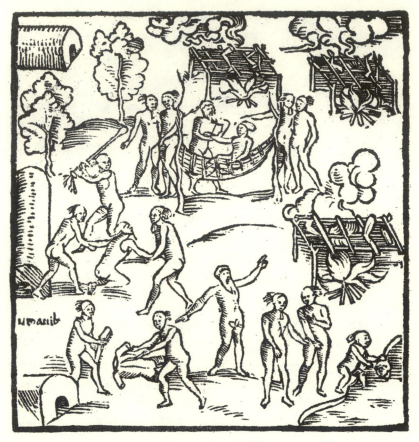

24 *The Death of the Carijó Slave*

this tooth, and when the blood is sluggish they cut the skin there with one of these teeth, so that the blood flows out. This is the same as when we bleed someone.

I took one of these teeth, intending to open the median vein. However, I could not cut it through, since the tooth was too blunt. The savages stood around me. As I left him, I saw that it was useless [to attempt to bleed him]. They asked me whether he would recover, and I told them that I had not been able to accomplish anything; as they had seen, no blood had flown. Yes, they said, he is going to die. We want to slay him before he dies.

I said: No, don't do it, he might recover. But it did not help. They dragged him in front of the hut belonging to the king Vratinge [Guaratinga]. Two of them held him, for he was so ill that he did not know what they were going to do with him. Then the man, to whom he had been given to kill, came over. He hit him on the head so that the brains spilled out. Then they left him lying in front of the huts and wanted to eat him. I told them that they should not do it. He had been a sick man, and they might also fall ill. Therefore, they could not agree on what to do. However, one man came out of the hut where I was staying, and shouted to the women to make a fire beside the dead slave. Then he cut off the head, for the slave had had only one eye, and looked terrible due to his disease, so he threw away the head. He singed the skin off [the slave's body] at the fire. After this, he cut him up and divided the flesh equally with the others, as they usually do. They ate all of him, except for the head and the intestines, which they loathed because he had been ill.

Afterwards, as I then went through the huts, I saw them roasting the feet in one of them, the hands in another hut, and a piece of his body in the third. Then I told them how this Cario whom they were roasting and wanted to eat, had always lied about me, saying that I had shot several of their friends while I was among the Portuguese, and that had been a lie, for he had never seen me before. Now, as you well know that he has been several years with you and never grew sick. But now my God has become angry with him because of the lies he fabricated about me, and He made him sick and made you decide to kill and eat him. My God will do the same to all evil persons, who have done or will do me evil. Many of them were terrified at my words. I thanked God for having been so mighty and merciful towards me throughout all of this. I therefore ask the reader to pay attention to what I write. For I do not take the trouble to write because I want to write something [which is] novel, but only to bring the blessings that God gave me to the light of day.

Then the time now approached when they wanted to wage the war that they had prepared for during the past three months. I constantly hoped that they would leave me at home with the women, when they departed. I wanted to escape while they were away.

CHAPTER 40

HOW A FRENCH SHIP ARRIVED TO TRADE WITH THE SAVAGES FOR COTTON AND BRAZIL WOOD; I WOULD HAVE LIKED TO BE ON THIS SHIP, BUT GOD DID NOT WANT IT TO BE SO. CAPUT XLI.

Some eight days before the savages planned to set out for war, a French ship had arrived in a harbor, which the Portuguese call Rio de ienero [Rio de Janeiro] and which is called Iteronne [Niterói] in the language of the savages. There, the French usually load brazil wood. Thus, they now also arrived with their boat at the village where I was kept, and bargained with the savages for pepper, long-tailed monkeys, and parrots. One of the crew came ashore from the boat. He was called Jacob and knew the language of the savages. While he was trading with them, I begged him to bring me along to his ship. However, my master said that no, they would not send me there like that. Rather, they wanted to have many goods [as a ransom] for me. Then I told them to bring me to the ship themselves; my friends would give them plenty of goods. They said no, these are not your real friends.

For those who have arrived with the boat would surely have given you a shirt, since you walk around naked; but they do not care about you at all (which was true). Yet, I told them that they would clothe me when I reached the big ship. They said that the ship would not depart right away; they first had to go to war, but when they returned, they would take me there. Now the boat [with the French traders] then wanted to travel on, because it had already anchored for one night at the village.

Now when I saw that they wanted to sail off again with the boat, I thought: O merciful God, if the ship now also sails away without taking me along, I am surely going to die among them [the savages], for this is a people one cannot trust.

With these thoughts [in mind], I left the hut, going towards the water, but the savages saw me and came after me. I ran in front of them, and they wanted to catch me. The first man that caught up with me, I struck down. The whole village was running after me, but I escaped them and swam to the boat. When I tried to climb into the boat, the Frenchmen pushed me away, for they thought that if they took me along without the consent of the savages, these might rise against them and become their enemies. De-

25 The Maria Ballete refuses Staden [page 99]

pressed, I swam back to the shore and thought: now I see that it is God's will that I should [*sic*] remain in misery for some time. If I had not tried to escape, then I should have blamed myself afterwards.

As I now returned to shore, they rejoiced and said: Look at that, he is coming back. Then I got angry with them and said: Do you think that I wanted to run away from you like that? I went to the boat to tell my people that they should prepare themselves. Thus, they will have gathered a lot of goods to give you when you return from war and bring me here [to the ships again]. This pleased them and they were once again content.

CHAPTER 41

HOW THE SAVAGES WENT TO WAR AND TOOK ME ALONG, AND
WHAT HAPPENED DURING THE EXPEDITION. CAPUT XLI.

Four days later, several canoes began to assemble at the village where I
stayed, to go to war. Then the chief king, Konyan Bebe [Cunhambebe], also
arrived [there] with his own canoes. Then my master said that he wanted to
take me along. I told him to leave me at home, and he would probably have
done so. However, Konyan Bebe told him to take me along. All this time, I
pretended to go along unwillingly, so that they would not think that I was
going to run away when they reached the enemy country. They would have
thought so, if I had gone along willingly. I hoped that they would guard me
less closely. I had also decided to run away to the French ship, if they had
left me at home [in the village].

However, they took me along. They numbered 38 canoes, and each
canoe carried 18 men, more or less. Using their idols, several of them had
foretold the outcome of the war by dreams and the other [kinds of] foolery
that they use. Thus, they all felt confident about the matter. Their intention
was to travel to the area around Brikioka where they had captured me, and
to hide in different places in the forest near the settlement. They would then
[capture and] bring back those who fell into their hands in this manner.

When we commenced this war expedition, it was about the 14th of August, in the year 1554. As I have already mentioned, this month usually witnesses the passage of a species of fish, which is called Doynges in Portuguese
[Taínhas], Liesses in Spanish [Liesses], and Bratti [Piratís] in the language
of the savages.[37] They leave the ocean for the fresh waters in order to spawn
there, and the savages call this season Pirakaen [Piracema]. When this happens, all savages, both they and their enemies, usually go to war in order to
catch and eat the fish while they are sailing. On the journey out, they travel
slowly, but on the journey back, they travel as fast as they can.

All the while, I hoped that the friends of the Portuguese would also be on
their way, for the Portuguese in the ship had previously told me that these
people planned to attack the others in their lands.

While travelling, they constantly asked me whether I thought that they

37. The mullet or dogfish (*Mugilidae*).

26 *Meyen Bipe War Camp*

would capture anyone. To avoid making them angry, I said yes. I also told them that the enemy would engage us. Thus, one night we lay at the place called Uwattibi where we caught many of the fish called Bratti [Piratís], which are as large as a good-sized pike. That night, the wind blew mightily and they chattered away and wanted to ask me many questions. Then I said: this wind blows over many dead people. Now another party [of Tupinambás] had also set out by water and had entered the lands on a river called Paraibe [Paraíbe]. Well, they said, they have probably already attacked enemy territory, so that several of them are dead. (I later heard that this had actually happened.) When we were a day's travel from the place they planned to attack, they made camp in the woods close to an island, which is named Sancte Sebastian by the Portuguese, but is called Meyenbipe by the savages [São Sebastião; Maembipe].

85

27 *The Pursuit of the Tupiniquins from Brikioka*

Towards evening, the chief called Konyan Bebe walked through the camp. He preached and said that they were now close to enemy territory. Each man was to take note of the dreams that he had that night, and they were all to see to it that they were going to dream something fortunate. When his speech was over, they danced with their idols until far into the night; then they slept. As my master laid down to sleep, he told me to dream about something pleasant. I said: I don't take heed of any dreams, they are false. Well, he said, you should nonetheless work out things with your God, so that we capture enemies.

At daybreak, the chiefs gathered round a bowl full of boiled fish and while they ate them they recounted their dreams, in so far as they were pleased with them. Several of them danced with their idols. Their decision was to travel closer to enemy territory that day, to a place called Boywassu kange [Boiçucanga], where they would wait until the evening.

As we were now leaving the place called Meyenbipe, where we had spent the night, they once more asked what I thought about it. Then I wished them good luck, saying: the enemy will meet us near Boywassu Kange, but be brave. I planned to run away from them when we arrived there, for it was only six miles away from the place where they had captured me.

As we were now travelling along the coast, we saw a number of canoes approaching us from behind an island. Then they [my captors] called out: Here come our enemies, the Tuppin Ikins. But they wanted to hide themselves and their canoes behind a rock, so that the others would pass without noticing them. They [the Tupiniquins] nonetheless became aware of us and fled back towards their homes. We rowed after them as fast as we could, for about four full hours, until we caught up with them.

They were five, fully manned canoes. They all came from Brikioka, and I knew all of them. In one of the five canoes, there were six Mamelukes who had been baptized. Among them were two brothers, one called Diego de Praga, the other, Domingus de Praga. They both defended themselves stoutly, one with a gun, the other with a bow. These two in their canoe held out strongly against our canoes, numbering about thirty men, for all of two hours. But when they had shot off all their arrows, the Tupin Inba attacked and captured them; some were slain or shot immediately. The two brothers were not wounded, but two of the six Mamelukes were very badly wounded, as were also several of the Tuppin Ikin, among them also a woman.

CHAPTER 42

HOW THEY TREATED THE CAPTIVES ON
THE RETURN JOURNEY. CAP. XLIII.

The place where they were captured was two full miles away from land, out on the sea. They hurried back towards the land as fast as they could, in order to camp once again [at the place] where we had camped the night before. When we reached the land [called] Meyen bibe [Maembipe] it was evening and the sun was setting. Then each man took his captive into his hut; those who were gravely injured, however, they took ashore and killed immediately. They cut them up according to their custom and roasted the flesh. Among those who were roasted that night were two Mamelukes who were

28 *The Treatment of Captives at Meyen Bibe*

Christians: one was a Portuguese named George Ferrero [Jorge Ferreira], the son of a captain who had fathered him with native woman.

The other was called Hieronymus [Jerônimo]. He had been captured by a savage who was from the hut where I stayed and was named Parwaa [Para-guá]. This savage spent the night roasting Hieronymus, about a step away from the place where I lay. This same Hieronymus (God rest his soul) was a blood relation of Diego de Praga.

That night, after they [the savages] had now camped, I went into the huts where they kept the two brothers. I wanted to talk with them, for they were good friends of mine from Brikioka, where I was captured. They asked me whether they were also going to be eaten. I told them that they had to trust in our Heavenly Father and in His dear Son Jesus Christ, who was cru-cified for our sins, and in whose name we have been baptized in His death.

I believe in Him, I said, and He has also protected me for so long among them [the savages]. We have to be content with the things that Almighty God decides to do to us.

The two brothers furthermore asked me how their cousin Hieronymus was doing. I told them that he lay by the fire roasting, and that I had already seen them eat a piece of Ferrero's son [the other Mameluke]. Then they wept and I comforted them, saying that they well knew that I had now been about eight months among them [the savages], and God protected me. He is also going to do that with you; trust in Him. Then I continued to say that, properly speaking, this ought to affect me more than them: I come from foreign lands and am not accustomed to the dreadful acts of these people. You have always been here, in these lands; you have been born and raised here. Well, they said, I had been so hardened by misery that I did not take notice of it anymore.

As I was talking to them like that, the savages told me to leave them and go to my hut, asking me why I was having such a long talk with them. I was sorry that I had to leave them, and I told them to put all their trust in the will of God; now, they ought to be able to see what kind of [great] suffering we have in this vale of sorrows. They replied that they had never experienced this as clearly as now, adding that they had to die once for God; now they would die all the more happily, since I was with them. With this, I left their hut and passed through the whole camp, visiting the captives. Thus, I walked around alone and no one took notice of me, and I could probably have escaped on this occasion, for the island called Meyenbipe was only some ten miles from Brikioka. However, I refrained on account of the Christian captives, of whom four were still alive. For I thought: if I escape, the savages will get angry and will kill them very soon. Maybe God will meanwhile preserve us all. I decided to remain with them and comfort them, which I did. All the same, the savages were very favorably disposed towards me, since I had predicted that they have luck when the enemy would encounter us. Since it had now turned out to be true, they said that I was a better prophet than their Maraka.[38]

38. See also chapter 23 in the second book.

29 *The Dance with the Captives at Occarasu*

CHAPTER 43

HOW THEY DANCED WITH THEIR ENEMIES ON THE
NEXT DAY WHILE WE WERE CAMPING. CAP. 44.

On the next day, we reached a big mountain called Occarasu [Ocaraçú], not far from their country. They camped at this place to spend the night there. Then I went to the hut of the chief king (called Konian bebe) and asked what he wanted to do with the Mamelukes. He said that they were to be eaten and forbade me to speak with them, for he was very angry with them: they should have stayed at home, instead of joining his enemies to wage war on him. I told him to spare their lives and sell them back again to their friends. He [repeated himself and] said that they were going to be eaten.

This same Konyan Bebe had a great basket full of human flesh in front of him. He was eating a leg and held it to my mouth, asking whether I also wanted to eat. I said [to him]: a senseless animal hardly ever eats its fellow; should one human then eat another? He took a bite, saying: Jau ware sche [Jauára ichê]. I am a tiger [jaguar]; it tastes well. With that, I left him.

That same evening, he gave orders that each man should bring his captive to an open place by the water, in front of the woods. This was done. They gathered together and formed a large circle, with the captives standing in the center. The captives were all forced to sing and rattle with the idols Tammaraka [Maracás]. Once they had sung, the captives began to speak provocatively, one after the other saying: Well, like brave people we set out to capture you, our enemies, and to eat you. Now you have gotten the upper hand and have captured us, but we do not care about that. Brave people who are fit to fight die in enemy territory. And our land is also big: our people will avenge our deaths on you. Well, the others said, you have already finished off many of our people. We want to take revenge on you for this.

Once these speeches had ended, each took his captive back to his lodgings.

Then on the third day, we arrived in their country. Each man brought back his captive to his home. Those from the village of Uwattibi, where I was staying, had captured eight, five savages, and three Christian Mamelukes: namely, Diego and his brother, and another Christian called Andonio [Antônio]. The latter had been captured by my master's son. They brought two other Christian Mamelukes back roasted, to eat them there. The journey back and forth had taken us eleven days.

CHAPTER 44

HOW THE FRENCH SHIP TO WHICH THEY (AS STATED ABOVE) HAD PROMISED TO BRING ME WAS STILL THERE ONCE THEY RETURNED FROM THE WAR ETC. CAP. XLV.

When we had returned home, I now asked them to take me to the French ship, saying that I had now gone to war together with them and had helped them to capture their enemies. This now ought to show them that I was not a Portuguese.

They said that yes, they would take me there, but first they wanted to rest and eat the Mokaen [Moquém], the roasted flesh of the two Christians.

CHAPTER 45

HOW THEY ATE THE FIRST OF THE ROASTED CHRISTIANS, GEORGE FERRERO, THE PORTUGUESE CAPTAIN'S SON. CAP. 46.

Now there was a king who ruled a nearby hut, opposite to my hut. He was called Tatamiri [Tatámiri]. He had one of the roasted Christians and had drinks made according to their custom. Many of them gathered, drinking, singing, and making merry. The next day, after the drinking, they reheated the roasted flesh and ate it. But the flesh of the other one, Hieronymus, hung in the hut where I was, in a basket above the fire, in the smoke for about three weeks until it was as dry as wood. The reason why it hung above the fire for so long without being eaten was that the savage called Parwaa [Paraguá], to whom it belonged, had gone off to another place. He went there to gather the roots necessary to make the drink that was to be served when the flesh of Hieronymus was eaten. Thus time passed by. They would not take me to the ship until they had feasted on Hieronymus' flesh. In the meantime, the French ship had departed. It had been anchored about eight miles from the place where I was.

When I heard this news, I became depressed, but the savages told me that they [the French] usually came back there every year. They told me to content myself with this.

CHAPTER 46

HOW ALMIGHTY GOD SENT A SIGN. CAPUT XLVII.

I had made a cross out of sticks and set it up in front of the hut where I stayed. I often said my prayers to the Lord by this cross, and I had ordered the savages not to remove it, lest some misfortune should befall them; but they did not pay heed to my words. Once while I was away fishing with them, a woman tore up the cross and gave it to her husband. Since the sticks were rounded, she told him that he could use them for rubbing down the

30 *Weather Shamanism and The Cross*

shells of sea snails which they use to make a kind of rosary. This made me very angry.

Soon after, it began to rain heavily, a rain which lasted for several days. They came to my hut and asked me to make my God stop the rain, for if it did not stop, it would spoil their planting season that had begun. I told them that it was their own fault. They had angered my God by removing the wooden stick, for I used to speak with my God at this piece of wood. Since they now thought this to be the cause of the rain, they helped me erect another cross for the Son of my Lord. Judging by the sun, it was about an hour after noon. As soon as the cross had been set up, the weather began to improve at once. Before mid-day, it had been very stormy. They all marveled and thought that my God did what I wanted Him to do.

31 *Weather Shamanism and The Fish*

CHAPTER 47

HOW GOD WORKED A WONDER WITH ME DURING
A RAINSTORM ONE EVENING, WHEN I WAS OUT
FISHING WITH TWO SAVAGES. CAP. XLVIII.

I was standing with one of the most prominent among them called Parwaa,
the one who had roasted Hieronymus. And as I stood fishing with him and
another man at the close of day, a great rain and thunderstorm arose. It
began to rain not far from where we stood, and the wind blew the rain in
our direction. Then the two savages begged me to speak with my God, so
that the rain would not hinder us and we might catch more fish. For, they
said, as I could see, we had nothing to eat in the hut. These words moved

me and I prayed to the Lord from the bottom of my heart, to use me to demonstrate His power, since the savages desired this from me.

Make them realize how you, my God, are with me at all times. Right after I had finished my prayer, the wind comes [*sic*] soaring with the rain, and it rained some six feet away from us, but on the place where we stood, we felt nothing. Hence, the savage Parwaa said: Now I see that you have indeed prayed to your God. And we did catch a number of fish.

Now as we returned to the hut, both of them told the other savages that such things had happened when I spoke to my God. This amazed the others.

CHAPTER 48

HOW THEY ATE THE SECOND ROASTED CHRISTIAN CALLED HIERONYMUS. CAPUT XLIX.

When the savage Parwaa had gathered all the necessary things together, [which he had set out to gather] as mentioned above, he had the drink made that was to be served with the flesh of Hieronymus. While they were drinking this, they brought the two brothers to me along with another man named Anthonius [Antônio], who had been captured by my master's son. Thus, we were four Christians sitting together. We were forced to drink with them but before we drank, we prayed to God to have mercy on the soul [of Jerônimo] and also on our [souls], when our hour would come. The savages chattered away with us and were merry, but we expected great misery. The next day, early in the morning, they boiled the flesh again and ate it; they devoured all of it right away. The same day, they took me away to present me as a gift. Now as I was parting from the two brothers, they begged me to pray to God for them. I gave them the directions that they should take in the mountains, in case they could escape, so that they [the savages] would not be able to follow their tracks—for I knew my way in the mountains. They also did as I had told them, for, as I later heard, they had escaped and run away. However, I do not yet know whether they were recaptured.

CHAPTER 49

HOW THEY TOOK ME OFF TO BE GIVEN AWAY. CAPUT 50.

The savages led me to a place called Tackwara sutibi [Taquaraçú-tiba] where they wanted to give me away. When we were at some distance from the shore, I looked back towards the huts and there was a black cloud hanging over the huts. I pointed the cloud out to them and told them that my God was angry with the village for having eaten Christian flesh, etc. Once they had taken me there [to Taquaraçú-tiba], they handed me over to a king called Abbati Bossange [Abatí-poçanga]. They told him that he should not burden me or allow others to do so, for my God was very vengeful towards those who hurt me. This they had seen while I was still with them. And I also admonished them, saying that my brother and friends would arrive shortly with a ship full of goods. If only they took care of me, I would give them the goods. I knew for certain that my God would soon bring my brother's ship. This pleased them. The king called me his son, and I went hunting with his sons.

CHAPTER 50

HOW THE SAVAGES OF THIS PLACE TOLD ME
ABOUT THE DEPARTURE OF THE ABOVE-MENTIONED
SHIP FROM FRANCE. CAP. 51.

They told me how the above-mentioned ship, the *Maria Bellete* from Depen [Dieppe in France] that I would have liked to be on, had taken in a full cargo of brazil wood, pepper, cotton, feathers, long-tailed monkeys, par-rots, and other similar things that cannot be found there [in France]. Then they had captured a Portuguese ship in the harbor of Rio de Jenero [Rio de Janeiro], and had given a Portuguese to a savage king called ItaWu [Itavú], who had eaten him. The Frenchman who after I had been captured had told the savages to eat me, was also onboard this ship and wanted to go home. It was this ship, which I had tried to reach, when I made my escape, and where they would not take me as I reached their boat. This ship sank on the voyage home. When I then reached France in another ship, no one had heard what had happened to it. I will tell of this presently.

CHAPTER 51

HOW ANOTHER SHIP ARRIVED FROM FRANCE SHORTLY
AFTER I HAD BEEN GIVEN AWAY, THE KATHERINA
DE VATTAVILLA [CATHERINE DE VATTEVILLE], WHICH,
THROUGH GOD'S PROVIDENCE, BOUGHT ME FREE;
AND HOW THIS HAPPENED. CAP. 52.

I remained some fourteen days in the settlement Tackwara sutibi with King Abbati Bossange. One day it so happened that several of the savages came to me and told me that they had heard shooting. It must have come from the harbor of Iteronne which is also called Rio de Jenero [Niterói; Rio de Janeiro]. As I now heard with such certainty that a ship was there, I told them to bring me there, for this might be my brother's ship. They said yes, but nonetheless held me back for another couple of days.

In the meanwhile, it so happened that the Frenchmen, who had arrived there, had heard that I was [captive] among the savages. The captain sent two of his men from the ship, together with several native kings who were their friends, to the settlement where I was [held]. They [the Frenchmen] came to the hut of the king called Sowarasu [Coó-uara-açú], which lay close to the hut where I was kept. News was brought to me by the savages that two men had now arrived from the ship. I was happy and went to them and greeted them in the savage language. As they now saw me walking about so miserably, they were filled with pity and gave me some of their clothes. I asked them why they had come. They said that it was because of me; they had been given orders to take me to the ship, using whatever means necessary. Then my heart rejoiced at the mercy of God. I told one of them, who was called Perot and knew the savage tongue, that in order for the savages to take me to the ship, he had to pretend he was my brother, who had brought me several chests full of merchandise, which they [the savages] would then want to collect. He was also to tell the savages that I would then remain with them to gather pepper and other goods until the ship returned again, next year. After these words, they brought me to the ship; my master went along himself. Everyone aboard the ship had pity on me and showed me great kindness. After we had been some five days on the ship, the savage king Abbati Bossange, to whom I had been given, asked me for the chests

97

[of goods]. He said that I should have them give these to me, so that we might return home in time. I reported his intent to the commander of the ship. He ordered me to put him [King Abatí-poçanga] off until his ship had taken in a full cargo, so that they would not become angry and plan some mischief or plot some treachery when they saw that they were going to keep me on the ship; for they were a people that you could not trust. However, my master had set his mind on taking me home. Yet, I put him off with empty words for some time, telling him not to be in such a hurry: he ought to know that when good friends get together, they cannot part at once. However, once they [the Frenchmen] wanted to sail away with the ship, we would then also be on our way back to his hut. Thus I stalled him.

At last the ship was ready to set sail and the Frenchmen all gathered on the ship. I stood next to them and the king, my master, was also there together with those [savages] he had taken along. Then the ship's captain spoke to the savages through his interpreter: he was very pleased that they had not killed me after they had captured me among their enemies. He also told them (in order to get me away from them with more decency) that he had ordered me to be brought from land to the ship so that he might give them something in return for having taken such good care of me. He also wanted to give me goods and leave me, who was familiar with them, to collect pepper and other useful goods, until he returned again. We had arranged between us that some ten crewmen, who more or less resembled me, should now gather together and pretend to be my brothers, who wanted to take me home. This resolve was presented to them: these brothers of mine would on no account allow me to return on land with the savages. They wanted me to return home, for my father longed to see me once more before he died. Then the captain let them [the savages] know that he was the commander of the ship and wanted me to return to shore with them. However, he was also only one man, he said, and my brothers were many, so he could not oppose them. All this was done to enable them to part from the savages on friendly terms. I told the king, my master, that I very much wanted to return with him, but that, as he could see, my brothers would not allow me to do so. Then he began to shout all over the ship, saying that if they really wanted to take me away, I then had to return with the first ship, for he looked upon me as his son and was very angry with those from Uwattibi, who had wanted to eat me.

And one of his wives who was with him on the ship lamented over me, according to their custom, and I also cried as they usually do. After all of this, the captain gave them a number of goods; some five ducats' worth of knives, axes, mirrors, and combs. Then they went ashore towards their dwellings.

Thus the Almighty Lord, the God of Abraham, Isaac and Jacob, saved me from the hands of the tyrants. Praise, glory, and honor be to Him through Jesus Christ, His Son, our Redeemer. Amen.

CHAPTER 52

THE NAME OF THE COMMANDER OF THE SHIP; WHERE THE SHIP CAME FROM; WHAT HAPPENED BEFORE WE LEFT HARBOR; AND HOW LONG OUR JOURNEY BACK TO FRANCE WAS. CAPUT LIII.

The captain of the ship was named Wilhelm de Moner, the helmsman, Francoy de Schantz, and the ship, Catherine of Wattavilla [Catherine de Vatteville] etc. They prepared the ship to sail for France. Then one morning, while we still lay in the harbor of Rio de Jenero, a small Portuguese ship sailed by and wanted to leave the harbor. It had been trading with a group of the savages called Los Markayas [Maracaiás]. Their country is next to the country of the Tuppin Ikins [Tupiniquins], who are friendly to the French. These two nations of savages are great enemies.

This small ship was the one which, as I have recounted, came to buy me from the savages, and it was owned by a factor [an agent] named Peter Rösel. The Frenchmen armed their boat with cannons and drew closer, planning to capture it [the Portugese ship]. They took me with them, so that I could speak to them [the Portugese] and tell them to surrender. But when we attacked [the Portugese on] the small ship they beat us off and killed and wounded several Frenchmen. I was also nearly mortally wounded by a shot; far more severely than any of the others who recovered. In my fear, I cried out to my Lord for I felt nothing but the fear of death. I prayed the Merciful Father to keep me alive, since He had already delivered me from the hands of the [savage] tyrants. Thus I would be able to return to Christian lands and proclaim to others the mercy He had shown to me. I was completely restored to health. Glory be to God the merciful for ever and ever.

On the last day of October 1554, we set sail from the harbor of Rio de

32 *The Attack on a Portuguese Ship at Rio*

Jenero and headed to France. We had such fair winds at sea that the crew marveled and said that such weather must have been sent as a special gift from God (as indeed it was). The Lord also worked visible wonders for us at sea.

On [the 24th of December,] the day before the first day of Christmas, great numbers of fishes, of a sort called sea hogs [porpoises], surrounded the ship. We caught so many that for several days we could eat our fill. On the feast of the Three Kings [on the 6th of January] God did the same again, sending us enough fish to fill our bellies. Aside from this we did not have a lot to eat; [we] only [had] what God gave us from the sea. Later, about the 20th of February in the year [15]55, we reached the Kingdom of France and anchored at a small town called Honflor [Honfleur], which lies in Normandy. Throughout the voyage, for almost four months, we did not

33 *The Catherine de Vatteville's Providential Voyage*

see land. I helped to unload the ship, and once this was done I thanked them all for the good deed that they had done for me. Then I asked the captain for a passport. However, he would rather have preferred for me to go on another voyage with him, but when he saw that I did not want to stay he managed to get me a passport from the supreme commander in Normandy, [the] Moensoral Miranth [Monsieur Admiral]. Once he [the admiral] heard about me, he called me into his presence and gave me the passport; my captain gave me money for the journey. I took my leave and went from Henfloer [Honfleur] to Habelnoeff [Le Havre Neuf], and from Habelnoeff to Depen [Dieppe].

CHAPTER 53

HOW, IN DEPEN, I WAS TAKEN TO THE HOUSE OF THE CAPTAIN
OF THE SHIP BELLETE, WHICH HAD LEFT BRAZIL BEFORE US
BUT HAD NOT YET ARRIVED. CAPUT 54.

The aforementioned ship, the *Maria Bellete*, came from Dieppe. The interpreter (who had told the savages to eat me) wanted to sail back to France in this ship. It was also these people who did not want to take me on board their boat when I escaped from the savages. The captain of this ship was also the one whom the savages told me had given the [other] savages a Portuguese sailor to eat, when they had captured the Portuguese ship, as mentioned above.

These people from the ship Bellete had not yet reached land when I arrived there—although, judging by the voyage of the ship from Wattavilla [Vatteville] that had arrived after them and had ransomed me, they should have returned home [some] three months before us. The wives, relatives, and friends of the men came to me and asked whether I might not have seen them. I said: I have indeed seen them. There are godless people on board the ship. I said that I could not care less, where they were. I told them how one of those who was on board the ship, who had been among the savages, had told the savages to eat me; yet the Almighty God had protected me. Furthermore, I told them that when they were in their boat by the huts where I was, trading with the savages for pepper and long-tailed monkeys, I had ran away from the savages and had swum out to their boat. Yet they had refused to take me in and I had been forced to swim back to land to the savages. This [refusal] nearly broke my heart. They [the sailors from Dieppe] had also given the savages a Portuguese, whom they [the savages] had [then] eaten. I told them how they [the sailors from Dieppe] had not wanted to show me any mercy at all. From all of this, I now clearly see that the dear Lord wanted to help me; hence—praised be the Lord—I am now here [in Dieppe] before you, and bring you the latest news [about them]. Let them come when they want; I will be a prophet unto you: God will not leave such mercilessness and tyranny, as they showed to me in these lands (may God forgive them) unpunished. This punishment will come sooner or later, for it is obvious that God, our Lord in Heaven, had mercy on my plight. Furthermore, I told them how good the journey back had been for those who had ransomed me free from the savages—which is also the truth. God sent us good weather and fair winds, and gave us fish from the depths of the sea.

They were angered by this, and asked me whether I thought they [their relatives and friends] were still alive. In order to comfort them a bit, I said that they might still return, even though most people, myself included, would have to assume that they had perished with the ship. After all these conversations, I left them, telling them that if the others arrived, they should inform them that God had helped me, and that I had been there.

From Depen [Dieppe], I traveled with a ship towards Lunden in Engellandt [London, England], where I stayed some days. Then I sailed from Lunden to Seelandt [Zeeland in the Netherlands], and from Seelandt towards Andorff [Antwerp]. Thus did the Almighty God, with whom all things are possible, bring me to my fatherland. May eternal praise be given to Him. Amen.

My prayer to God, our Lord, while I was in the hands of the savages, who wanted to eat me.

O Almighty God! You, who made heaven and earth; You, God of our forefathers, Abraham, Isaac, and Jacob; You, who with great might led the people of Israel through the Red Sea out of the hands of their enemies; You, who protected Daniel amongst the lions. I pray to You, eternal ruler, to deliver me from the hands of these tyrants, who do know not You, for the sake of Your dear Son, Jesus Christ, who has redeemed the captives from everlasting captivity. Yet if it is Your will, Lord, that I should suffer death at the hands of these people, who do not know You, and who, when I tell them of You, say that You do not have the power to take me out of their hands: then strengthen me in the last hour when they want to work their will upon me, so that I will not doubt Your mercy. If I am then to suffer so much in this great misery then give me peace afterwards and save me from the misery there which appalled all our forefathers. Yet Lord, You can certainly deliver me from their power. Help me, Lord, I know for sure that You can help me, and once You have helped me I will not ascribe it to good luck, but only say that Your mighty hand has helped, for now no human power can help me. When You have helped me out of their power, I will praise Your mercy and bring it to the light of day, among all peoples, and in all countries, wherever I may come. Amen.

I cannot believe that a man can pray from the
bottom of his heart,[39]
Unless a danger to his life, or another great cross, or
tribulation comes upon him.
For whenever the flesh can live according to its will.
The poor creature will constantly strive against its
Creator.
Therefore, whenever God places obstacles in the ways
of humans,
He truly has good, heartfelt intentions.
Let none doubt this.
This is a gift from God,
Comfort, protection, or weapons will never be found
at any time,
save by the one who is armed with the faith and with
the Word of God.
Therefore every devout man.
Cannot teach his children anything better,
Than to grasp the Word of God well, for in times of
trouble they can then trust in this.
So that you, dear reader, shall not think.
[That] I have taken these pains to gain a reputation
and that I consider myself to be someone important,
[Let it be known that] this happens for the glory and
praise of Almighty God,
Who knows the thoughts and hearts of all people,
To Him, dear reader, I commend you.
May He also protect me from now on.

THE END OF THE FIRST BOOKLET.

39. In the German original, this poem rhymes according to a simple "a-a, b-b, c-c" structure; the syn-
tax follows the poetical, inverted word order. For instance, the first two strophes sound thus: "Ich kan
nicht wol gleuben das von hertzen könne beten eyn man / Es sei dann das leibs gefahr oder ander groß
Creutz und verfolgung i[h]n treffe an. [. . .]." Staden's peculiar interpunctuation has been preserved in
this prose translation as it reflects the orality of the work overall.

[11]

A true and brief account of the manners and customs of the Tuppin Inbas
[Tupinambás], whose captive I was. They live in America. Their land lies
24 degrees on the southern side of the equinox. Their country is bounded by
[the mouth of] a river called Rio de Jenero [Janeiro].

CHAPTER I

WHAT THE VOYAGE BY SHIP IS LIKE FROM PORTUGAL TO RIO DE JENERO, WHICH LIES IN AMERICA, AT ALMOST 24 DEGREES AT THE HEIGHT OF THE TROPIC OF CAPRICORN. CAPUT I.

Lissabona, a town in Portugal, lies at 39 degrees north of the equinox. If you want to sail from Lissabona to the Province of Rio de Jenero in the land of Brazil, which is also called America, you first travel to islands called the Cannariae [Canary Islands], which belong to the King of Spain. 6 of them are mentioned here: the first is Grand Canaria; the second, Lanserutta; the third, Forte Ventura; the fourth, Il Ferro; the fifth, La Palma; the sixth, Tineriffe.[40] Then you sail for the islands called Los insules de Cape virde, that is to say the Islands of the Green Headland [Cape Verde]. This Green Headland lies in the country of the Black Moors, which is called also Gene [Guinea]. The abovementioned [Cape Verde] islands lie below

40. Gran Canaria, Lanzarote, Fuerteventura, Ferro, Palma, and Tenerifa.

34 *Tupinambás*

the tropic of Cancer and belong to the King of Portugal. From the islands, you sail south-south-west to the land of Brazil. It is a vast, great sea; you often sail for three months and more before reaching this land. First you cross the tropic of Cancer and leave it behind; then [you cross] through the equinoctial line. When you leave this behind to the north, you no longer see the North Star that is also called Polum articum. Then you come to the height of the tropic of Capricorn and sail under the sun, and once you have passed through the tropic of Capricorn you see that at noon the sun is to the north. The heat in the area between these two tropics is always severe. The aforementioned country of Brazil lies partly within the tropics.

CHAPTER 2

WHAT THE COUNTRY CALLED AMERICA OR BRAZIL, WHICH I HAVE PARTLY SEEN, LOOKS LIKE. CAP. II.

America is a large country, which contains many groups of savages who speak very different languages. There are many strange animals. It is pleasant to the eye. The trees are always green and there is no forest there that is similar to the forests in this country [in Hessia or in Germany]. The people walk naked. In the part of the country which lies between the tropics, it never gets as cold as it is here at the time of Michaelmas [on the 29th of September]; but the country lying south of the tropic of Capricorn is somewhat colder. The nation of savages called Carios [Carijós] lives there. These people use the skins of wild animals, which they prepare with great skill, to clothe themselves. The savage women of this nation make things [for clothing] from cotton yarn, resembling a sack below and open above; they wear these and call them Typpoy [Tipoi] in their language. There are several fruits from the earth and the trees in the country, which the people and the animals feed upon. Because of the sun that burns them so much, the people of this country are of a reddish-brown colour. They are a skilled people, expert in every kind of wickedness, and they are always inclined to pursue and eat their enemies, etc. Their land, America, stretches several hundreds of miles north and south. I have sailed some five hundred miles along [the coast] of this land and I have been in many places inland.

CHAPTER 3

REGARDING A GREAT RANGE OF MOUNTAINS IN THIS COUNTRY. CAP. III.

There is a range of mountains which reaches to within three miles of the sea, in some places closer and in some further away. It begins near Boiga de Todolos Sanctus [Bahia de Todos os Santos], a settlement built by the Portuguese who live there. This mountain range runs along the sea for a total of 204 miles, and ends at latitude 29 degrees south of the equinox. In some places, it is eight miles wide. There is also land on the other side of the mountain range. Many beautiful waterways emerge from these mountains and there is an abundance of game. A species of savages called Wayganna

[Guaianás] lives in the mountain range. Unlike the other savages living on both sides of the mountains, they have no fixed dwellings. These Wayganna wage war against all other nations, and when they capture them, they eat them—the others are similar to them in this respect. They track game in the mountains and are skilful at shooting game with their arrows. They are also very adept at using other things to capture game with, namely, slings and traps.

There is also lots of wild honey in the mountains, which they eat.

They normally also know how to imitate the cries of the animals and the singing of the birds, in order to track them down and more easily shoot them.

They make fire like the other savages, with two pieces of wood, and they normally roast the meat that they eat. They roam [the lands] with their wives and children.

When they set up their camps close to enemy territory, they surround their huts with sticks, so that you cannot rush and overrun them, and also in order to give protection against the tiger animals. They also surround the huts with sharp thorns called Maraga eibe Ju [Maracá-ibá], just as people here lay down caltraps. They do this for fear of their enemies. They burn a fire all night long, but when day breaks they extinguish it, so that you cannot see the smoke and track them down.

They let their fingernails and the hair on their head grow long. In addition, they, like the other savages, also have rattles called Maraka [Maracá] that they consider to be gods; they make [alcoholic] drinks and organize dances; they also use the teeth of wild beasts to cut with; and they use the stone wedges to chop with, which the other savages also used before they began to barter with the ships.

They frequently set out to pursue their enemies. When they want to capture them, they hide behind the dry thickets, near the enemies' huts. They do so in order to take captives whenever some of them come out of their huts to gather wood.

They also treat their enemies in a more tyrannical manner than their enemies treat them. The reason for this is their great envy, which often leads them to cut off an arm or a leg from a live captive. The others kill their enemies before they cut them up for eating.

CHAPTER 4

HOW THE SAVAGE TUPPIN INBA, WHOSE CAPTIVE
I WAS, BUILD THEIR DWELLINGS. CAP. 4.

They have their dwellings close to the sea, in front of the above-mentioned mountain range; [but] their homelands also extend some 60 miles behind the mountains. They have also settled at one place on the banks of a river that they call Paraeibe [Paraiba], which flows down from the mountains to the sea. [Furthermore,] they inhabit an area stretching for about 28 miles along the coast of this sea. They are pressed by enemies on all sides. To the north, they border the lands of the group of savages called Weittaka [Guiatacás] who are their enemies; to the south, their enemies are called Tuppin Ikin [Tupiniquins]; towards the interior their enemies are called Karaya [Carajás]; the Wayganna [Guaianás] live in the mountains close by; and yet another group of savages, who persecute them greatly, are called Markaya [Maracaiás] and live in between. These aforementioned tribes all make war amongst themselves, and when one of them captures an enemy savage, they eat him.

They prefer to set up their dwellings in places where they have both water and wood as well as game and fish nearby. When they have exploited one place, they move their dwellings elsewhere. When they want to set up their huts, a chief among them collects a party of some 40 men and women, as many as he can gather; they are usually friends and relatives.

These people set up a hut, which is about fourteen feet wide and, depending on how many they are, up to 150 feet long. These huts are about 2 fathoms[41] high and are round at the top like a vaulted cellar. They cover them thickly with palm branches to keep out the rain. Inside, the huts are all open; none of them have any particular separate chamber. Each couple of man and woman has a space about twelve feet long on one side of the hut, and on the other side another couple has a similar space; the huts are filled in this manner, each couple having its own fire. The chief of the hut has his dwelling in the centre of the hut. They normally have three small entrances, one at each end, and [a third] one in the middle, and they are so low that people have to stoop down when they go in and out.

---

41. 1 fathom = 6 feet = 1.829 m.

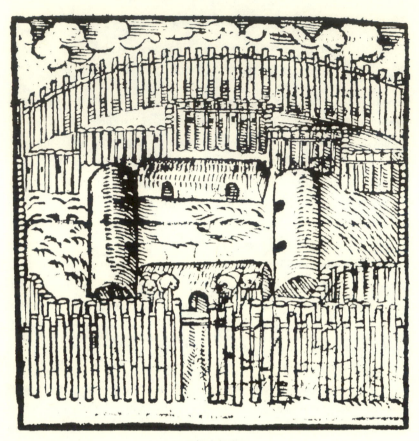

35 *Palisaded Village*

CHAPTER 5

FIGURE PICTURE OF THE HUTS AND
THE PALISADE FENCE. CAPUT V.

Few of their villages have more than seven huts. They leave a square place between the huts; there they slay their captives. They also tend to build fortifications around their huts as follows: They make a palisade fence out of palm trees, which they [first] split. This palisade fence is about one and a half fathoms high. They build it so thickly that no arrow can pierce it and leave little holes through which they can shoot. Surrounding this palisade fence, they build another fence out of big, high poles, which they do not place right next to each other, but only so close that a man cannot creep through. Several [groups] among them have the custom of spiking the heads of those, whom they have eaten, on the palisade fence in front of the entrance to the huts.

36 *Fire Sticks*

37 *Ini (hammock)*

CHAPTER 6

HOW THEY MAKE FIRE. CAPUT VI.

They have a type of wood called Urakueiba [Uraçú-iba], which they dry.
Then they take two small sticks that are as thick as a finger and rub them
together. This then produces dust, which is set on fire by the heat from the
rubbing. With this they make fire, as is shown in this figure.

CHAPTER 7

WHERE THEY SLEEP. CAP. VII.

They sleep in things called Inni [Ini] in their language, made of cotton
yarn. They tie them to two poles above the ground, and always keep a fire

Haben

burning nearby. They do not like to leave their huts at night to relieve themselves, without carrying fire; for they very much fear the Devil, whom they call Ingange [Anhanga] and often think they see.

CHAPTER 8

HOW SKILLED THEY ARE AT SHOOTING WILD ANIMALS AND FISH WITH ARROWS. CAP. VIII.

Wherever they go, whether in the forest or along the water, they always bring their bows and arrows with them. When walking in the forest, they keep their heads raised towards the trees. Every so often, when they hear the [sounds of] big birds, long-tailed monkeys, or other animals that live in the trees, they approach and try to shoot [the game], and follow it for as long as it takes to catch something. It seldom happens that a man returns empty-handed from hunting. They follow the fish along the seashore in the same way. They have keen sight. When, for instance, a fish comes close to the surface, they then shoot at it and seldom miss. As soon as a fish is hit, they jump into the water and swim after it. Several large fish sink to the bottom upon feeling the arrow, but they [the savages] dive down to a depth of six fathoms to bring them back up.

Furthermore, they have small nets. They make the yarn which they use to make the nets from long pointed [palm]leaves called Tockaun [Tucum, Latin: *Bactris setona*]. When they want to fish with the nets, several of them get together and form a circle in shallow water, so that each has his own area. Then several persons enter the circle and beat the water. If the fish wants to head for deeper waters, it is caught in their nets. He who catches the greatest number gives some to the others.

It often happens that those who live far from the sea come down and catch many fish, which they fry until they are dry, and then pound into flour. They dry this flour well, so that it can keep for a long time; [then] they carry it back home, and eat it with root flour. Otherwise, if they took the fried fish home, it would not keep for long, since they do not salt it. One can also fit more flour than whole fried fish into a container.

CHAPTER 9

WHAT THE PEOPLE LOOK LIKE. CAPUT IX.

As regards body and figure, they are a fine people, both women and men. They are like the people of these [German] lands, except that they are brown from the sun because they all walk around naked, both young and old; they do not even have anything to cover their sex and they decorate themselves by painting. They do not have any beards, since they pluck out the hair by the roots as soon as it grows. They make holes in their mouth and ears, in which they hang stones; this is their ornament. They [also] wear feathers.

CHAPTER 10

THE TOOLS THEY USE TO CUT AND HEW, IN THOSE PLACES WHERE THEY CANNOT GET ANY CHRISTIAN GOODS, SUCH AS AXES, KNIVES, AND SCISSORS. CAP. X.

Before the [Christian] ships began to arrive, the savages used a type of bluish-black stone shaped like a wedge, which they sharpened at its broadest end. In the many parts of the land where no ships arrive, they still use this [stone wedge]. It is about a span long, two fingers thick, and as broad as a hand; some are larger, and some are smaller. They then take a narrow stick and bend it around the top of the stone, binding it with bast.

The iron wedges, which the Christians provide them with in several places, have the same shape. However, they now make the shafts differently. They bore a hole, in which they stick the wedge, and this is their hatch with which they hew.

They use also the teeth of boars, which they whet in the center to sharpen them; then they tie them between two sticks. With these, they even their bows and arrows, making them as round as if they had been turned.

They also use the teeth of an animal called Pacca, which they sharpen at the tip. When they have an illness that arises from the blood, they scratch themselves on the spot where it hurts, which then bleeds; this is their way to bleed themselves.

CHAPTER II

WHAT THEY EAT FOR BREAD; WHAT THEIR FRUITS ARE CALLED; AND HOW THEY PLANT AND PREPARE THEM SO THAT THEY ARE EDIBLE. CAP. XI.

In the places where they want to plant [their roots], they cut down the trees and leave them to dry for about three months. Then they set fire to them and burn them down. They then plant their roots between the stubs. This root is called Mandioka [manioc], and they feed on it. It is a small tree about a fathom high, which has three roots. When they want to eat the roots, they pull up the tree and break off the roots; then they break off a branch from the tree and place it back in the earth. This then throws out roots, and in six months it grows big enough to be used for food. They use the roots in three ways.

First of all, they grind them to very small crumbs against a stone. Then they press out the juice from the crumbs with a thing called tippiti [tubular press], which is made from the peel of palm branches. When the crumbs are dry, they pass them through a sieve and use the flour to bake thin cakes.

The thing [container] in which their flour is dried and baked is made of burnt clay and shaped like a large bowl. They also, [secondly,] take the fresh roots and place them in water; there they let them rot. They then take them out and place them over the fire and let them dry in the smoke. They

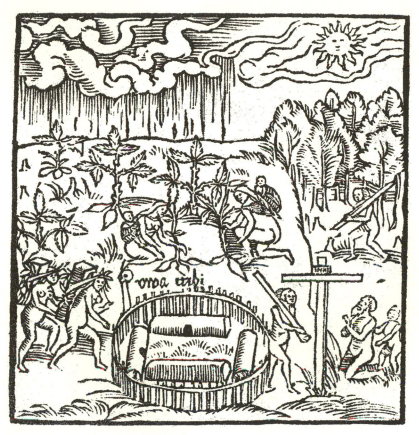

39 *Weather Shamanism and The Cross (ii)*

call this dried root Keinrima [Carimã], and it keeps for a long time. When
they want to use it, they pound it in a mortar made of wood. It then becomes as white as wheat flour, and with this they make cakes called Byyw
[Beijú].

They also take well-fermented mandioka [manioc] and instead of drying
it, they mix it with dry roots and green roots. They dry this into flour, which
keeps for a year and is just as good to eat. They call this flour V.Y.than [Uia-
tán].

They also make flour out of fish and meat. They do so in the following
manner: They roast the flesh or fish in the smoke over the fire and let it become quite dry. They pluck it to pieces, and then dry it once again over the
fire in pots called Yneppaun [Inhêpoan]. After this, they pound [the bits of]
it with a wooden mortar and press it through a sieve, reducing it to flour.
This keeps for a long time. They are, after all, not accustomed to salt their

fish or meat. They eat this flour together with the root-flour, and it tastes quite good.

CHAPTER 12

HOW THEY PREPARE THEIR FOOD. CA. XII.

Among these peoples there are many groups, who eat no salt. Some of those among whom I was a captive, ate salt. They had learned this from the Frenchmen who traded with them. But they told me how a nation of peoples called Karaya [Carajás], who live inland [in an area which lies] away from the sea and borders their country, make salt from palm trees and eat it. However, they also said that those who were used to eat a lot of it [the palm tree salt] did not live long. They make it in the following way—as I myself saw and helped them with: They cut down a thick palm tree and split it up into small chips. Then they make a pile of dried wood, place the chips on it, and burn them to ashes together with the dry wood. From the ashes they make a solution, which they boil until something, that looks like salt, is deposited. I thought it was salpeter and tested it in the fire, but it was not. It tasted like salt and was gray in colour. But most of the peoples eat no salt.

Whenever they boil something, whether fish or flesh, they usually add green pepper to it, and when it is quite well cooked, they take it out of the broth and make a thin mush with it. They call this Mingau [Mingáu], and drink it out of gourds, which they use for drinking vessels. Furthermore, when they cook food, which is to keep for some time, whether it be fish or flesh, they lay it upon small pieces of wood, 4 spans above the fire. They make a good fire beneath and let it roast and smoke until it becomes completely dry. When they then later want to eat it, they boil it up again and eat it, and they call this meat Mockaein [Moquém].

CHAPTER 13

WHAT KIND OF GOVERNMENT AND ORDER THEY HAVE REGARDING AUTHORITIES AND LAWS. CAPUT XIII.

They do not have any particular form of government or law. Each hut has its chief, who is the king. Now all their chiefs belong to one tribe, one area, and one government; you may call this what you want. When one of them has more experience in going to war than the other, he will be listened to more than the others when they wage war, as in the case of the aforementioned Konyan Bebe [Cunhambebe]. Otherwise I have not noticed any particular privileges among them, except that the young are supposed to obey their elders in matters where their customs demand it.

If one person strikes or shoots another person dead, his friends are ready to kill [the murderer], but this happens rarely. They also obey the chief of the hut: when he commands, they comply, but alone out of good will, without compulsion or fear.

CHAPTER 14

HOW THEY MAKE THE POTS AND VESSELS
THAT THEY USE. CAP. XIIII.

The women make the vessels that they use, as follows: They take clay and make it into a kind of dough, out of which they make whatever vessels they want. They leave them to dry for a time. They [also] know how to paint them well. When they want to fire the pots, they place them upside down on stones; then they arrange a lot of dried bark around them, which they then set on fire. This fires the vessels so that they become red-hot like hot iron.

CHAPTER 15

HOW THEY PREPARE THEIR DRINKS THAT THEY USE
TO BECOME INTOXICATED, AND WHAT THEIR ATTITUDE
IS TOWARDS DRINKING. CAPUT XV.

The females prepare the drinks. They take the Mandioca [manioc] root and boil it in great pots filled to the top. When it is cooked, they pour it out of the pot into another pot or vessel and let it cool a little. Then young girls sit down nearby, and chew it in their mouths; what is chewed, they set apart in a special vessel.

When the boiled roots are all chewed, they place the roots back in the pot again, which they refill with water, mixing the water with the chewed roots; then they reheat the mixture. They have special vessels, which they

40 *Preparation of Drink by Women* 𝕸𝖆𝖓𝖓

have half buried in the ground. They use them as you use casks for wine or beer here [in Germany]. They pour it [the mixture] into these [vessels] and close them tightly and it [the mixture] ferments of itself and becomes strong. They let it stand for two days, and then they drink it and become intoxicated. It is thick, and is also good to eat. Each hut makes its own drink, and when all the people of their village want to make merry—which normally happens once a month—they first all get together in a hut and drink everything there. This continues from one hut after another, until they have drunk everything in all the huts. They sit down around the vessels where they drink; some sit on firewood, others on the ground. The women serve them the drinks in an orderly manner. Some get up and sing and dance around the vessels, and they pass their water [urinate] right where they drink.

The drinking carries on all night, and they also dance around the fires, shouting and blowing trumpets; they make a terrible commotion when they are drunk, [but] you rarely see them quarreling. They are also very generous: when one of them has more food than another, he shares it with him.

CHAPTER 16

WHAT THE ADORNMENT OF THE MEN LOOKS LIKE, HOW THEY PAINT THEMSELVES, AND WHAT THEIR NAMES ARE. CAPUT XVI.

They make a shaved space on their head, leaving a circle of hair around it, like a monk. I often asked them where they had this haircut from. They told me that their forefathers had seen it on a man called Meire Humane, who had worked many miraculous deeds among them; people claim that he was a prophet or an apostle.

Furthermore, I asked them how they had cut their hair [in the time] before the ships brought them scissors. They told me that they had used a stone wedge and had held another thing underneath; then they had cut off the hair. They had made the bare space in the middle with a sliver of crystal, which they use frequently for shearing. Furthermore, they have made a thing [an adornment] called kannittari [acangatara] out of red feathers, which they tie around the head.

They also have a large hole in the lower lip of their mouths, which they make in their youth. When they are still boys, the savages pierce a small hole through their lips with a sharp staghorn. They then insert a small piece of stone or wood in this hole, and then rub it with their ointment. The small hole then stays open. When they have then grown big enough to bear arms, they enlarge this [lip hole] for them, and he [the young man] then inserts a large green stone in it. This stone is shaped like this [picture shows]. The narrower end at the top goes inside [the mouth] to hang on the lips, and the larger end sticks out. Their lips always hang down with the weight of these stones. They also have another small stone in each cheek, on both sides of the mouth. They whet the stones to a long and round shape. Several of them wear stones made out of crystal, which are narrow but just as long. They have another ornament, which they make from the shells of the large sea snails that they call Matte pue [Matapú]. This ornament is shaped like a half-moon, and they hang it round the neck. It is snow-white and

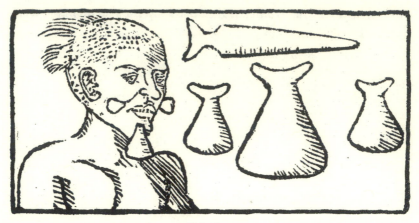

41 *Male Adornment*

is called Bogessy [Bojecí]. They also make small white discs from the sea snails, which they hang round the neck. These are about as thin as a straw, and producing them takes a great deal of work.

They paint themselves black and bind plumes to their arms. They mix red and white feathers together and stick these feathers to their bodies with a substance that comes from the trees. They smear themselves with this substance where they want to feather themselves, and then they press the feathers on, so that they stick fast. They also paint one arm black and the other red, and do the same to their legs and body.

They also have an ornament made of ostrich plumes, which is a large round thing made of feathers. They tie this to their buttocks when they set out to wage war against their enemies or when they have a celebration. It is called Enduap [Enduape].

The picture of the Enduape.

They call themselves by the names of wild animals and give themselves many names, but with one distinction: When they are born, they are given one name. They only keep this [name] until they are fit to bear

Die Figur Enduape.

42 *The Enduap—worn in war and feasting*

arms and able to slay their enemies, and each man has as many names as he
has killed enemies.

CHAPTER 17

WHAT THE ORNAMENT OF THE WOMEN IS. CAP. 17.

The women paint the lower part of their faces and their bodies in the same
manner as the men paint themselves, mentioned above. But like women
elsewhere, they let their hair grow long. Otherwise, they have no adornment, apart from the holes they have in their ears; they hang things there
that are about a span long. They are round and about as thick as a thumb,
and they call them nambibeya [Nambipai] in their language. They also
make them from the sea snails called Mattepue [Matapús].

They are named after birds, fishes, and fruits from the trees. When they
grow up, they only have one name, but for every slave killed by the men,
the women also give themselves another name.

When one woman rids another of head lice, they eat the lice. I have often
asked them why they do so. They told me that the lice are their enemies who
are eating their heads, and they wanted to take vengeance upon them.

There are no particular midwives there. When a woman is in labor, the
nearest person, whether man or woman, runs to help her. I have seen them
walk around, about four days after they had given birth.

They carry their children on their backs in cradles made of cotton, and
carry on their work with them [tied to their backs]. The small children sleep
and are very content, regardless of how much the women stoop and move
about.

CHAPTER 18

HOW THEY GIVE THE SMALL CHILDREN
THEIR FIRST NAMES. CAP. XVIII.

The wife of one of the savages, who had helped to capture me, had given
birth to a young son. A few days later, he called his neighbors together in
the hut and asked them what kind of courageous and terrifying name he
could now give to the child. They suggested a lot of names that did not
please him. He wanted to name the child after one of his four forefathers,

and he said that children with such names prospered and had good luck in catching slaves. He listed his forefathers: the first was named Krimen [Kirimā]; the second Hermittan [Eíamitā]; the third Koem [Coema]; I cannot recall the name of the fourth. When he spoke of Koem, I thought that he must have meant Cham, but Koem means "the morning" in their language. I told him to give this name to his son, since that had surely been one of his forefathers;[42] and this was the name given to the child. Thus they name their children, without any baptism or circumcision.

CHAPTER 19

HOW MANY WOMEN ONE OF THEM HAS, AND HOW HE DEALS WITH THEM. CAP. XIX.

Most of them only have one woman, but some have more, and several of the kings have 13 or 14 women. The king called Abbati Bossange [Abatípoçanga] (the last person to whom I was given, and from whom the Frenchmen bought me) had many women, and the one who had been his first woman had the highest rank among them. Each of them had her separate place in the hut, her own fire, and her own [manioc] roots. He [Abatípoçanga] lived in the space of the woman with whom he was doing things [having sex] with at a given moment.[43] She gave him food to eat, and this went on in turns. As for their children, the boys go hunting when they grow up. Each brings his catch back to his mother, who cooks it and shares it with the others; the women get along well with each other. They [the savages] also have the custom that one man gives away a woman to another man, when he is tired of her. They also give each other, say, a daughter or a sister.

42. According to Genesis 9:18–10, 32, Cham was one of the three sons of Noah, who populated the world after the Flood. While his two brothers Shem and Japheth were said to be the progenitors of the peoples in Europe and Asia, Cham was seen as the ancestor of all Africans. The sons of Noah appear again in Chronicles 1, and in Luke 3:23–38, which tracks the genealogy of Jesus back through David, Abraham, Shem, and Adam, to God.
43. The phrase "doing things" is also unspecific in the original, *mit welcher er zuthun hatte*. Judging by its use below, it most likely refers to sexual intercourse.

CHAPTER 20

HOW THEY BECOME ENGAGED. CAP. XX.

They betroth their daughters when they are still young. When they [the daughters] have reached the age when they begin to share the customs of women [when they begin to menstruate], they [the savages] then cut off the hair from the heads of the young women, scratch peculiar marks on their backs, and tie the teeth of wild beasts around their necks. Afterwards, when their hair has grown out again, and the cuts have healed, you can still see the scars where they were cut, for they put something in there [in the wounds], so that they remain black when they have healed, and they consider this to be a [sign of] honor.

When these ceremonies have come to an end, they hand her [the young woman] over to the man, who is meant to have her, without any further ceremonies. The men and women also do as is fitting and do their things in private.[44]

I have also seen one of their chiefs go through all the huts early in the morning, scratching the children's legs with a sharpened fish tooth in order to frighten them. [This is done] so that when they are unruly the parents can silence them by telling them that this man is going to come back [and scratch them again].

CHAPTER 21

WHAT THEY POSSESS. CAP. XXI.

There is no trade among them and they do not know anything of money either. Their treasures are the feathers of birds. He that has many of them is rich, and he who has rare stones in his lip is also among the richest of them.

Each couple of man and woman among them has its own roots to eat.

---

44. Staden again uses an unspecific phrase to refer to sexual intercourse; the original reads: *machen ire sachen heymlich.*

CHAPTER 22

WHAT THEIR GREATEST HONOR IS. CA. XXII.

This is what they consider honor to be: when someone has captured and slain many enemies—for this is customary among them. Each person has given himself as many names as the number of enemies that he has killed. The most prominent among them are those who have a lot of these names.

CHAPTER 23

WHAT THEY BELIEVE IN. CAP. XXIII.

They believe in a thing, which grows like a pumpkin; it is the size of a pint pot[45] and is hollow inside. They put a stick through it and cut a hole in it like a mouth; then they put in small pebbles so that it rattles. They rattle it about when they sing and dance, and they call it Tammaraka [Maracá]. It is shaped like this:

43 *The Tammaraka*

Each male has his own [maracá]. Now there are also several among them, whom they call Paygi [pajé], and these are looked up to [in the same manner] as we revere soothsayers. These [pajé] people travel through the land once a year, visiting all the huts. They pretend that a spirit from a foreign, far-off place has been with them and given them power to make all the

45. The original reads *eyn halb maß döppen*. Since the German beer-measure *Maß* has never been standardized, half a *Maß* may be either 0.25 or 0.5 liter.

rattling Tammaraka—as many as they want—speak and grow powerful; if [only] they [the pajé] ask the spirit to do so, this power would be granted. Then everyone wants his rattle to become powerful, and they make a great feast with drinking, singing, and prophesying, and perform many strange ceremonies. Afterwards, the soothsayers choose a special day. They clear out a hut; no women or children are allowed to stay there. Then the soothsayers order everyone to paint his Tammaraka red, decorate it with feathers, and come to the hut. Then [one of the pajé] says that he will grant them [the Maracá] the power to speak. After this they go to the hut, and then the wise men sit down at the upper end and have stuck their Tammaraka into the ground around them. The others also place their Tammaraka there, and each man gives the soothsayer a present—such as arrows, feathers, and the things they hang in their ears—so that his Tammaraka will not be forgotten. When they are then all gathered together, [one of the pajé] takes each and every Tammaraka separately and fumigates it with a herb called Bittin [Pitim, tobacco]. Then he holds the rattle close to his mouth shaking it and saying to it: Nee Kora [Né cora], now speak and let yourself be heard. Are you there? Then he says a word in [such] a low voice and so fast that you cannot understand it, and the people think that the rattle is the one speaking. Nevertheless, it is the soothsayer who speaks; he does the same with all the rattles, one after the other. Then everyone thinks that his rattle holds great power. Then the soothsayers tell them to make war and capture enemies, for the spirits who are in the Tammaraka crave the flesh of slaves. Then they set off to war.

After the soothsayer, the Paygi, has made gods out of all the rattles, each person takes his rattle away. He calls it his beloved son and builds a separate, little hut where it is kept. He places food before it and asks it to provide him with everything that he needs, just as we pray to the true God. Such are their gods. They do not care about the true God, who has made heaven and earth. They take it to be common knowledge that the earth and the heavens have always been there. Apart from this, they do not know anything particular about the beginning of the world. Now they say that there was once a great flood that drowned all their ancestors, except for some who escaped in a canoe and others who stayed in high trees. I think this must have been the Flood.[46]

46. The story about the Flood and the rescue of Noah and his family is found in Genesis 6–9.

Now when I first arrived among them and they told me about it [the Maracá-rattle], I thought it had to be a diabolic spirit, for they often told me how these things were speaking. Now as I entered the hut, where the soothsayers were staying—those who were supposed to make the things speak—they all had to sit down. But as I saw the deceit, I walked out of the hut and thought to myself: what a poor, beguiled people they are.

CHAPTER 24

HOW THEY TURN THE WOMEN INTO SOOTHSAYERS. CAP. XXIIII.

They first go into a hut and take all the women from the hut and fumigate them, one after another. Afterwards, each woman has to scream, jump, and run about until she becomes so exhausted that she falls down to ground, as if she were dead. Then the soothsayer says: Look: now she is dead. Soon, I will bring her back to life again. When she then recovers, he says that she is now able to foretell future things. When they go out to war, the women have to prophesy about the war.

One night, the wife of my master (to whom I had been presented to be killed) began to prophesy. She told her husband that a spirit had come to her from a foreign country. It wanted to know when I was to be killed, and had asked where the club was, with which I was to be killed. He answered her that it would not be long and that everything was prepared; only it seemed to him that I was not a Portuguese, but a Frenchman.

After the woman had ended her prophecy, I asked her why she was striving for my death, when I was no enemy; and whether she was not afraid that my God would punish her with a plague. She said that I should not bother about it, for it was the foreign spirits [and not her] who wanted to know about me. They have many such ceremonies.

CHAPTER 25

HOW THEY SAIL ON THE WATER. CAPUT XXV.

There is a species of tree in the country called Yga Ywera [Igá-ibira]. They cut off all the bark of the tree in one piece, from the top to the bottom, by building a special scaffold around the tree so that they can remove the entire bark intact.

Afterwards, they take the bark and carry it from the mountains to the sea. They heat it at the fire and bend it upwards at the rear end and at the front end. But they have first lashed it together with wood at the middle, so that it does not stretch. Out of this, they make canoes, in which thirty men can go to war. The bark is as thick as a thumb, about four feet wide, and forty feet long; some are longer, some are shorter. They paddle these [canoes] quickly and travel as far as they want. When the sea is rough, they beach the canoes until the weather improves. They do not venture more than two miles from shore, but travel long distances along the coast.

CHAPTER 26

WHY ENEMIES EAT EACH OTHER. CAPUT XXVI.

They do not do this from hunger, but from great hate and jealousy. When they skirmish during war and are filled with hate, one will call out to the other: Dete Immeraya, Schermiuramme, beiwoe:[47] May all misfortune fall upon you, my food. De kange Juca eypota kurine:[48] On this very day, I will smash your head to pieces. Sche Innamme pepicke Reseagu[49]: I am here to take vengeance on you for the death of my friends. Yande soo, sche mocken Sera, Quora Ossorime Rire[50] etc.: This day, before sunset, your flesh shall be my roast meat. They do all this because of their great hatred [for one another].

CHAPTER 27

HOW THEY MAKE THEIR PLANS WHEN THEY WANT TO SET OUT TO MAKE WAR IN ENEMY TERRITORY. CAP. 27.

When they want to go to war in enemy territory, the chiefs gather and deliberate how to do this. They make the decision [to go to war] known in the huts with regular intervals, so that they [the men in the hut] may arm themselves. They choose a certain fruit and say that when it ripens, they will leave; for they do not reckon by the day or year. [Sometimes] they also

47. *Debe marã pá, xe remiu ram begué.*
48. *Nde akanga juká aipotá kuri ne.*
49. *Xe anama poepika re xe aju.*
50. *Nde roó, xe mokaen serã kuarasy ar eyma riré.*

decide to leave when the species of fish, which they name Pratti [Piratí] in their language, spawns; they call the spawning time Pirakaen [Piracema]. Prior to this time, they ready themselves with canoes, arrows, and the dried root-flour that they call V Ythan [Uiatan] and use for provisions. After this they consult the Pagy [pajés], their soothsayers, [and ask] whether they are then going to be victorious. They [the soothsayers] then will probably say yes, but they order them to take heed of those dreams, where they dream about the enemies. If most of them dream and see the flesh of their enemies roasting, that means victory. But if they see their own flesh frying, that does not bode well; it means that they should then stay at home. If their dreams please them, they now arm themselves, prepare much drink in all of the huts, and drink and dance with their idols, the Tammaraka. Each of them beseeches his own idol to assist him in capturing an enemy. Then they set off [to war]. When they then arrive near the enemy territory, their chiefs then, on the evening before they attack the land of their enemies, once more direct the men to remember the dreams that they are going to dream during the night.

I [once] accompanied them on an expedition. Then, as we were right next to enemy territory, on the evening before they wanted to attack the land of their enemies, the chief was walking through the camp telling the men to take note of the dreams that they were going to dream that night. He furthermore ordered the young men to set off at daybreak to hunt game and catch fish. This was done, and the chief had the food cooked. He then summoned the other chiefs, who gathered in front of his hut, and they all sat down on the ground in a circle. He gave them [food] to eat, and after they had eaten, they told [each other] their dreams, insofar as they had been pleasant. Afterwards, they danced for joy with the Tammaraka. They spy on the enemies' huts at night and attack in the early morning, at dawn. If they capture someone who is badly wounded, they immediately kill him, roast him, and carry home the meat. But those [captives], who are still healthy, they take back alive; then they kill them in their huts. They attack with loud shouts, stamping on the ground and blowing trumpets made of gourds. They all carry cords bound about their bodies, to tie their enemies up with, and they adorn themselves with red feathers, so that they may distinguish themselves from the others. They rapidly shoot both arrows and fire-arrows into the enemy huts to set them on fire. If one of them is wounded, they have their special herbs that they use to heal themselves with.

CHAPTER 28

WHAT THEIR WEAPONRY IS. CA. 28.

They have bows. The points of their arrows are made of bone, which they sharpen and bind to the arrows; they also make them from the teeth of a fish, which they catch in the sea and call Tiberaun. They also take cotton and mix it with wax; [then] they bind it at the heads of the arrows and set them on fire: these are their fire-arrows. They also make shields of bark and the skin of wild beasts, and they set sharpened thorns into the ground just like [we use] caltraps here.

They also told me that when they wish to do so, they can drive their enemies away from fortifications by means of the pepper that grows there; however, I did not see this myself. It is done in the following manner: if the wind is blowing, they make great fires and throw a whole bunch of pepper into the flames. If the smoke reaches those who are in the huts, they are forced to leave them. I do believe this to be true, for, as related above, I was once with the Portuguese in a province called Brannenbucke [Pernambuco]:[51] then we stranded with our ship in the shallows of a river, because the tide had left us. Many savages approached and intended to capture us, but they were not able to do so. Then they piled a great amount of bushes between the ship and the shore and also planned to drive us out with the pepper fumes, but they could not ignite the wood.

CHAPTER 29

THE CEREMONIES AT WHICH THEY KILL AND EAT
THEIR ENEMIES. THE THINGS THEY USE TO SLAY THEM,
AND HOW THEY HANDLE THEM. CAP. XXIX.

When they bring home their enemies, these are first beaten by the women and the children. Then they decorate him [the captive enemy] with gray feathers, shave off the eyebrows above his eyes, and dance around him,

---

51. See chapters 3 and 4 in the first book.

44 *Induction of the Captive—Aprasse Dance*

45 *The Dance with the Arasoya*

46 *Iwera Pemme*

binding him tight so that he cannot escape. They give him a woman who attends to him and is also doing things with him.[52] If she becomes pregnant, they raise the child until it is grown. If it then enters their minds [to do so], they kill and eat the child.

They feed the captive well and keep him for some time, while they make preparations: they make many vessels, which they use to make drinks in, and they fire special pots, where they prepare the things with which they paint him [the captive]; they make tassels, which they tie to the club, with which he is to be killed; and they [also] make a long cord, called Mussurana, to bind him when he is going to die.

When they have made all these things ready, they then decide when he is going to die and invite the savages from the other villages, so that they come there at the given time. A couple of days in advance, they then fill all the vessels with drinks. Before the women make the drink, they lead the captive once or twice to the [open] place [between the huts] and dance round him. When all those [guests] who come from outside have now gathered together, the chief of the hut bids them welcome and says: Now come and help to eat your enemy. The day before they begin to drink, they tie the cord Mussurana about the captive's neck; on this day, they also paint the club called Iwera Pemme [Ibira-pema] with which they want to kill him. This figure picture shows what it looks like:

It is more than a fathom long. They [first] cover it with sticky stuff. Then they take the eggshells of a bird called Mackukawa [Macaguá], which they grind to a powder and spread upon the club. Then a woman sits down and scratches in the eggshell-powder. While she is painting, a lot of women surround her and sing. When the Iwera Pemme is as it is supposed to be—with tassels and other things—they hang it upon a pole in an empty hut, and then gather around it and sing all night.

---

52. Here, Staden again uses an indirect expression *ein weyb, das [. . .] mit ime zu tun hat* to refer to sexual intercourse.

They paint the face of the captive in the same manner; the women are also singing, while one of them is painting him. And when they begin to drink, they take their captive along and chat with him, while he drinks with them.

When the drinking has now come to an end, they rest the next day and build a small hut for the captive, on the place where he is going to die. There, he spends the night under close guard. Then, towards the morning, some time before dawn, they come and dance and sing around the club, with which they wish to slay him, until day breaks. They then take the captive away from his small hut, which they tear down and clear away. Then they remove the Mussurana from his neck, tie it around his body, and draw it tight on both sides. He is standing tied in the middle; on both ends, many of them are holding onto the cord.

They let him stand like this for a while and place small stones next to him, so that he can throw them at those women, who run about him and threaten to eat him. Now these women are painted, and when he is going to be cut up, they are meant to take the first four pieces and run with them around the hut. This provides amusement to the others.

When this [mocking and dancing] has now come to an end, they make a fire about two paces away from the slave. He has to look upon the fire. After this, a woman comes running with the club Iwera Pemme. In order to make him see it, she waves the tassels in the air, shrieks with joy, and runs past the captive.

After this has happened, a man now takes the club, goes to stand in front of the captive, and holds the club in front of him, so that he will look at it. Meanwhile, the one, who is going to slay him, goes forth with 13 or 14 others, and they all paint their bodies gray with ashes. Then he [the executioner] and his henchmen come to the place where the captive is, and the other person, who is standing in front of the captive, gives the club to this person [the executioner]. Then the king of the hut comes and takes the club, and thrusts it once between the legs of the person who is going to slay the captive.

This is a great honor among them. Then the one, who is going to kill him, takes back the club and then says [to the captive]: Well, here I am. I will kill you, since your friends have also killed and eaten many of my friends. He answers: When I am dead, I will still have many friends, who are

47 *The Women Drinking and Feasting*

48 *The Women Adorn and Carouse with the Captive*

49 *The Dance with Iwera Pemme*

50 *The Women Carouse with the Captive*

51 *The Women Taunt the Captive*

52 *The Dismemberment of the Flayed Body by the Men*

53 *The Women's Feast*

54 *The Youngsters' Feast*

certainly going to avenge me. The executioner then strikes him on the back of his head and beats out his brains. The women immediately seize him and put him over the fire, where they scrape off all his skin, making him all white; they place a piece of wood in his arse to prevent a discharge.[53]

When he [the dead captive] has then been skinned, a man takes him and cuts off the legs above the knees, and the arms at the body. Then the four women come and seize the four pieces and run around the huts with them, screaming loudly with joy. After this, they part the back, including the buttocks, from the front part and divide this [rear part] amongst themselves.

However, the women keep the innards, simmer them, and make a type of mush, called mingau [Mingáu], in the broth. They and the children drink this [mush] and eat the innards. They also eat the flesh from the head. The brain, the tongue, and whatever else is edible, is eaten by the youngsters.

When this is all done, everyone returns home, and each of them brings their piece [of meat] along. The one who has killed this [captive] gives himself another name. The king of the hut scratches him [the executioner] on the upper arm with the tooth of a wild animal. When this wound has healed properly, you can see the scar; this is the [sign of] honor for this act. He then has to lie all that day in a hammock, but they give him a small bow and an arrow, so that he can pass the time by shooting into [a target made of] wax. This is done to prevent his arms from becoming feeble from the shock of the slaying. I was present and have seen all of this.

Moreover, they do not know how to count beyond five. If they have to count further, they use their fingers and toes. When they want to speak about greater numbers, they point to four or five persons, referring to the number of fingers and toes that these persons have.

CHAPTER 30

REPORT CONCERNING SOME ANIMALS IN THE COUNTRY. CAPUT XXX.

In this land, there are the same country deer that are found here [in Germany]. There are two species of wild boars. One species is like the ones

---

53. Sousa (1851: 318) indicates that this was the usual method of cooking game: "They do not skin the game but scorch it or whitewash it with hot water. They eat it broiled or boiled with the tripes hardly washed. They do not scale off the fish nor remove the insides and they boil or broil it as it comes from the sea."

[that live] here. The other is as small as a young piglet and is called Teygasu Dattu [Tanhaçú-tatu]. They are very difficult to catch in the traps that the savages use for game.

There are three species of long-tailed monkeys. One species is called Key [Cai]. This is the one, which has been brought to these [German] lands.

Then there is another species called Ackakey [Acacai]. They normally jump about in the trees in great numbers and make great noise in the forest.

Then there is another species called Pricki [Buriqui]. These [monkeys] are red, bearded like goats, and are as big as a medium-sized dog.

There is also a species of animal called Dattu [Tatú; armadillo]. It is about a span high, and a span and a half long. It is armored all over its body, except on the belly where it has no protection. This armor resembles horn, and is linked together with joints like a suit of armor. The animal has a long, pointed little mouth and a long tail. It likes to walk around rocks and lives on ants. Its flesh is fat, and I have often eaten it.

CHAPTER 31

THE FIGURE OF THE DATTÚ. CAP. XXXI.

55a *The Armadillo—Dattu*

CHAPTER 32

SERWOY. CAP. XXXII.

55b *The Possum—Serwoy*

There is another species of game called Serwoy [Sarué, the possum]. It is as big as a cat, and has whitish-gray or dark gray hair, and a tail like a cat. When it breeds, it has about six young ones. It has a pouch on its belly, about half a span long, in which there is a second skin, for the belly is not open. The nipples are in this pouch, and wherever it goes, it carries its young in the pouch between the two skins. I have often helped to catch them and take the young out of the pouch.

There are also many tiger animals in the country.

They kill the people and do much damage.

There is also a kind of lion, which is called Leoparda—that means: gray lion. And there are many other strange animals.

There is also an animal called Cativare, which lives [both] on land and in water.[54] These eat the reeds that are found by the shore of fresh waters. Whenever they fear something, they flee to the bottom of the water. They are bigger than sheep and have a head like a hare, only larger and with short ears. They have a stubby tail and fairly long legs. They move quickly over land, from one [area with fresh] water to another. Their hair is blackish-gray and they have three toes on each foot. Their meat tastes like the flesh of pigs.

54. Capybara (*hydrochoerus capybara*).

Moreover, there is [also] a species of big lizards that [both] live in water and on land. They are good to eat.

CHAPTER 33

CONCERNING A SMALL INSECT, SIMILAR TO SMALL FLEAS, WHICH THE NATIVES CALL ATTUN. CAP. 33.

There are small insects, similar to fleas, only smaller, which are called Attun [Tunga] in the savage language. They come from the huts, and breed on the filth of the people. These insects creep into the feet and it only itches when they creep in. Then they eat their way into the flesh, [but in such a manner] so that you scarcely feel them. If you do not notice and remove them at once, the insect lays a nit as round as a pea, and when you then notice it and remove it, a small hole remains in the flesh, about the size of a pea. When I first came there to this the land with the Spaniards, I saw how they ruined the feet of several of our companions, because they did not pay attention to them.

CHAPTER 34

CONCERNING A SPECIES OF BATS IN THIS COUNTRY, AND HOW IT BITES THE TOES AND THE FOREHEADS OF THE PEOPLE WHEN THEY ARE ASLEEP AT NIGHT. CAP. XXXIIII.

There is species of bats in the country, which is bigger than the ones here in Germany. At night, they fly around hammocks in the huts where the people are sleeping. And when they sense that someone is asleep and will let them do what they want, they fly to the feet and bite [and suck] a mouthful [of blood], or they bite them in the forehead; then they fly away again.

When I was among the savages, they often bit me on my toes, and when I woke up, I found my toes to be bloody. But they normally bite the savages on the forehead.

CHAPTER 35

CONCERNING THE BEES OF THE COUNTRY. CAPUT XXXV.

There are three species of bees in the country. The first is almost like those in these [German] lands.

The second is black and as large as flies.

The third is as small as mosquitos. All of these bees have their honey in hollow trees, and I have frequently chopped out the honey from all three species, together with the savages. In general, we found the honey among the smallest bees to be better than that of the others. Furthermore, they do not sting as severely as the bees in these [German] lands. I have often seen that the bees swarmed on the savages because they were taking the honey, so that they had enough to do with brushing them off their naked bodies. I have also taken the honey when I was naked, but the first time I had to run to a stream in great pain and wash the bees off, to get them off my body.

CHAPTER 36

CONCERNING THE BIRDS OF THE COUNTRY. CAP. 36.

There are also many strange birds in this place. One species is called Uwara Pirange [Scarlet Ibis]. These [birds] seek their food by the sea, and they nest in the rocks that lie close to the shore. The bird is about the size of a hen, with a long beak and legs like a heron, but not as long. Naturally, the first feathers on the young birds are light gray. Later, when they are fledged, the feathers become dark gray. As is well known, they then fly about with these feathers for a year. Then, the feathers change again and the whole bird becomes red, as red as any red color can be. It stays like this, and the savages value its feathers greatly.

CHAPTER 37

AN ACCOUNT OF CERTAIN TREES IN THE COUNTRY. CAPUT XXXVII.

There are trees there, which the savages call Junipapeeywa, where a fruit not unlike an apple grows.[55] The savages chew the fruit and press the juice into a vessel. They paint themselves with this [juice]. When they first spread it on the skin, it is like water. After a while, the skin then becomes as black as ink, and so it remains until the ninth day. Then it wears off—but not before this time, regardless of how much they wash themselves in the water.

55. Genipape (*Genipa brasiliensis*).

HOW THE COTTON PLANT AND THE BRAZILIAN PEPPER PLANT GROW, AND SOME OTHER ROOTS, WHICH THE SAVAGES PLANT FOR FOOD. CAP. 38.

The cotton grows upon small trees that are about a fathom high and have many branches. When they blossom they get capsules, and when these ripen, they open; the cotton is found in the capsules, covering black kernels. These kernels are the seeds from which the trees are planted. The small shrubs are full of these capsules.

There are two kinds of pepper in the country: one is yellow, the other is red, but they grow in the same way. When green, it is about the size of the rosehips that grow on thorn bushes. The pepper tree is a small little tree, about half a fathom in height, and has little tiny leaves. It is full of pepper, which burns the mouth. They gather the pepper when it is ripe, and dry it in the sun. And there is another kind of small pepper, which is somewhat similar to the aforementioned, and which they dry in the same way.

There are also roots called Jettiki, which taste good [Jetica, sweet potato]. When they plant them, they cut the roots into small pieces and place these in the ground. This [piece of root] then takes root and spreads over the ground like the hopvines do, throwing off lots of [other] roots.

[III]

Hans Staden wishes the reader mercy and peace in the name of God.

Kind reader. To make this account of my voyage and journey as short as possible I have only described its beginning, how I fell into the hands of a tyrannical people. [I did this] to show how mightily our Lord and God, the Helper in all Need, delivered me from their power, when I was without hope. Everyone shall know that Almighty God still protects and directs His faithful Christians among the godless heathen people in a most wondrous manner, just as He has done right from the beginning. May all join me in my gratitude to God for doing so, and may all rely upon Him in times of trouble. For [in Psalm 50:15] He himself says: Call on me in the day of trouble; I will deliver you, and you glorify me, etc.

Now some may say that I should have printed all that I have experienced and seen. Then I would have to make a thick book. It is true that I could indeed have told a lot more, if it were fitting. But it is not fitting. I have already frequently made my intention—what made me write this little book—sufficiently clear: how very much we owe it to God to praise and thank Him for having protected us, right from the first hours following our birth up to the present hour in our lives.

Furthermore, I can imagine that the contents of my little book will seem strange to many. This cannot be helped. Nevertheless, I am neither the first, nor shall I be the last, who experiences such voyages and becomes familiar with strange lands and peoples. Those who have had similar experiences did not do so laughingly, nor will they do so in the future.

But that he, who has stood face to face with death, should be in the same state of mind as those, who view it from afar or who hear about it, is not to be expected, as everyone knows. Moreover, if all who sailed to America were to fall into the hands of the tyrannical enemies, who would then want to go there?

But this I know for certain: there are many honest men in Castile, Portugal, and France, and also some in Antdorff [Antwerp] in Brabandt, who have been in America and can testify that matters are as I describe them.

Confronted by others, to whom such matters are unknown, I call upon these witnesses[56]—and above all, I call upon God:

My first voyage to America was made in a Portuguese ship. The captain's name was Pintyado [Penteado]. There were three of us Germans on board. One came from Bremen and was called Heinrich Brant; the second was called Heinrich von Bruchhausen; I was the third. My second voyage was from Civilien in Spain [Seville] to Rio de Platta [Rio de Plata], a province that lies in America. The commander of this ship was named Don Diego de Senabrie [Sanabria]. No Germans traveled [with me] on this voyage. After much exertion, fear, and danger on land and at sea during this one voyage which, as I have stated, lasted for two years, we finally suffered shipwreck upon the island of S. Vincente [São Vicente], which lies close to the mainland of Brazil and is inhabited by the Portuguese. There I found a countryman, a son of the late Eobanus Hessus, who received me kindly. One of the merchants from Antdorff [Antwerp] named Schetz also had a factor [an agent] there, who was called Peter Rösel. Both of them can testify how I arrived there and also how I was, in the end, captured by the tyrannical enemies.

Furthermore, the ship's crew, who ransomed me from the savages, came from Normandy in France. The captain of the ship came from Watavilla

56. Short biographical information on most of the following persons is given in the index to the modern German version of Hans Staden's account, edited and transcribed by Karl Fouqet.

[Vatierville] and was named Wilhelm de Moner. The navigator's name was Francoy de Schantz from Harflor [Harfleur]. The interpreter was from Harflor; his name was Perott. These honest men (may God reward them in eternal blissfulness), they, second after God, have helped me in France. They have helped me to get a passport, and have clothed and fed me. They can testify where they encountered me.

Then I left Dippaw [Dieppe] in France and came to Lunden [London] in England. There, the ship's captain with whom I traveled told the merchants from the Dutch Exchange what my situation was. They invited me to be their guest and gave me money for my journey. Then I sailed for Germany.

At Antdorff [Antwerp] I came to the house von Oka, owned by a merchant called Jaspar Schetzen. This man's factor [agent] at sancto Vincente [São Vicente] was, as mentioned, the said Peter Rösel. I brought him the news of how the French had attacked his factor's small ship at Rio de Jenero, but had been beaten off. This merchant gave me two Imperial ducats for my sustenance. May God reward him.

Now if there is any young fellow, who is not satisfied with this description and these witnesses, then let him, with God's help, undertake the voyage himself, lest he should live in doubt. I have given him information enough; let him follow the tracks. The world is not closed to one whom God assists.

May praise, honor, and glory for ever and ever be given to Almighty God, who is everything, Amen.

ERRATA.

Line 15 on the front of page B III. reads "gollicht" [tallow candle]; this should be "eyn unschlicht liecht" [a simple candle].

Likewise, five woodcuts were [accidentally] turned around during the production of the moulds.[57]

[Printed] In Marburg at the Kleeblatt, by Andres Kolben, on Shrove Tuesday 1557.

57. The reversed woodcuts are found in the first part of the book, in chapters 2 (at Kap Ghir), 12, 18, 47, and possibly also in chapter 9.

The Ceremonial Order in Tupinambá Anthropophagic Ritual

extracted from the Warhaftige Historia

I. INDUCTION

beaten by women and children

decorated with feathers / shaved

bound, danced with wearing the feather headdress *arasoya*

2. INVIGILATION

given a woman, whose progeny might also be sacrificed

fed and treated well

other preparations made—pots, paint, tassels for club, the cord *mussurana*

3. INGESTION

a. Ritual Production

invitations to other villages

painting of head of sacrifical club Iwera Pemme [Ibira-pema] with Macaguá bird egg-
    shell, inscriptions, and tassels added to the handle

painting of captive in same manner as club, "remaking" him as the enemy

women drink and dance with him, just as in the dance with the *arasoya*

special hut where he is secluded overnight as they sing to him and the club

mussuruna moved from neck to waist and he is held

women now threaten him

fire is lit and Iwera Pemme displayed by women
executioner comes and hut-chief makes ceremonial possession of captive
captive is killed

b. Ritual Consumption

skinned and anus plugged by women
butchered on the fire by men; legs/arms distributed, spliced along back
distribution of innards, head flesh, brain, and tongue
return of the rest of the body to hosts' huts
receiving of new "beautiful" name by executioner, also scarified by chief
killer retreats to hammock and nurses "feeble arms" which are strengthened by wearing
    of victim's severed lips and eyeball ganglions

The Destiny of the Sacrificed Body
after Combès 1992: 62–63

HEAD / SKULL

smashed if captive was sick or had been "married" by woman of captors village
trophy impaled on wooden palisade
drinking cup
lips and eyeball ganglions to executioner (Cardim)

BRAIN

not eaten according to Léry
eaten by women and/or youngsters with the flesh of the head (Thevet, Staden)

TONGUE

to the women

ENTRAILS

always boiled to make *mingau* for women, young girls, and infants

INTESTINES AND STOMACH

both boiled and grilled
for the young men
also added to *mingau*

SEXUAL ORGANS

male organs given to women
served to men by women, according to Sousa

ARMS AND LEGS

the barbecued flesh, *mokaen*, for men

VARIOUS "CHOICE CUTS"

to the hosts of the ceremony; specifically mentioned are the finger tips, liver, and heart

BLOOD

at the execution, drunk warm by the women
rubbed on the breasts of lactating women and on young children

TEETH

necklaces for men and women

BONES

war-flutes, arrow points, used to threaten the enemy

NOTES

Preface

1. *True History and Description of a Land belonging to the wild, naked, savage, Man-munching People, situated in the New World, America.*

2. The term "Tupi" is a collective term applied to a number of Tupí-Guarani speaking tribes such as the Caeté, Potiguara, Tamoyo, Timino, Tupinambá, and Tupiniquin, who in the sixteenth century occupied extensive areas of the Brazilian Atlantic coast from southern São Paulo to the mouth of the Amazon River. Now extinct, although other Tupian speakers persist in Brazil, these widely dispersed tribal groups showed considerable uniformity in language and culture (see map 1). For these reasons the Tupinambá (Tuppin Imba), Staden's captors, and the Tupinquin (Tuppin Ikin), allies to the Portuguese, are not always distinguished and the generic term "Tupi" is used unless such a disaggregation of particular groups is relevant to the discussion. For a general summary of the ethnology of the Tupinambá and related peoples see Métraux 1948.

3. For example, among the most recent works of this kind, see Barker, Hulme and Iversen 1998, Creed and Horn 2001, Conklin 2001, Goldman 1999, Lestringant 1997, Madrueira 2005, Petrinovich 2000, Sanborn 1998, Turner 1999, Yue 1999, Zheng 1996.

4. Karl Fouquet's 1941 transcription of the Staden's original text has been a source for translations since then. Our translation likewise in part utilized Fouquet's transcription, but not uncritically, since we were careful to assess its fidelity to the original. In fact, although it is in general a highly accurate transcription there are some notable changes that were not made overt by Fouquet, such as the replacement of Staden's term "konig" (king) with "hauptling" (leader). Other German-language

editions were Reinhard Maack and Karl Fouquet's 1964 edition (following closely on a 1963 edition of Fouquet's 1941 work) and Gustav Faber's 1982 edition, of which there was a second edition in 1984 and a third in 1988. We have not modernized Staden's spellings and orthography for place names or Tupi phrases in our introductory discussion; rather, modern equivalents are noted in the text of the translation itself.

5. However, we have been aware of the distortions introduced in earlier translations into English. The version by Richard Burton is fairly loose and expressive of the literary styles of his day but in the case of Malcolm Letts's edition of 1928 there were more active distortions. For example, at the end of the first part of the work, the *Historia* proper, Letts notes of some verses by Staden: "I cannot attempt a literal rendering of these doggerel verses, but I give the gist of them" (Letts 1928: 179, n. 62), thereby failing to appreciate and alert his readers to the particular poetic form that Staden followed and the oral nature of the construction of the text overall. No less significantly, Letts took it upon himself to edit Staden's description of Tupi anthropophagic ritual, merely indicating in a rather cryptic manner, "I have suppressed a few details" (Letts 1928: 182, n. 86).

6. Harbsmeier 1994, Whitehead 2002a, 2002b, 2004a, 2004b.

Introduction

1. EA = *European Americana: A Chronological Guide to European Printed Works on Americas, 1493–1776*, 6 vols., ed. John Alden and Dennis Landis (New Canaan, Conn.: Readex Books, 1982). Three of the woodcuts that appear in Part I of the work are reused in Part II (figs. 30 and 39, 17 and 44, 18 and 45) and one appears three times in Part I (figs. 4, 9 and 33), so that there are in fact only fifty distinct woodcuts, while the paired illustrations of the possum and armadillo are printed from one original wood block, so that there are fifty-one separate images.

2. The Frankfurt 1557 pirated editions include a number of illustrations from a previous printing of a German translation of Ludovico de Varthema's Oriental and African travels—*Die ritterlich vnd lobwirdig Raiss des gestrengen: Vnd über all ander weyt erfarnen Ritters vnd Lantfarers* (Augsburg: E. Öglin, 1518). The pictures of Turkey and the Levant might be taken as indicative of further similarities between Varthema and Staden, as Menninger (1995: 171ff) argues in an attempt to decry the original authorship of Staden. Although Varthema certainly writes about cannibals on the island Java and describes in detail how his miraculous healing powers allowed him to escape his captivity, it will be apparent that the shamanic potential of a culturally strange captive is entirely consistent with native thought in the Americas, as the case of Cabeza de Vaca (discussed below) clearly demonstrates. Michel de Montaigne (also discussed below) certainly did associate Turks with cannibals through his imitation of Postel's work on the Ottoman (see Lestringant 1997:53), but then he lacked the first-hand experiences of Staden.

3. In the intervening years between the first two editions of the *Warhaftige Historia* in 1557 and the inclusion of a Latin translation of the text in de Bry's (1592) collection, eight further reprints and editions appeared in 1557 (Marburg, Frankfurt), 1558 (Dutch translation, Antwerp), 1561 (Low German translation, Hamburg), 1563 (Antwerp), 1567 (Frankfurt—as part of a collection edited by Sebastian Franck), and 1567 (Frankfurt), if one is to believe the not always reliable list compiled by Karl Fouquet. From 1592 to 1736, Fouquet has registered further twenty-two Dutch, nine German, and three Latin printed editions, counting a total of no less than eighty-three editions between 1557 and 1964 (Fouquet 1964).

4. Wynkelmann published a portrait of Hans Staden in that edition (reproduced in Fouquet 1963: 167) and also claimed to have discovered some thirty-four of the original wood blocks, made for the illustrations that appeared in the first edition of 1557, during his preparation of the work, but, as Letts drily noted; "Winckelmann . . . printed a portrait of the traveller, which presents him as a long-bearded, solemn-looking elderly man clasping a book in his left hand, but I do not reproduce it, since a portrait produced for the first time a century after the sitter lived is open to a good deal of suspicion" (Letts 1928: 13).

5. *Véritable histoire et description d'un pays habité par des hommes sauvages, nus, féroces et anthropophagessitué dans le nouveau monde nommé Amérique, inconnu dans le pays de Hesse, avant et depuis la naissance de Jésus Christ, jusqu'à l'année dernière*, ed. Henri Ternaux (Paris, A. Bertrand, 1837).

6. *N. Federmanns und H. Stades Reisen in Südamerica, 1529 bis 1555* (Stuttgart: Litterarischer Verein, 1859).

7. *Hans Staden, suas viagens e captiveiro entre os selvagens do Brazil: Edição commemorativo do 40. centenario* (São Paulo: Casa eclectica).

8. A search on the WorldCat / OCLC bibliographic Internet engine reveals 104 different publications since 1736, being either translations, new editions, facsimile editions, or subsequent editions of earlier translations. This does not include redacted versions or the inclusion of materials from Staden's account in collections on discovery or exploration and so forth. In short, the text has an impressive and continuous publication history and has even been translated into Japanese, as *Bankai yokuryuki: Genshi Burajiru hyoryu kiroku* (Tokyo: Teikoku Shoin, 1961).

9. In the work of the anthropologist Isabelle Combès (1992) Staden's account is not used to elucidate the complexities of Tupian ritual practice per se, since Combès is far more concerned with the secondary interpretations that have been made of the sixteenth-century source materials. Where and how the *Warhaftige Historia* is used by Combès thus becomes all the more enlightening as to the character of Staden's text, in that the principal use of the *Warhaftige Historia* is as a credible visual reference for Tupian cultural practice. This underlines the fact that Staden's text is exceptional not only for its textual narrative and description but also for the ethnological quality of its visual materials, which have rarely been the subject of critical

consideration. Many editions of the *Warhaftige Historia*, as was the case even with the second printing in Frankfurt in 1557, omit the woodcuts or supplant them with quite spurious materials, as Richard Burton noted, or the versions promulgated by Théodore de Bry. As a consequence the original woodcuts in the *Warhaftige Historia* of 1557 are often overlooked.

10. Dryander was a professor of anatomy and medicine at Marburg until his death in 1560 and took a close interest in ethnological description as an example of observational knowledge, akin to that produced by the astronomer or anatomist — see further discussion below.

11. It should be noted here that the differing interpretations and editorial strategies of Richard Burton and Malcolm Letts are often germane to precisely this issue. In the passage under discussion the Burton edition suggests that corrections were only made "if necessary" and the implication of heavy revision by Dryander is absent (Burton 1874: 158–59). Letts, as already noted, also took it upon himself to spare his readers some of the details of the cannibalistic rites.

12. Landgrave Philip von Hesse, called the Magnanimous (1504-67), to whom the book is dedicated, was one of the main protagonists of the Lutheran Reformation in Germany, founder and protector of the first Protestant University in Marburg, and a key figure in the alliance of Protestant forces known as the Schmalkaldic League. After having suffered defeat by the forces led by the Holy Roman Emperor Charles V, Philip was held in captivity in the Netherlands from 1547 until 1552. Dedicating his book to Philip, to whom he also had given an oral report about his adventures in the presence of Johannes Dryander, Staden perhaps also wanted to allude to this captivity.

13. This actually was the name of a working group formed by Eduard Grimmell, Karl Meers, Hilmar Milbradt, Wilhelm Winter, Heinrich Ruppel, and other members of the Gesellschaft für Familienkunde für Kurhessen und Waldeck in 1956 — see Harbsmeier 1997: 85-86.

14. See Menk (1989). The first of these two documents was discovered by Hilmar Milbradt (1956). Further evidence as to the oral character of the text of the *Warhaftige Historia* is sociolinguistic and is based on an analysis of the frequency of certain semantic patterns in the text, particularly the use of connectives. Bradley (1993) argues that analysis of the use of connectives in the text strongly suggests that the text as written directly reflects the spoken language of Staden's time, because it shows aspects of fragmentation which are to be identified with the characteristics of spoken language. This bears on both the issue of authorship and the issue of Dryander's editing of the account. Following Ratzel (1893), Bradley concurs that Staden may therefore have dictated his account but that this also suggests that the influence of Dryander on the text would have been minimal and likely confined to those aspects he openly indicates, that is, in Dryander's words: "Hans Staden, who now commits this book and story to print, asked me whether I would first

take a look at his work and written stories, correct them, and wherever necessary, improve them (before publication)."

15. Staden elaborates: "the savages among whom the Portuguese dwell had waged war on the Tuppin Imbas and had captured a whole village, killing and eating the grown men. But the young ones had been carried off and bartered to the Portuguese for goods, and among them was this young man" (*Warhaftige Historia* I, chap. 25).

16. See Combès (1992: 83–118) for a fuller discussion of the significance of the moon and sun in Tupian cannibal cosmology.

17. See TenHuisen (2005).

18. Compared to the impressive amounts of energy spent on research into the biographical details about Hans Staden and his family, and the relationship of his account to other examples of early Tupi ethnography, strikingly little has been written about the importance of Johannes Dryander for the *Warhaftige Historia*. Having been suspected and suggested many times as the "true author" of the text, especially the second, descriptive part, and also as the interlocutor responsible for the transformation of Staden's primarily oral performance into a written and then a printed text (Ebersohl 1965, Harbsmeier 1994: 112 ff.), the extent of the contribution of Dryander's wide-ranging active interests in medicine, anatomy, astronomy, cartography, mathematics, and instrument making to Staden's book still needs to be assessed. Dryander, whose original German family name was Eichmann but who, like many other contemporary humanists, preferred a translation into classical Greek of this name, was born in 1500 in Wetter and studied in Erfurt and Paris. After a short time as physician-in-ordinary he became, in 1535, professor at the first Protestant university, that of Marburg, which had been founded by Phillip of Hesse, to whom the *Warhaftige Historia* was dedicated, some eight years previously. From 1548 to his death in 1560, Dryander served as vice-chancellor of the university and also involved himself in political and medical issues. Among his numerous publications in both German and Latin one can find whole series of texts which in one way or another point to issues central to the *Warhaftige Historia*. In his more popular medical treatises written in German, Dryander fought against the prejudices and superstitions which he also mentions in his preface; through the public dissections, for which he was responsible in 1535, 1536, 1539, and for a last time one year after the publication of Staden's book. In his illustrated anatomical works partly based on these dissections (see bibliography), Dryander clearly shows a focus on the human body, so prominent in Staden's text as well as his illustrations; in his works devoted to astronomy and cartography, Dryander was as much concerned about geography, the shapes of the landscape and the distances between various places, as was Staden in his concern to locate his experiences correctly in time and space; in his mathematical works and his activities as designer and maker of a wide range of different scientific instruments, which runs through most of his works

155

from the very beginning (Schachtner 1999), Dryander was attempting to develop the means to apprehend landscapes as a series of fields to be measured, studied, and described by scientific means. Schachtner (1999: 809) has emphasized Dryander's obsession with developing a single multifunctional instrument, which could serve as both a sundial and a quadrant for the determination of angular distances and the indirect measurement of height and longitude. In Hans Staden, Dryander apparently had found the man to realize his dreams of scientific study "out there" in the field. Seen from the perspective of a history of fieldwork cutting right across all disciplinary boundaries, Staden and Dryander together can be claimed to have made a major step forward in the early history of both fieldwork and anthropology. As Joan-Pau Rubiés (2004) reminds us, there certainly can be found many further examples of similar kinds of collaboration between humanist scholars at home and travelers out there.

19. A concept originated by Harbsmeier (1994, 1997).

20. Vespucci indicates in the account of his first voyage that "of four voyages which I have made in discovery of new lands: two [were] by order of the king of Castile, King Don Fernando VI, across the great gulf of the Ocean-sea, towards the west: and the other two by command of the puissant King Don Manuel King of Portugal, towards the south." It was on the latter journeys that Vespucci made certain observation of Tupi peoples. However, on his claimed first journey, from Cadiz in May 1497, he reached the mainland, possibly south of the Amazon River, returning to Spain in October 1498. The relation of this first voyage was in a letter addressed to Piero Soderini, *Gonfaloniere* of Florence (quoted above). Because Vespucci mentions in this letter that "they called us in their language Carabi, which means men of great wisdom," it seems plausible he encountered Tupi people, since "Karaiba" became the general name by which Tupi people referred to the Europeans. On May 16, 1499, Vespucci apparently sailed from Cadiz on his second voyage, with Alonzo de Ojeda and Juan de la Cosa. The ships coasted the Guianas and the continent, from the Gulf of Paria to Maracaibo and Cape de la Vela, passing the Amazon River, returning to Spain in September 1500. These were the two expeditions undertaken in the service of Spain. On May 14, 1501, Vespucci sailed in service of Portugal as far as the Rio de la Plata, returning to Lisbon in September 1502. On his fourth voyage, Vespucci sailed with Gonzalo Coelho in June 1503, to what he named Bahia de Todos Santos. Thereafter, he coasted nearly to the Rio de la Plata and then returned to Lisbon in June 1504. Vespucci made a fifth voyage with Juan de la Cosa, between May and December 1505, to the Gulf of Darien. Various controversies surround the veracity of Vespucci's claims to have made these four voyages (see Vespucci 1894: i-xliv) but the interest here is in the way his letters establish a rhetoric of depiction rather than the credibility of his claims to discovery.

21. In fact "cannibalism" as a word derives from the Columbian voyages to the Caribbean where the native term "caniba" comes to stand for a European notion of

the eating of human flesh in the letters of Columbus and other contemporary commentators (see Hulme and Whitehead 1992). It is notable that Vespucci uses the term "canibali" in his accounts of the regions to the north of the Amazon but not in regard to Brazil (Vespucci 1894: 23). Hans Staden does not use the term at all, nor do other commentators on the Tupi such as Nóbrega—quoted below. This underlines that fact that indigenous ritual practices, including funerary custom and sacrifice, were actively read for "evidence" of such a behavior which thereby reduced its meaning to this one key moment of the consumption of human flesh. Moreover the cultural idiom of "eating" is wider than a relationship with food, as in Staden's comment: "They told me that the lice are their enemies who are eating their heads, and they wanted to take vengeance upon them" (*Warhaftige Historia* II, chap. 17).

22. An anonymous account from 1584 also somewhat spreads the blame for the exercise of gratuitous cruelty: "Naturally they are inclined to kill, but they are not cruel; because ordinarily they do not torture their enemies at all, since if they do not kill them in battle, afterwards they treat them very well, and content themselves with breaking their heads with a club, which is a very easy death, considering that usually the blow either kills or at least stuns them, so that they loose their senses. If any cruelty existed, even though the instances were rare, it was by the example of the Portuguese and the French" (Anonymous 1844: 438).

23. See Monteiro 2000 for a thorough discussion of the significance of Sousa's ethnology and its role in the nineteenth-century "invention" of the Tupi.

24. See the important work of Hélène Clastres (1975, 1995) on the messianic search for a "Land-without-Evil" by the Tupi karai, and discussion below.

25. Sousa also remarks on other aspects of Tupi subjectivity, noting for example, "The Tupinamba do not inflict any punishment on their children and do not admonish them or scold them for anything they may do. . . . They are carried until seven or eight and the girls as well. Children are nursed until their mothers give birth to another child and therefore they suckle up to the age of six or seven" (1974: 170–71).

26. "They put neatly made cords around the waist and neck of their prisoners. They feed them well so that they can get fat and they give them the prettiest girls of the village. These girls give them food all the time and they treat them well. If the girls get pregnant, they raise the children to an age at which they may be eaten and offer them to their closest relatives, who are very grateful. They break the child's skull on the plaza and take a new name. The child is roasted and eaten at a big feast and the mother is the first to taste the flesh. No child born from such unions can escape [see also remarks of Anchieta quoted above]. The mother who does not eat her own son, called *cunhambira* or son of the enemy, is looked down upon, and it is worse if her brothers or parents do not give the child away. Some women run away with the captives after having cut their ties and given them food. Such women do not hand over their children, but if they protect them until they are big enough to escape

the fury of their enemies they are safe. Often the Tupinamba do not kill their prisoners, because they were taken when small and can be used. They treat them well and these men could run away if they wanted to, but they do not try to because it is optional with them. Since contacts with the Portuguese, the Tupinamba like to have slaves in order to sell them. Often also after having brought up a child, they kill them with these ceremonies.

"The day before the execution of a prisoner they sing and dance, and on the very day they drink many drinks in the morning, singing verses referring to the man who will die and who drinks with them. The themes of these songs are insults against the man who will suffer and praises of the killer. Before they drink they smear the captive with honey and cover him with bright feathers. They paint the rest of his body with genipa [a black dye] and his feet with rucu [a red dye]. They put a club in his hand so that he may defend himself as well as he can. The prisoner boasts of his deeds and tells how he slaughtered the relatives of the executioner and he threatens the village with the vengeance of his relatives. They take the prisoner to a field where he is placed between two posts, stuck in the ground at a distance of 20 palms. These posts have holes through which the cords which hold him are passed. Old women tell him to look at the sun for the last time since his end is near. He answers with courage that since he is so sure to be avenged he accepts death with fortitude.

"The killer is painted with genipa and wears a bonnet of yellow feathers, a diadem, bracelets and anklets of feathers and bunches of white shell beads across the chest and a wheel of feathers on the buttocks. He has in his hand a heavy club inlaid with white shell beads and decorated with egg shells of different colors, arranged in designs according to their style on a layer of wax, in which they set in nice order. At the end of the club there are tassels of long feathers hanging from the handle and called *embagadura* [see also figure 46]. When the killer is ready to receive that honor which is the greatest to be had among these pagans, his relatives and friends gather and fetch him from his house. They accompany him with lengthy songs and with the playing of trumpets, flutes and drums, calling him a fortunate man; for he has gained the great honor of taking revenge for the death of his ancestors and of his brothers and relatives. Amid this noise he arrives at the field of execution where the victim has been waiting for him, a club in his hand and full of courage. The killer stops in front of him and tells him to defend himself since he has come to kill him. The prisoner answers with a thousand invectives. The other man, holding his club with two hands attacks him and the prisoner tries to dodge, but those in charge of the ropes pull them so that he has to receive the blow. It happens sometimes that the prisoner before dying reaches the killer with his club and injures him, though he is prevented by the cords. This is of no avail, however, for he only prolongs his life for a short while and finally the executioner breaks his skull with his club. After the execution the corpse is dragged to the place where it is divided. The killer adopts a new name and he declares it with the ceremonies already described. He retires into his hut where he throws away all his array. Those who took the prisoners in war change their names with the same festivities and rites and this is done with no less pomp than for the one who actually kills the prisoner" (1974: 182–83). A similar description also appears in Pedro de Magalhães Gandavo's "History of the Province of Santa Cruz" (1922: 102–7) and in Fernão Cardim's "A Treatise of Brasil" (1906: 4312–440).

27. Vespucci indicates here that they have no sounds in their language unknown to European organs of speech, all being either palatals or dentals or labials.

28. See Whitehead 2002c for further discussion of this issue in the Caribbean region.

29. As early as 1503 a French trader from Normandy, Paulmier de Gonneville, spent some five to six months living among the Carijó, a coastal Tupi people, initiating a system of Norman "interpreters" living for extended periods among native peoples in order to organize and promote trade. However, as their moment of political significance passed, the "squaw-men," as they were also known, became conflated with the other hybridic creations of the early colonial moment, the half-breed Tapuyas, remnant Tupi mercenaries, and denationalized white adventurers such as *El Tirano*, Lope de Aguirre, as featured in the film by Werner Herzog, *Aguirre—Wrath of God*. By the end of the sixteenth century the presence of such unnatural and asocial categories of persons invited and induced renewed discursive efforts to tidy up the terms of ethological classification, which had been derived from initial contacts, with the invention of *Guaymures*—the tribe of white cannibals—lineal descendants of the "squaw-men," a new New World marvel where European conceptual continence was broken down by American categorical incontinence (see Whitehead 2005a).

30. According to Léry (1990: 33–50) Villegagnon did not formally take either a transubstantialist or consubstantialist view that the sacramental wine and wafer were to be literally or in part identified physically with the body and blood of Christ. Nonetheless Léry uses the context of Tupian ritual to suggest that "they [Catholics] remained obstinate; to the point that, without knowing how it might be done, nevertheless they wanted not only to eat the flesh of Jesus Christ grossly rather than spiritually, but what was worse, like the savages named *Ouetaca* . . . they wanted to chew and swallow it raw" (41).

31. As Léry's most recent translator, Janet Whatley (1990: xxi), notes. "Léry's long, impassioned, and sometimes difficult Preface is his attempt to set the record straight. But it becomes clear over the ensuing decades that more is at issue than clearing the record on that one ten month encounter. With successive editions of the *Voyage*, together with the works of other writers, we see Protestants staking out their ground of moral and intellectual influence over how the experience of discovery and expansion in the New World would be assimilated by Europe." This is indeed the case for Staden's text as well.

32. Two issues exist of the same original edition, one dated 1557 and the other 1558. The 1558 copies are the remainder of the 1557 edition with a new title page—see Moraes's (1983: 857–58) lengthy notes on this.

33. Lestringant (1997: 46, 58, 65–66) suggests that "these particularities give the ethnographic tableau a vivid impression of truth" and that this was "raw information probably gathered in the course of his voyage to Brazil." But, taking Lestringant's own example of this supposed ethnographic veracity, we find that the description and depiction of the decoration of the execution club *iwera pemme* was already in Staden—see fig. 46—as Gaffarel (1878: 200, fn. 1) acknowledged in his edition of Thevet's *Les Singularitez* (1558). This issue of the ethnographic, that is, dialogic and cross-cultural, basis of ethnology was explicitly considered in a published dialogue between Claude Lévi-Strauss and Frank Lestringant in the latter's 1994 edition of Jean de Léry's *Histoire d'un Voyage*. For Lévi-Strauss, however, it was Léry who figured as the anthropologist's "breviary"—at least in matters of Tupinology. Given the theological nature of dispute between Léry and Thevet, reference to an item of Catholic ritual equipment to characterize the militant Calvinist Léry is ironic indeed, even if not so intended.

34. Thevet (1928: 246) evokes this theme as follows: "In our presence was committed an act by an old woman which was the most horrible, and most cruel one had ever heard of. She would have been better known as a dog. You must believe me—there were children only seven years old present; children of one of the girls married to the executed prisoner—as soon as he was dead, she [the old woman] cut off his head, and through the hole, sucked out the brain, and the blood had not been cooked. The girl was six years old and the boy seven, whose father was killed in their presence."

35. Thus Nóbrega writes. "When they capture someone, they take him to a great feast, . . . and begin to raise him as they would a pig, until the time for killing him arrives" (1988: 100), while Cardim notes, "The poore wretch beeing dead they carrie him to a bone-fire . . . and bringing the bodie neere the fire, touching him with the hand, flay off a skinne somewhat thicker then the rinde of a Onion, till he remaineth cleaner and whiter than a scalded Pig. Then it is delivered to the Butcher which maketh a hole beneath the stomacke according to their use" (1906: 438–39), though Sousa ironically writes, "These people do not eat the flesh of pigs which they raise in their houses, only the slaves brought up among white people do it, but they do eat the flesh of the wild boars" (1851: 318). Léry pursues the analogy and demonizes the women: "they will keep these captives for greater or lesser periods of time, . . . after being fattened them like pigs at the trough, the captives are finally slain and eaten, with the following ceremonies" (1990: 122); "They [the women] come forward with hot water that they have ready, and scald and rub the dead body to remove the outer skin, and blanch it the way our cooks over here do when they prepare a suckling pig for roasting" (126).

36. Written ca. 1587–88, the original is in Paris (Biblioteque Nationale MS fr. 15454) and was transcribed and published by Susan Lussagnet (1953: 237–310).

37. For a discussion of the wider meanings of this and other indigenous notions of attacking spirits and malignant demons, see discussion in Whitehead 2002a: 46–53.

38. Even though Lestringant (1997) may have not wished to stray beyond the Francophone texts he is utterly silent on how Staden's account, and particularly its visual materials, may (or may not) also have had a significant impact on French accounts, and at the very least a direct bearing on their interpretation.

39. In fact, "The draft was lost, rewritten, lost again and found later in its original version" (Whatley 1990: xvii).

40. "By the time he wrote the version to be published, he [Léry] had experienced twenty more years, which included some of the most hideous in French history. The St. Bartholomew's Day Massacre had flooded across the land in waves of such violence that Frenchmen were to be seen roasting and eating other Frenchmen's hearts. Léry himself had lived through the siege and famine of Sancerre. The period gave occasion for a focused meditation on the differences and similarities between the ways of Europeans and the ways of 'savages,' and indeed the growth of a nostalgia for the Brazilian forests and for his Tupi friends" (Whatley 1990: xvii).

41. As similar transformation is evident in the reworking of Staden's illustrations for the visual compendium *Americae* published in 1592 by Théodore de Bry (see further discussion below).

42. In this vein Léry also emphasized the relish with which old women among the Tupinambá engaged in cannibalism being: "all assembled beside it [the roasting corpse] to receive the fat that drips off along the posts of the big, high, wooden grills, and exhort the men to do what it takes to provide them always with such meat. Licking their fingers, they say 'Yguatou'; that is, "It is good" (1990: 126). Equally, the relish for certain kinds of meat and the semiophagic aspects of eating particular foods is nicely illustrated by the following contemporary description of the Waiwai of Guyana; "In my family, the female head of the household was a Wapishana woman who had lived for a long time among the Waiwai. She was always very careful to point out to me that her family ate differently than 'real' Waiwai families. One of the most meaningful differences for her was that they did not cook and serve monkey meat. Other Waiwai families, and most especially those of the older generations routinely ate monkey as part of a range of available game animals. . . . The divisions between eaters and noneaters did not simply fall between Waiwais and Wapishanas, though part of this distinction was due to the Wapishana residents constant assertion that they were 'more Christian' than their Waiwai neighbors and also 'more sophisticated.' Unlike most of the behaviors that Waiwais and Wapishanas performed as part of being Christian, a restriction on consuming monkey meat does not find reinforcement in the Bible. The idea that 'true Christians' do not eat monkeys seems to generate from the village having con-

tact with various biological researchers, who cautioned that monkeys need to be preserved and that they might carry diseases that could be transferred to humans if eaten. The line was also not strictly drawn between either the old and the young or males and females. . . . My personal experience with this situation began with a visit to an elderly couple as I was in search of the male head of my household, . . . 'Yes!' his uncle chuckled, 'We are eating good tonight, while they are punishing with bare farine and . . . fish! Kaywe will come soon, he knows we are eating monkey tonight'! . . . 'Quickly Wachana' said his uncle, 'You must take the head before he comes'! Wachana reached in for the head and began sucking it from the back of the skull. He explained that he was sucking out the brains and that this was the sweetest part. . . . The scene was always the same: various family members would hunch over the pot in the dark and eat quietly, in contrast to other family meals. In addition, there were always moments when there would be a loud smacking of the lips, grunts and an over exaggerated bearing of the teeth. I asked several times why someone would act this way and got the same reply every time. 'We are eating monkey meat Weparu'! 'It is very sweet and we are not eating fish or *poniko* (bush hog).' 'The meat makes us smack our lips and show our teeth, that is what monkey meat makes you do.' Why? I asked several times. *'Because when we eat monkey, maybe we are eating someone'!"* (Stephanie Weparu Aleman, personal communication; my emphasis).

43. Staden tells us that a captured Cario(Carijó) slave "urged the savages constantly to kill me" and that when this man fell ill Staden told them "on account of his lying stories about me my God was angry and smote him with sickness and put it in your minds to kill and eat him. So will my God do to all evil persons who seek or have sought to injure me" (*Warhaftige Historia* I, chap. 34).

44. See Arens's 1979 book and 1998 chapter, both of which argue that most of the European evidence of cannibalism was in fact hearsay and second-hand, an aspect of colonial domination rather than sound ethnological accounts of exotic ritual practice. Indeed there are very few eyewitness accounts of ritual cannibalism, which has made Staden's text something of a lightning rod in this debate. It seems undeniable that charges of cannibalism were indiscriminately made in order to justify and morally extenuate the colonial project as a whole—see also Whitehead 1984—but Arens's rhetorical conjecture, that ritual anthropophagy has never taken place, seems misguided and was the basis for quite surprisingly strong invective against him—suggesting that the cannibal sign remains as potent as ever.

45. The supposed demonstration of Anasazi cannibalism—whatever the view one takes of the "evidence" presented—cannot be divorced from the wider politics of Native American oppression in the United States. The Anasazi have functioned as an example of the "ancient wisdom" of southwestern cultures, a fit emblem of indigenist fantasies for Euro-American tourists. Such a dramatic reversal in that image—they were really cannibals along with all the other "savages"—must therefore be under-

stood alongside such equally ideological laden scientific discoveries—as in the case of Kennewick man, a supposed ancestral Caucasian skeleton found along the Columbia River and conveniently fulfilling the wishes of those who would picture the aboriginal inhabitants of the Americas as but the first in a line of immigrants, and so with no special claims to affirmative action in their favor.

46. See also discussion in Viveiros de Castro 1992: 304.

47. For example, in his discussion of Thevet's tale of the Tabajare Indian, who, having traveled to France and been baptized, was hacked to pieces by enemies on his return to Brazil, Lestringant (1997: 62) notes, "For once, they did not eat their victim," as if want of opportunity or inclination held them back even as the victim was "butchered" as if for consumption. But as Darling (1999) recently has shown with regard to the peoples of the southwestern United States, including the Ana-sazi, this may well be misinterpretation of the purposes for which human bodies might be dismembered and defleshed, since "witches" and "sorcerers" might be so treated in order to ensure their metaphysical, as well as physical, death: and in this case cannibalism is not appropriate See also Rautmann and Fenton 2005 on the archaeological forensics of "cannibalism," and Whitehead 2002a and Stewart and Strathern 1999 for contemporary examples of mutilating and "cannibalistic" assault sorcery.

48. See discussions in Basso 1995, Combès 1992, Hendricks 1993, Viveiros de Castro 1992.

49. A "tupinambization" of the Caraïbe can also be recognized in the sixteenth-century French sources through the way in which the previous French encounters in Brazil led to a transliteration of certain native terms and a similar framework of expla-nation for the cannibal rite, although this does not in itself preclude ethnological relatedness (Whitehead 1995a: 93 n. 4).

50. However, Isabel Combés (1992: 81) has offered a forceful argument for resisting this generalization, lest we lose the particularity of Tupian cultural praxis, which she originally formulated contra René Girard (1977: 383) who sees in Tupian human sacrifice only an exemplum of the universal notion of the scapegoat.

51. Although the separation of cannibal consumption and oratory was a distinction already present in Tupian thought (see Viveiros de Castro 1992: 293).

52. See note 3, section 4 on Léry. Nationalist politics also were very evident from the way in which the spectacle of the Tupi was created for Henry II's royal entry ritual into Rouen in 1550 where "in the events of the festival, just as the French [in another battle tableau] responded to the unprovoked Portuguese attack, the Tupinamba (*Toupinabaulx*), who were allied with the French, responded to the un-provoked attack of the Tabajarc (*Tabagerres*), who werc allied with the Portuguese. And just as the French viciously defeated, burned and sank their foe's ship, so too the Tupinamba overran their enemies and burned their lodges to the ground. The similarity of the narratives structuring these two battles points to the efforts of the

festival's organizers to raise their particular local interest in trade with the New World to a national level by tying it both to on-going inter-European conflicts and to Henri II's well known imperial ambitions" (Wintroub 1999: 396).

53. For example, Hakluyt's 1582 collection, *Divers voyages touching the discouerie of America, and the Ilands adiacent vnto the same, made first of all by our Englishmen, and afterward by the Frenchmen and Britons* . . . or his better-known 1589 work, *The principall navigations, voiages and discoveries of the English nation . . . Whereunto is added the last most renowmed English nauigation, round about the whole globe of the earth.* In a more sinister development Staden's account, principally because of its association with Richard Burton, who is billed as "Explorer—Racialist—Man of the West," is posted online as "A White Nationalist Literary Resource" at JR's Rare Books and Commentary (http://www.jrbooksonline.com/HTML-docs/ Staden_preface.htm). The "Statement of Purpose" for this site reads, "This site's purpose is to bring to the fore many old works of literature you may not be aware of. Certainly, if you grew up in the past 30 years, went through an 'establishment' education and did what you were told, chances are you were never allowed to examine the works presented herein. These books and essays all deal in some way with White solidarity and White Nationalism. . . . The Establishment has taken great pains to ensure that you never look at these books, articles and essays. Many old books disappear off library shelves, conveniently 'lost' or 'misplaced.' Some are bought out for the sole purpose of destruction. Many are now quite rare. A few titles can be seen in your local bookstore—but invariably the text is altered in some way. They are presented here as an act of preservation, and in defiance of 'Political Correctness.'" Although it is Malcolm Letts's 1928 edition that is actually posted online—fittingly enough, perhaps, since Letts was in fact a member of the American pro-Nazi "Deutsche Bund." He also published an apology for the Nazi regime based on a visit he made to Heidelberg (Letts 1933).

54. Sir Richard Francis Burton's travels in Brazil are relatively obscure when compared to his famous explorations of Africa and his interests in Indian and Arab culture, although he did also travel to the western United States. In 1861 Burton was appointed consul in Brazil. In his journeys in Brazil Burton was accompanied by his wife and they also published translations of Brazilian literature—*Iraçéma, The Honey Lips: A Legend of Brazil by J. De Alencar and Manuel de Moraes, a Chronicle of the Seventeenth Century by J.M. Pereira da Silva* (London: Bickers and Son, 1886). Iraçéma, a Tupi woman, is pictured in the Alencar work as the mother of the Brazilian nation. In the story, based on a myth from Ceará, she copulates with a nonindigenous man, gives birth to the first "Brazilian," and then dies. The name Iraçéma is an anagram of "America."

55. Robert Southey's judgment that "the history of his [Staden's] adventures is a book of great value, and all subsequent accounts of the Tupi tribes rather repeat than add to the information which it contains" was quoted by Burton in the conclusion

to his introduction to the volume (1874: xciv), and this was substantially the same judgment which Malcolm Letts came to in his 1928 edition also: "The fact is that in every page of his book Hans Staden stands out as his own witness for truth. That he saw what he tells us he saw, and suffered the vicissitudes which he describes, cannot, I think, be doubted by anyone who has read his narrative with attention." (13)

56. In particular, following up on Erwin Frank (1987), Annerose Menninger in a number of publications (1988, 1992, 1995, 1996a, 1996b) has tried systematically to put together all the available evidence and arguments to disprove the claims of Hans Staden and other witnesses of cannibalism. However, other recent commentators such as the ethnologists Eberhard Berg (1988), Mark Münzel (2001), and Michael Harbsmeier (1994: 97-118), or the literary historians Wolfgang Neuber (1991, 1995), Franz Obermeier (1999-2000, 2000, 2001, 2002), and, in a more deconstructionist mood, Christian Kiening (2000), have been more interested in the literary aspects of Staden's work as a piece of early travel writing and ethnography, rather than as an exemplar of textual deceit.

57. The recent work by Sanborn (1998) suggests that Melville was a pivotal figure in establishing and using the "sign of the cannibal" to radical purposes. By rehearsing and implicitly critiquing key European ideas about cannibalism in his stories, Melville, according to Sanborn, drew attention to the way in which his readers' own fears and fascination went toward constructing the idea of a "savage cannibalism," supplying thereby the grounds for a critique of colonialism itself. The papers collected by Creed and Hoorn (2001) demonstrate the richness of this approach for the Pacific region by linking, as in this work, cannibals, captivity, and the body as a polyvalent site for the reproduction and destruction of colonialism; see also the collection by Barker et al. (1998), many of the individual papers being discussed in this work.

58. Menninger (1995, 1996) and Neuber (1991) most clearly take up the arguments of Arens in suggesting the counterfeit nature of Staden's account and stressing the market for tales of the monstrous and marvelous in sixteenth-century Europe.

59. See Beaver 2002 for a comprehensive review of recent anthropological literature on cannibalism and Forsyth 1985 and Whitehead 1984 for some initial reactions to Arens's treatment of South American historical and ethnographic materials. The fact that Hans Staden's account occupied a whole chapter of Arens's book underlines the critical nature of the *Warhaftige Historia* as a contemporary source for anthropology, while the recent account of Wari' funerary cannibalism by Beth Conklin (1995, 2001) shows that this is an issue which can still be researched ethnographically.

60. So much is evident from the case of the Yanomami of Brazil and Venezuela, whose representation by anthropologists as "fierce" may have served also to legitimate and justify military and criminal actions against them (Ramos 1998, Whitehead

1998b) and have created a mythology of fieldwork which has clearly undermined the professional standing of anthropology itself—see discussions in Borofsky and Albert 2005.

61. See, for example, Claude d'Abbeville 1614 and Yves d'Evreux 1985, in addition to the Portuguese materials discussed above.

62. Although, as Viveiros de Castro (1992: 277) points out, it was an observation made by Thevet, to the effect that the sacrificial victim had to "renew the grave" of the dead man in whose memory he was to be executed that provided Fernandes with the motor to drive the system of revenge, which the sacrifice represented, since the eating of the victim restored the energies of the dead to the group.

63. Bellei (1998: 107) quotes Benedito Nunes, the editor of the works of Oswald de Andrade, who was the founder of the *antropofagistas* movement, that it seems "difficult to understand how . . . *antropofagia*, potentially open to the glorification of force, to technological barbarism, and to Hitler, led many of its sympathizers in the direction of Marxism." In fact this possibility is evident in the use of Staden's text, via Richard Burton, by contemporary "White Nationalists"; see note 2 above.

64. As Madrueira (2005: 11) also points out, this leads to an insoluble dilemma for radical postcoloniality as to whether or not the local can adequately grasp the systemic nature of the global relations which modern capitalism has created, or whether the "local" itself, as a direct artifact of that systemic global process of economic differentiation and cultural homogenization, is necessarily trapped within forms of capitalist reproduction, being in fact a "symptom" of postcolonial modernity itself.

65. Nostalgia for the primitive is prevalent enough to be almost unremarkable, but perhaps Ray Bradbury's line from his screenplay for John Huston's film *Moby-Dick* can aptly, if cynically, stand for all such fantasies of a wild majesty, as Ishmael says to Queequeg at their first meeting; "Many a Christian has longed to be a dark man on a cannibal island."

66. In similar vein, the deployment of the cannibal motif as a means of social and political critique was certainly part of Léry's writing (Lestringant 1997: 73–74) and could service conservative no less than radical political purpose. For example, George Fitzhugh published the tract *Cannibals All! or, Slaves Without Masters* in Richmond, Virginia, in 1857 with the intention of examining "the subjects of Liberty and Slavery in a more rigidly analytical manner." Fitzhugh discusses classical and historical accounts of slavery and cites the Bible as evidence and presents the poor working- and factory-class conditions in England as evidence that the feudalistic Southern institution of slavery is economically justifiable. The progressive capitalism of Europe and the Northern states results in a moral cannibalism, by making capitalists and the professional class into the masters and free labors into exploited slaves, leaving them far more disenfranchised than their slave counterparts. Black slaves in contrast to free labor's "White Slave Trade" are pictured as

happy and free. They enjoy those comforts and necessities granted them under a mutually beneficial, supportive system and community (see also note 11).

67. For example, the journal *Ethnohistory* (Duke University Press) contains many such examples of this kind of hermeneutic approach to colonial archival and printed materials; see also Whitehead 2003. Examples of particular studies of textual materials that utilize this approach include Salomon and Urioste 1991, Whitehead 1995b and 1998a, Zamora 1988.

68. See Basso (1995), Conklin (2001), Hendricks (1993), Viveiros de Castro (1992), Whitehead (2002a), Whitehead and Wright (2004).

69. However, other modern appropriations of the Tupi and related indigenous peoples are evident in the adoption, as in the United States, of the names of such conquered, yet "wild and savage," peoples as in the names of weapons and military hardware. For example, the Brazilian Navy's submarine force, near Niteroi, just across the bay to the east of Rio de Janeiro, named their first rank submarine *Tupi* (S30), which was designed and built in Kiel, Germany, by Howaldtswerke-Deutsche Werft (HDW) and commissioned into the Brazilian Navy in 1989. The naval shipyard in Rio de Janeiro itself constructed the *Tamoio* (S31), commissioned in 1994, *Timbira* (S32), commissioned in 1996, and *Tapajo* (S33), commissioned in 1999. The *Tikuna* (S34), an improved *Tupi*-class submarine, was scheduled for commissioning in 2004, followed by the *Tapuia* in 2005. However, budget cuts by the Brazilian Ministry of Defense led to a halt in construction of the *Tikuna* and the *Tapuia* was cancelled.

70. For a long time Hans Staden has also had a special place in the memories of the German immigrants in Brazil. This interest is documented not only by the long series of Portuguese translations and serialized and shortened versions of Staden's story but more particularly by the use of Staden's name for a series of societies and institutions concerned with German Brazilian interests. The Union of German Teachers of São Paulo took Staden's name in 1935 on the initiative of Karl Fouquet, who also took part in the founding of the Hans Staden Institute in 1938, which after a break in its activities during World War II reopened in 1951 and since 1953 has been responsible for the publication, every year, of a new issue of the *Hans Staden Jahrbuch*. The Instituto Hans Staden de Ciências, Letras e Intercâmbio Cultural Brasilieiro Alemâo, for a long time functioning much as the "Goethe-institutes" in other parts of the world to promote German culture, arts, and science, was renamed in 1997 as the Instituto Martius-Staden, marking the nineteenth-century presence of another important German traveler and ethnologist. See Spix and Martius 1824.

71. See especially *Sick Societies* (Edgerton 1992), *War before Civilization* (Keeley 1996), *The Anthropology of Cannibalism* (Goldman 1999), and *Man Corn* (Turner 1999).

72. For analyses of cannibal serial killers, see Duclos 1998;, Seltzer 1998, 2005, and Tithecott 1997; for discussion of postcolonial violence, terrorism, and its impact

on the cultural imagination, see Whitehead 2004a and 2005b; and for discussion of resurgent forms of traditional violence, see Hoskins 1996, Stewart and Strathern 1999, Taylor 1999, Yue 1999, and Zheng 1996.

73. As Elaine Scarry (1985) has stressed, the "irreducibility" of the body as an experiential locus in the material world make this an always potent site for the production and inscription of meaning.

74. The eerie irony of the case of Armin Meiwes—eerie because he came also from the state of Hesse, like Staden, ironical because, as often with Tupian sacrifice, the victim was a consensual actor in the performance—was reported by, for example, the Canadian Broadcasting Company in 2004 as follows: "German cannibal sentenced to 8 years in prison. Kassel, Germany—A 42-year-old German man who confessed to killing, dismembering and eating another man who he said agreed to the grisly act was sentenced to eight and a half years in prison. A German court convicted Armin Meiwes of manslaughter on Friday, ruling he had no 'base motives' in the crime and sparing him a murder conviction. The prosecution, who had been looking for a murder conviction and a life sentence, said they would appeal the verdict. Prosecutors had argued that Meiwes, who met his victim over the internet, was satisfying a sexual impulse. They said he filmed himself dismembering the victim before he ate him so he could 'admire himself as a human butcher.' But Meiwes' lawyer argued that the slaying was a 'homicide on demand.' He said it was a form of mercy killing—because the victim gave his consent to be killed and eaten. In his trial, Meiwes confessed in detail to the March 2001 killing of 43-year-old Bernd Juergen Brandes at his home in the nearby town of Rotenburg. Brandes had traveled from Berlin in reply to an internet advertisement seeking a young man for 'slaughter and consumption.'" Meiwes testified that Brandes wanted to be stabbed to death after drinking a bottle of cold medicine to lose consciousness. "'Bernd came to me of his own free will to end his life,' said Meiwes in a closing statement Monday. 'For him, it was a nice death.' Meiwes said he regretted the killing. 'I had my big kick and I don't need to do it again,' he said. 'I regret it all very much, but I can't undo it.'" CBC News Online, Friday, January 30, 2004.

75. The phenomenon of "dark shamanism," as both an expression of profound spiritual traditions and a radical vehicle for countering the blithe faith in "development" as a means of political and social redemption, is discussed extensively in Whitehead 2002a and Whitehead and Wright 2004. For a discussion of the contemporary meaning of cannibalism in this kind of context see Conklin (1997, 2001).

76. See Allwork (1976), Handelsman (1977), Hanigan et al. (1990), Pirsig (2002). Johannes Dryander's interests also extended to globes (*Spherae materialis* 1539) and mechanical devices. Indeed, Dryander wrote the first dedicated treatise on one particular instrument (*Das Nocturnal oder Die nachtvhr* 1535), a night dial for determining the hour of the night by means of the position of the stars. The instrument could be constructed using four detachable pages appearing in the work. The trea-

tise was begun by J. Koebel (1460–1535) and completed after his death by Dryander, his student. Dryander thus also became famous as an instrument maker, and the plates in this book, his first such essay, were meant to be used for constructing the evening dial, or night clock. His interest in celestial observation also found its way into publication, through the translation and editing of a twelfth-century Arabic work on navigation (*Abraam Iudaei—De nativitatibus* 1537b), and in his introduction to the *Warhaftige Historia* he directly compared such observation of the stars to the eyewitness cultural reporting of Hans Staden.

77. Isabelle Combès (1992: 62–63) provides a summary of the information to be derived from the sixteenth-century sources on this; see Appendix.

78. Staden directly quotes the chief Konyan Bebe to this effect (see above under "French Texts") and also notes that when he asks a boy to stop gnawing the legbone of the slave, "both he and the others grew angry with me, saying that this was their *proper food*. So I let it be" (63; my emphasis). See also Viveiros de Castro (1992: 262–72) for an extended discussion of such ontological transformation through anthropophagy.

79. Wandel (2006:7) also suggests that this would represent a direct challenge to the Aristotelian physics which had allowed these two notions to be united through the argument Aristotle made that "substance" and "accident" were distinct, the latter an aspect of phenomenological appearance, the former the real or true cause and occasion for the "accidents" of the appearance of the eucharistic substances.

80. Wandel (2006: 33) notes that the term "Host," which very early on in Christian history supplanted words for the unleavened bread of Passover, thereby translated the "bread" of Christ's supper into a context of sacrificial death and bodily violence. This literal view of the Host as appearance and substance of Christ was, then, a fruitful ground for ideas of its "kidnap" by "the Jews," recalling in turn Christ's treatment prior to his crucifixion, to which Staden also likened his own treatment by the Tupi (*Warhaftige Historia* I, chap. 42).

81. The forms and meanings of anthropophagy were not new to theological debates or the wider cultural imaginary. As Price (2003) copiously illustrates, there were many uses to the term "cannibalism" in medieval as well as early modern Europe, although he fails to recognize the historicity of the term itself. Nonetheless Price nicely illustrates (7–11) that the public anthropophagy of the flesh of "Saracens" by Richard I, the Lionheart, was not just a rhetorical claim of the French chroniclers but an overt tactic of personal intimidation and self-aggrandizement; altogether making Richard lion-heart seem quite temperamentally and ontologically analogous to the jaguar-heart Konyan Bebe.

82. Karen Gordon-Grube (1988, 1993) documents the use of human body parts, particularly blood, heart tissue, and flesh, within Paracelsian medical practice. Ironically, this movement was favored by Puritans in England, perhaps recovering thereby some of the mystery of the transubstantiation that was theologically excluded for

them. The English College of Physicians endorsed this practice throughout the seventeenth century and human blood was still recommended as a treatment for epilepsy into the eighteenth century. Indeed, Merck Pharmaceuticals, makers of the notorious drug Vioxx, still listed "mummy" in their pharmaceutical catalog as late as 1909: "genuine Egyptian mummy, as long as supply lasts, 17 marks per kilogram" (quoted in Gordon-Grube 1988: 407). The idea of human blood and flesh as restorative and medicinal was certainly reported from antiquity by Pliny but it is important to note that the preparation "mummy / mummia" was distinct from this tradition, also being considered the more effective when taken from a corpse that had suffered a violent death. This made the gibbets and execution grounds of England excellent places for collecting such material, even as the executioners and torturers of the condemned retained the right to sell the warm blood of their victims.

83. Especially since public executions in Europe, particularly England, were the scene not only of a sacrificial cannibalism (see note 11) but also the source of civil disorder, especially where the condemned were also (and humiliatingly) sentenced to "dissection" by the newly professionalizing surgeons. The rioting and rescuing of the condemned from the gibbet was sufficiently frequent to eventually require that this state performance of its power was taken inside the prison walls (Lindebaugh 1975, 2003).

84. As Wandel (2006: 44) writes, "In the particular forms of abstinence—from meat and sex in particular—the Lenten season brought depth and density to mediaeval understandings of 'the flesh.' Lent was preceded by and paired with Carnival. . . . The 'flesh' as it was defined in Carnival encompassed wine and eat in abundance, sexuality . . . as well as gambling, dancing, card games and ribaldry."

85. There is a Rabelais-inspired rendering of the story of Staden, published in 1625 in Strasbourg, called *Florians von der Fleschen wunderbarliche seltzame, abenthewerliche Schiffarten und Reisen*, which puts Staden's adventures in comical and satirical light not unrelated to the way in which the genre of travel writing as such was looked at in a text which was to become a classic in German literature, Christian Reuter's Schelmuffky's *Warhafftige Curiöse und sehr gefährliche Reisebeschreibung zu Wasser und Lande* from 1696 (Harbsmeier 1994: 11-34). Sabine Wagner (1995) has also commented on this; see also Schlechtweg-Jahn (1997).

86. Lestringant (1994), in his introductory essay to Jean de Léry's *Histoire d'un Voyage*, explicitly discusses the "laughter of the Indian," suggesting that Léry himself is proto-Rabelaisian for his appreciation of the nature of Tupian sacrifice in this regard. See also Viveiros de Castro (1992: 271) on the "Zen" humor of Konyan-Bebe, quoted above.

87. This is exactly the starting point for Pierre Clastres in his 1987 work *Society against the State*. Not only was the power and influence of leaders limited and made contingent through the necessity of community participation in the sacrificial ritual,

but so too the messianic influence of the *karai* (prophet-shamans) undermined the stability of the political order, as also shown by Hélène Clastres (1975, 1995). This meant that political power and hierarchy could not be institutionalized the way it had in feudal Europe, where a military class likewise dominated the social order, and for whom the Christian Church provided theological justification.

88. The central reference here is to the medieval and early modern state in Europe, but the example of the Roman Empire, and its spectacles of death in the arena (Kyle 2001), is no less germane. State power in the Americas was similarly instituted through Aztec and Mayan rituals and spectacles of sacrificial death.

89. In this way the "rescue" by vengeful whites of cannibal victims, and their sale as plantation slaves, actually did a double violence to the reproduction of indigenous society (Whitehead 1993a), first through this commercialization of war and second through the resulting commodification of the captive. However, simply seeing cannibalism in this aspect, as a structure and function of society, or as an act of hyper-resistance to colonialism, is to precisely constrain ethnographic experience in the ways suggested earlier. But this is also the very reason why cannibalism—even the blood-frenzy that accompanies it—cannot be reduced to some form of maniacal exaggeration of a symbolic necessity (revenge) that might be satisfied in more "civilized" ways.

90. As TenHuisen (2005) writes in his analysis of the broad influences of the medieval *passio* literary form on the *Warhaftige Historia*: "As with other early modern chronicles, the hagiographic discourse in *Warhaftige Historia* is often ignored or dismissed as merely fictitious or artificial by contemporary readers, relegating the religious language, biblical allusions, and miracles to unconvincing attempts on the part of the author to manipulate his readers. The influence of hagiography, however, cannot be disregarded. In fact, hagiographic language is the principal lens through which Staden both frames and interprets his experience, and the discourse of martyrdom also determines his view of the indigenous peoples that he encounters." See also Obermeier 2002: 54ff.

91. Staden first quotes Jeremiah after the French trader, Karwattuware, refuses to say he is not Portuguese and encourages the Tupi to sacrifice him: "Then I remembered the saying in Jeremiah Chapter XVII [17.5] where he says: Cursed are those who trust in mere mortals" (*Warhaftige Historia* I, chap. 26). According to TenHuisen (2005), "Staden's response follows the narrative strategy of quoting one line and allowing his audience to recall the appropriateness of the whole. He extends the lessons Jeremiah learns while in captivity with the Babylonians to his own experience. By placing his hope for escape in the Frenchman, Staden is like the shrub in the desert (who puts his trust in man), rather than the tree by the water (who trusts in God). And the crucial concept of God's anger, introduced in this Psalm, extends to Staden as well: 'Through your own fault you will lose the inheritance I gave you. I will enslave you to your enemies in a land you do not know, for you

have kindled my anger, and it will burn for ever.' . . . But ultimately, the closing of the Psalm reiterates the image of Staden as stalwart in his faith and suggests the direction of the narrative to come. That is, God will reward the faithful and punish the wicked. . . . This lesson carries with it the directive to maintain alterity and construct barriers between self and Other. Israel can only receive God's grace as long as she refuses to take on the culture of the Babylonians. Thus in order for Staden to receive God's mercy he must resist the Other as godless and barbaric. Although Staden, like Jeremiah, has been punished in captivity, Staden demonstrates that the Tupinamba mock God as well as Staden. As the enemy of God, the Tupinamba are the true Other" (18–20).

92. As Peter Parshall (1999: 555) notes, "In the sixteenth century the importance of artistic invention migrated to the centre of critical debate, and in certain circles the classical model of *mimesis* came to be reformulated in such a way that for a time the operations of art and nature were paralleled to one another and their separate products esteemed on similar and equal terms." Parshall (1993: 560–64) suggests that the German-speaking regions of Europe were particularly significant during the sixteenth century in contributing to this intellectual environment. The authority of the eyewitness, and the aesthetic form of the printed image, were in turn central to such questions. Notably the phrase to indicate this epistemological status was *warhafftig ab conterfeit*, for which textual accompaniment provided a constant insistence as to the veracity of the image, as in Staden's *Warhaftige Historia*.

93. A wonderful collection of these woodcuts is reproduced in Strauss 1974 and 1975.

94. As Dryander remarks in his introduction: "His intention is both honorable and fitting—if this were not so, he would surely have spared himself this time-consuming effort and labor, and the considerable expense of printing this work and cutting the blocks [for the woodcuts]," although Dryander clearly employed a better block maker for his 1542 publication *Der Gantzen Artzenei*.

95. Parshall (1993: 566) also indicates that as various civil and ecclesiastical authorities tried to censor such productions for both factual accuracy and religious and political propriety, judgments were increasingly made, from the 1530s onward, on the basis of "verifiability by sensory means, and eye-witness accounts became the legitimate test of their genuineness." Hence the relevance of Dryander's introduction to the *Warhaftige Historia*, stressing the eyewitness status of Staden in the matters he describes.

96. A graphical depiction of this scene is reproduced in Honour 1975(63) and in Boorsch 1976 (fig. 78).

97. "The king himself talked to them a good while, and they were made to see our fashions, our pomp, and the form of a great city. After which, some one asked their opinion, and would know of them, what of all the things they had seen, they found most to be admired? To which they made answer, three things, of which I have forgotten the third, and am troubled at it, but two I yet remember ." (Montaigne 1580, IV, "Of Cannibals").

98. It should be emphasized that the modern sin of "plagiarism" is connected to historically and culturally specific ideas of individual creativity and the financial economics of creative production in a world of copyright law and massive investment in networks of distribution by recording companies, publishers, and retailers. In Staden's day the issues were less prominent and focused more on depiction and discussion of natural phenomena. As Parshall (1993: 56) notes, "How can one be accused of copying what is, after all, simply the face of nature itself?"

99. Honour (1975) reproduces and discusses many of these illustrations. William Sturtevant (1976) also provides a very useful, if incomplete, survey of the earliest images of indigenous peoples of the Caribbean and South America.

100. The various *tableaux vivants* already discussed could conceivably have supplied visual tropes for Brazilian Indians, but it is striking that the representational aesthetic present in the *Warhaftige Historia* is quite different from other woodcuts of the time, while certain elements, particularly the *enduap*, as opposed to the imaginative "feather skirt," as well as the lip-plugs and other facial piercings, are present in the *Warhaftige Historia*'s graphics and also appear in Thevet's publication *Les Singularitez* of 1557.

101. A similar hermeneutical approach was taken by Whitehead (1998a) in his edition of *Discoverie of the Large, Rich and Bewtiful Empire of Guiana by Walter Ralegh*, an account that was also subject to immediate and persistent accusations that it was a purely imaginative or fictional work.

102. Figs. 17–18 and 30 are repeated in Part II of the work, appearing as figs. 44–45 and 39.

103. Staden's account has recently been realized as a comic book, or graphic novel, by Jô Oliveira (2005), in which many of the iconic scenes of the original illustrations are redrawn or reworked. The visual power of the original illustrations is again testified to by the way in which certain visual elements—Staden's nakedness, the impaled skulls, the palisaded village, the massed canoes, the butchery of the corpse—are repeatedly used in this contemporary version. Otherwise Oliveira presents a gentler and less obsessed Hans, although key events are retained, such as the incidents with the French, the prophecy of the angry moon, his curing of the sick, the dialogue with Konyan Bebe, and the help given to other Portuguese prisoners. Oliveira also hints that Staden was better integrated into Tupi life than the *Warhaftige Historia* suggests, as he is shown somewhat tenderly saying goodbye to Abbati Bossange's village (64–66).

104. Despite his depiction of himself with a beard in all the illustrations, in fact the beard was removed after his initial protests (*Warhaftige Historia* I, hap. 22).

105. Life-size cardboard figures of Staden and his hosts, apparently exhibited for the first time in Sâo Paulo in 1954 on the occasion of the four-hundredth anniversary of that city (Fouquet 1956, 1957: 9), can now be found at the museum in Wolfhagen.

106. Especially the scene in fig. 35, a palisaded village, devoid of all life and suggesting a

stark severity and aesthetic regularity to the indigenous art of war. The layout of the composition is detailed and accurate, with a line of skulls at the entrance passage to complete the intimidating vision.

107. Alexander (1976: 90) suggests that this was also done since the original woodcuts would not have been adequate for long print runs. For general discussions of de Bry's collections and print making practices, see Keazor 1998 and Bucher 1981.

108. Bernadette Bucher (1981: 46–64) elaborates on this trope within de Bry's reworking, offering a structuralist style analysis of the interrelation between gender, age, and cannibal proclivity in his copperplates. Greve (2004:134-73), discusses the "third part" of de Bry's *Americae*, relating to Staden and Léry in particular. For general discussions of the de Bry collections, see also Duchet 1987, Burghartz 2004, and Obermeier 2000.

109. It is also notable that fig. 53 (168), *The Women's Feast*, is the most often reproduced woodcut in both the original and de Bry versions and is the sole reproduction, for example, in the Japanese translation (Staden 1961).

110. Such is the case with Lestringant (1997: 56–57, fig. 5), who appears to treat de Bry as a source independent of Staden and somewhat misleadingly suggests that Thevet's illustration adds details not present in Staden's text, such as the use of the *boucan* and the cooking of the entrails and the head. In fact these details do appear in other woodcuts in the Staden series, though not in the particular illustration from the *Warhaftige Historia* he reproduces—see figs. 24, 26, 28, 47, 53 and 54. Menninger (1995: 209-19) also discusses what Thevet appears to have added to Staden both in the text and in the illustrations of the *Les Singularitez*. She concludes that three features in particular—the wife giving herself to mourning once "her" prisoner has been killed; the notion that small children are smeared with the blood of the victim to strengthen them; and that women taken as prisoners are put to work as slaves in the field—are part of a standard repertoire of popular images of the barbarian savage of the time (216).

111. The Tupi were classic examples of an indigenous people caught in the tribal zone (Whitehead 1999) of colonial intrusion. Encapsulated by the progressive encroachment of permanent colonial settlement and fortification, the Tupinambá, Tupinikin, and other ethnic formations of coastal Brazil were inevitably sucked into the politics of colonial rivalry. The war-complex on which Staden reports was thereby deeply affected and its purposes and practices subtly intensified and altered to accommodate their alliances with the various European factions—see also Whitehead's (1993a) particular account of this process in Brazil and more generally Monteiro (1999), Whitehead (1999a-c).

112. Parshall (1993: 572) characterizes such borrowing and changing as legitimate for compilers like de Bry for whom it is likely that "the identity of the primary witness is no longer as important as the self-sufficiency of that which is witnessed." In the seventeenth century Baconian epistemology proposed that proper scientific obser-

vation would require the progressive elimination of the variables associated with the observer.

113. Issued by the Brazilian publisher Editora Terceiro Nome with a subsidy from Deutsche Bank and support of the Brazilian Ministry of Culture. This may be understood as a part of a revival and renewed interest in the work of Candido Portinari as well as evidence, alongside Oliveira's comic book and Luis Alberto Pereira's 2000 film *Hans Staden*, of the continuing relevance of the *Warhaftige Historia*. Editora Terceiro Nome also issued a Portuguese translation of the *Warhaftige Historia*, with the original illustrations, in an edition of 1999, edited by Mary Lou Paris and Ricardo Ohtake and overtly paired with the Portinari volume. An introductory essay to this edition by the historian Fernando A. Novais reinscribes Hans Staden as a foundational figure for modern Brazil, much as is suggested by the current revival of the work of Portinari, and that essay also appears in the *Portinari Devora Hans Staden* volume.

114. Malcolm Letts (1928: xvii) suggested that the only clue we have as to the possible identity of the woodcut maker is contained in this illustration, since the initials "DH" appear on the flag fluttering from the main mast. This certainly was a common way of indicating authorship but no woodcut maker of with those initials is recorded working in Marburg or adjacent cities at this time (see Strauss 1974, 1975).

115. Sturtevant (1976) discusses the establishment of this particular visual convention, which is apparent form the earliest woodcuts, as well as map illustrations.

116. It is uncertain whether the illustrations reproduced in the Terceiro Nome volume are all that are extant. The website <http://www.portinari.org.br> for the *Projeto Portinari*, being organized and overseen by Candido's son Joao Portinari, certainly had three other illustrations posted. However, we were not able to secure permission to reproduce any of Portinari's works for this volume and requests for information on the scope and archival holdings for original project of an edition of the *Warhaftige Historia* were not forthcoming. A limited edition catalogue of all Portinari's works is in preparation by Joao Portinari, there apparently being some 5,000 artworks and 30,000 pages of documentation relevant to the artist's career.

117. In both native cosmology and in modern Brazil the parrot is not merely an example of natural wonder, since the red plumage of, for example, the Scarlet Macaw recalls the western sunset and blood. Wilbert (2004: 33) informs us: "The Land of Darkness and its ruler have existed since the universe began. And when, in early times, the Lord of Death decreed that heretofore spiritual humans were henceforth to become embodied mortals, the Ancient Hoebo manifested as the red macaw (*Ara chloroptera*) and claimed the new terrestrial species as his and his relation's staple food. In time, the parrot people built a settlement of humble houses near Macaw's colossal iron (or aluminum) mansion and gathered there with their lord to drink of human blood from a thirty-foot canoe and feast on human flesh from well-stocked

larders. The blood container, like the parrots' houses and their furniture, is made of human bones. A gagging stench of putrefaction saturates the air, and blowflies carpet the environs, sodden with coagulating blood. Wind instruments of human tibias and skulls are playing, and partakers in the banquets are attired in their feather coats adorned with necklaces of human costal bone." Equally the Brazilian *pau de arara* (parrot's perch) is a horizontal bar used as an instrument of torture, the victim being suspended upside down with his or her legs bent over the bar.

118. The ambiguous status of the returning captive is an important trope in the genre of captivity literature more widely and was the key dramatic element in the screenplay of that modern reworking of the "savage captivity" tale, John Ford's *The Searchers*. The scene of the final rescue of the woman taken by the Indians is a moment of high drama and tension, as it is unclear if the obsessed "Ethan," played by John Wayne, who has pursued her and her captors for years, will kill her for the savage she might have become or bring her back to the world which no longer knows her. Exactly this dilemma was expressed in the memoir of John Tanner (1994), known as Grey-Hawk or The Falcon, first published in 1830. Tanner was taken as a child by the Ojibwe but, when he finally made his return after some twenty years, he was at best barely tolerated since he had by then become a "savage" himself. He in fact went back into Ojibwe territory and was never heard from again.

119. Neuber (1991), Pratt (1986: 33–34), and TenHuisen (2005) all mention that the *Warhaftige Historia*, in its division into two distinct parts—Part I, the "*Historia*" proper, and Part II, the "*Bericht*"—conforms precisely to particular literary forms of the day, the medieval *passio* and the humanistic *apodemic*. In fact the *Warhaftige Historia* adheres very strictly to the apodemic form according to Neuber and Ten-Huisen, "even appearing in order in the 38 chapters, starting with the name and location of the Tupinambás and ending with descriptions of flora and fauna" (Ten-Huisen 2005: 216). This point was first made by the geographer Friedrich Ratzel in his article about Hans Staden in the *Allgemeine Deutsche Biographie* (1893: 364–66) and has often been noted by later commentators.

120. See in particular the articles by Harbsmeier (1989, 1993) concerning the "magic of writing," which further consider the case of Hans Staden.

121. Indeed, Knivet even claimed to have met Abbati Bossange, by then a very old man. Knivet was accompanying a punitive Portuguese expedition against the Wataquazes (Ouetacas) when they came across the place that Abbati Bossange had taken refuge with "fortie or fiftie of his Countrimen" after he had been driven from the coast by the Portuguese some twenty years previously. Encircled and captured by the punitive expedition, he was given the chance to lead the attack on the Ouetacas, with whom he was already at war. Declaring, when they asked his advice on how to make an effective attack on the Ouetacas, that "he had no policie but to fight in open field, and if we would, we should see how he made warre against his enemies . . . Abausanga came forth . . . [and] hee ran into the thickest of his enemies, with

all his companie, where eighteene of his companie were presently killed, . . . he himselfe being shot in one and twentie parts. . . . This Abausanga assone as he perceived the Portugals to stand amazed of him, desired then to tell him somewhat of God, for he said, that the Frenchmen had told him that there was a God, and that he which beleeved in him should be saved . . . and desired to be baptised, and had his name given John. For the space of two houres that this Indian lived, hee did nothing but call upon God, and so ended his life, being one hundred and twentie yeeres of age, as he shewed us by signs" (1625: 253–54).

122. He did stay at least one night, retiring to his bed, while the "cannibal feast" raged around him. However, he refused the offer of a roasted foot (already a standard incident of American travelogues), rather less sturdily than did Hans in the face of Konyan Bebe, and rather presumptuously imagines that he might be their next victim. Certainly he happily contextualized this evidence of his naiveté with a sound and detailed discussion of Tupi cultural practice, but the contrast with the elaborate and cunning stratagems of Staden, informed by his long experience in Brazil, could not be greater; especially since Léry was guided by an "interpreter," probably someone much like the French trader Karwattuware in Staden's account, "who had been off carousing with those raskals of savages all night long in other village houses" (1990: 163), as should have been the would-be "ethnographer" Léry.

123. "Nine and a half years" being the total length of Staden's two voyages, service in Brazil, and captivity with the Tupi, as suggested on the contents page of the *Warhaftige Historia* (11). The text of the *Warhaftige Historia* gives April 29, 1547, as the date of his first departure from Kampen in Holland, and February 20, 1555, as the date he arrived in Honfleur following his captivity with the Tupi. This is less than nine and a half years but he subsequently traveled from Dieppe to London, then, after a "few days," to Zeeland and finally Antwerp. Also Staden may have counted his time in traveling at the beginning of his voyage from Homberg to Bremen to Holland (at Kampen), where he embarked on salt ships bound for Portugal on April 29, 1547. If we also count the time from Honfleur to Antwerp on his return, then this itinerary might well have been nine years or more.

124. A Hellenizing neologism deriving from the Greek word for traveling (*apodemein, apodemeo*) and from 1577 on used to name a genre of books and treatises dealing with the "art of traveling," often entitled *Art apodemica.* See Stagl 1995.

125. This is very evident from many of the essays collected in the *Cambridge Companion to Travel Writing*, ed. Peter Hulme and Tim Youngs, 2002; see Whitehead 2002b: 134–35 for discussion of this in South America. The essays collected in Creed and Horn (2001) map these themes in the Pacific context.

126. A German textbook introduction to anthropology written by Anton Blok and Klaus Schomburg (1985) makes use of Hans Staden and the *Warhaftige Historia* as a kind of organizing principle for discussion of fieldwork and participant observation and the relationship between ethnography and anthropological theory.

127. This was the subject of much debate within anthropology and while no consensus has emerged it would be fair to say that ethnography has undergone a transformation from the kind of writing that Malinowski initiated to accounts in which the position of the author is much more prominent as a context for understanding the interpretations of cultural practices that are being made (Clifford and Marcus 1986, Clifford 1988, Geertz 1973, Marcus 1992). This change was also consistent with the "new historicists" working from historical texts (Greenblatt 1993) who likewise saw the contextualization of those texts in the historical and cultural particularities of their production, especially that of colonialism (Asad 1973, Comaroff and Comaroff 1992), not issues of their "truth," as key to their interpretation. The crossover between these methodological changes in both history and anthropology was also related to the perceived lack of, respectively, culture and time (Fabian 1983, Fox 1991). In both cases the answer to such issues begun with a recognition of the relevance of literary critique of text to the texts of the archive as well as the "text" of social and cultural behavior (Derrida 1967 and Ricoeur 1971). For further discussion, see Whitehead 1995b.

128. It should be realized, however, that part of this "invention" of the fieldwork method was necessitated by the fact that, as a Polish citizen, Malinowski faced difficulties in leaving an Australian colony during the First World War. He was not formally interned by the British but certainly his ethnographic engagement shared aspects of a more overt physical captivity.

129. The conjunction of captivity and modern ethnography is perfectly exemplified by Etorre Biocca's 1965 recording and transcription of Helena Valero's account of her captivity among the Yanoáma of southern Venezuela in the 1930s. Biocca explicitly indicates that, while he tried to preserve Valero's own phrasing and emotive reactions in the account of her captivity, he also pushed her toward certain kinds of topics that were ethnographically significant to him. This may be how others have also construed Dryander's role in the production of the *Warhaftige Historia*, despite the evidence to the contrary as discussed above.

130. In fact two of these captives, the de Praga brothers, did later escape, as Staden tells us: "Several Mameluke brothers were stationed at this point to prevent the savages from passing through. Their father was a Portuguese, and their mother a Brazilian woman, and they were Christian. They were skilled and experienced in both the Christian and the savage languages and manners of fighting" (*Warhaftige Historia* I, chap. 15).Undoubtedly they were very well versed in survival skills and the geography of the region.

131. As Fausto (1999: 938) remarks. "The binding control established by the killer over his victim's subjectivity should be compared to the relation between shamans and familiar spirits. Both are conceived of as an adoption, as the transformation of a relationship of predation (real or virtual) into control and protection, modeled as the passage from affinity to consanguinity. The familiarization of animal young in

hunting and the abduction of children in warfare are particular cases of this wider relational structure which articulates predation and familiarization, affinity and consanguinity, exterior and interior." See also Viveiros de Castro 1992: 280–82.

132. Staden's behavior on his return, however, also hints that he might have been transculturated to some degree, at least into the vengeful aspects of Tupi life, as his behavior on arriving in Dieppe suggests. See *Warhaftige Historia* I, chap. 54; the full passage is quoted above.

133. Cabeza de Vaca served in the 1527 expedition of Pánfilo de Narvaez which left Spain with five ships and over six hundred men. They were sent to establish a colony in North America. But, in the event, less than three hundred men and some forty horses actually landed in southern Florida, from which point they headed north. They encountered persistent local hostility and suffered from malaria and dysentery. The remnants of the expedition then built rafts and turned west along the Gulf Coast toward Mexico, Spain's nearest outpost. Two of the rafts, containing some eighty sick, were wrecked on East Island, Louisiana. All but fifteen of these survivors died due to hunger and disease. Cabeza de Vaca spent six years on East Island before heading west again, traveling through Texas, New Mexico, and Arizona. Passing from village to village, eating off the land, Cabeza de Vaca and three others performed as shamanic healers as a means of approaching and relating to the native peoples. In this they were, as in the case of Staden, apparently successful. In 1536 they finally arrived in Mexico City, where Cabeza de Vaca wrote the first version of his account.

134. A number of authors have considered Cabeza de Vaca's accounts and their meaning for analysis of the cultural interface between Europe and America. The discussions of transculturation by Mary Louise Pratt (1992) and of identity blurring by Tzvetan Todorov (1984) are particularly useful in this, as is José Rabasa's (2000) examination of the contrary writing of violence as the mode of interaction with the native. See also Whitehead 2001 for a review of the Adorno and Pautz edition of Cabeza de Vaca's account.

135. In 1571 Miguel de Cervantes fought at the Battle of Lepanto against a Turkish fleet, where he was wounded in his left hand by an arquebus shot. The following year he took part in Juan of Austria's campaigns in Navarino, Corfu, and Tunis. On his way back to Spain in 1575, the galley *El Sol* on which he was traveling was attacked by Turkish ships and Cervantes was taken captive to Algeria. During his five years of captivity he wrote the *Epístola a Mateo Vázquez*. Juan Gil obtained Cervantes's freedom in 1580 in exchange for 500 ducats and he returned to his family in Madrid.

136. See the works written and edited by Vaughan and Clark (1981), Stodola and Levernier (1993), Ebersole (1995), and Strong (1999). Vaughan and Clark do an admirable job of outlining the main themes present in the captivity genre and make use of the idea of "rites of passage" to analyze the literary structure and narrative form of captivity tales. The latest volume edited by Gordon Sayre (2000) breaks

179

with the solely North American orientation of the other volumes and introduces selections from Letts's edition of Staden. In reference to another kind of oversight in the scholarship so far, Sayre (2000: 422–43) also includes the Apache leader Geronimo's account of his captivity and imprisonment by the United States government at the end of the nineteenth century. Strong (1999) also includes a consideration of native captives, which, as she rightly points out, was the much more prevalent experience in colonial America.

137. I was very much helped in thinking about this theme through participation in a panel on Japanese and Korean castaways and their role in ethnic and territorial discourses, organized by Michael Wood for the Association of Asian Studies meeting in Chicago, 2005.

BIBLIOGRAPHY

Abbeville, Claude d.' 1614. *Histoire de la mission des Pères Capucins en l'Isle de Maragnan et terres circinfines [. . .].* Paris: François Huby.

Abler, Thomas S. 1999. "Beavers and Muskets: Iroquois Military Fortunes in the Face of European Colonization." In *War in the Tribal Zone: Expanding States and Indigenous Warfare*, 2nd ed., ed. R. B. Ferguson and Neil L. Whitehead, 151–74. Santa Fe: School of American Research Press.

Adorno, Rolena, and Patrick Charles Pautz. 1999. *Álvar Núñez, Cabeza de Vaca: His Account, His Life, and the Expedition of Pánfilo de Narváez.* Lincoln: University of Nebraska Press.

Alexander, Michael. 1976. *Discovering the New World.* London: London Editions.

Allwork, Sally P. 1976. "Dryander of Marburg's Woodcut (The Oldest Transposition?)." *European Journal of Cardiology* 4(1): 105–7.

Anchieta, José de. 1846. "Information on the Marriage of the Indians of Brazil." *Revista trimensal de historia e geographia* 8: 254–62.

———. 1988. *Cartas, informaçoes, fragmentos históricos e sermoes.* Sao Paulo: Editora da Universidade de São Paulo.

Andrade, Oswald de. 1972 [1928]. "Manifesto Antropófago." In *Obras completas*, vol. 6, ed. Benedito Nunes, 11–19. Rio de Janeiro: Civilização Brasileira.

Anonymous. 1844. "Enformação do Brazil, e de suas Capitanias." *Revista trimensal de historia e geographia* 6: 412–43.

Arens, William. 1979. *The Man-Eating Myth: Anthropology and Anthropophagy.* New York: Oxford University Press.

———. 1998. "Rethinking Anthropophagy." In *Cannibalism and the Colonial World*, ed. Francis Barker, Peter Hulme, and Margaret Iversen, 39–62. Cambridge: Cambridge University Press.

Asad, Talal, ed. 1973. *Anthropology and the Colonial Encounter*. Atlantic Highlands, N.J.: Humanities Press.

Bakhtin, Mikhail. 1968. *Rabelais and his World*. Translated by Helene Iswolsky. Cambridge: MIT Press.

Barker, Francis, Peter Hulme, and Margaret Iversen, eds. 1998. *Cannibalism and the Colonial World*. Cambridge: Cambridge University Press.

Basso, E. 1995. *The Last Cannibals: A South American Oral History*. Austin: University of Texas Press.

Beaver, Dan. 2002. "Flesh or Fantasy: Cannibalism and the Meanings of Violence." *Ethnohistory* 49(3): 671–85.

Bellei, Sergio L. P. 1998. "Brazilian Anthropophagy Revisited." In *Cannibalism and the Colonial World*, ed. Francis Barker, Peter Hulme, and Margaret Iversen, 87–109. Cambridge: Cambridge University Press.

Berg, Eberhard. 1989. "'Wie ich in der tyrannischen Völcker Gewalt kommen bin': Hans Stadens Reisen in die Neue Welt." In *Der Reisebericht: Die Entwicklung einer Gattung in der deutschen Literatur*, ed. Peter J. Brenner, 178–96. Frankfurt: Suhrkamp.

Blok, Anton, and Klaus Schomburg. 1985. *Anthropologische Perspektiven: Einführung, Kritik und Plädoyer*. Stuttgart: Klett-Cotta.

Boorsch, Suzanne. 1976. "America in Festival Presentation." In *First Images of America: The Impact of the New World on the Old*, ed. Fredi Chiapelli, 503–15. Berkeley: University of California Press.

Borofsky, Robert, and Bruce Albert. 2005. *Yanomami: The Fierce Controversy and What We Might Learn from It*. Berkeley: University of California Press.

Bradley, JoBeth. 1993. "The Use of Connectives in Hans Staden's *Warhafftig Historia* and *Warhafftiger Kurtzer Bericht*. M.A. thesis, University of Tennessee.

Bry, Théodore de. 1592. *Americae Tertia Pars*. Frankfurt.

Bucher, Bernadette. 1981. *Icon and Conquest: A Structural Analysis of the Illustrations of de Bry's "Great Voyages."* Translated by B. M. Gulati. Chicago: University of Chicago Press.

Burghartz, Susanna. 2004. *Staging New Worlds: De Bry's Illustrated Travel Reports, 1590–1630*. Basel: Schwabe.

Burton, Richard F. 1874. *Veritable Historie and Description of a country belonging to the wild, naked, savage, man-eating people, situated in the New World, America*. First Series, 51. London: Hakluyt Society.

Caminha Pedro Vaz de. 1938. *The Voyage of Pedro Alvares Cabral to Brazil and India*. London: Hakluyt Society.

Cardim, Fernão. 1906. "A treatise of Brasil and articles touching the dutie of the kings majestie our lord, and to the common good of all the estate of Brasill." Translated by Samuel Purchas. *Hakluytus posthumus* 16: 417–51. Glasgow: J. MacLehose and Sons.

Carneiro de Cunha, Manuela, and Eduardo Viveiros de Castro. 1985. "Vingança e temporalidade: Os Tupinambás." *Journal de la Société des Américanistes* 71:191–208.

Carvajal, G. de. 1934. "Discovery of the Orellana River." In *The Discovery of the Amazon according to the Account of Friar Gaspar de Carvajal and Other Documents*, ed. J. T. Medina, trans. B. T. Lee, 167–235. New York: American Geographical Society.

Chartier, Roger. 2005. *Inscrire et effacer: Culture écrite et littérature (XIᵉ–XVIIIᵉ siècles)*. Paris: Le Seuil.

Clastres, Hélène. 1975. *La terre sans mal: Le prophétisme tupi-guarani*. Paris: Le Seuil.

———. 1995. *The Land-without-Evil: Tupi-Guaraní Prophetism*. Translated from the French by Jacqueline Grenez Brovender. Urbana: University of Illinois Press.

Clastres, Hélène, ed. 1985. *Yves, d'Evreux, Voyage au nord du Bresil fait en 1613 et 1614*. Paris: Payot, 1985.

Clastres, Pierre. 1972. *Chronique des Indiens Guayak: Ce que savent les Aché, chasseurs nomades du Paraguay*. Paris: Plon.

———. 1974 *La société contre l'État: Recherches d'anthropologie politique*. Paris: Éditions de minuit.

———. 1980. *Recherches d'anthropologie politique*. Paris: Le Seuil.

———. 1987. *Society against the State: Essays in Political Anthropology*. Translated by Robert Hurley in collaboration with Abe Stein. New York: Zone.

———. 1994. *Archeology of Violence*. Translation of *Recherches d'anthropologie politique* by Jeanine Herman. New York: Semiotext(e).

———. 1998. *Chronicle of the Guayaki Indians*. Translated by Paul Auster. New York: Zone.

Clifford, James. 1988. *The Predicament of Culture: Twentieth-Century Ethnography, Literature, and Art*. Cambridge: Harvard University Press.

Clifford, James, and George E. Marcus, eds. 1986. *Writing Culture: The Poetics and Politics of Ethnography*. Berkeley: University of California Press.

Comaroff, J., and J. Comaroff. 1992. *Ethnography and the Historical Imagination*. Boulder: Westview.

Combés, Isabelle. 1992. *La Tragédie cannibale chez les anciens Tupi-Guarani*. Paris: Presses Universitaires de France.

Conklin, Beth A. 1995. "'Thus Are Our Bodies, Thus Was Our Custom': Mortuary Cannibalism in an Amazonian Society." *American Ethnologist* 22(1):75–101.

———. 1997. "Consuming Images: Representations of Cannibalism on the Amazonian Frontier." *Anthropological Quarterly* 70(2):68–78.

———. 2001. *Consuming Grief: Compassionate Cannibalism in an Amazonian Society*. Austin: University of Texas Press.

Conley, Tom. 1996. *The Self-Made Map: Cartographic Writing in Early Modern France*. Minneapolis: University of Minnesota Press.

———. 2000. "Thevet Revisits Guanabara." *Hispanic American Historical Review* 80(4): 753–81.

Creed, Barbara, and Jeanette Hoorn, eds. 2001. *Body Trade: Captivity, Cannibalism and Colonialism in the Pacific*. New York: Routledge.

Darling, J. Andrew. 1998. "Mass Inhumation and the Execution of Witches in the American Southwest." *American Anthropologist* 100(3): 732–52.

Davis, Darien. 2001. Film Review—Hans Staden, How Tasty Was My Little Frenchman. *American Historical Review* 106(2): 695–97.

Deneke, Bernward. 1974. "Kaspar Goltwurm:. Ein lutherischer Kompilator zwischen Überlieferung und Glaube." In *Volkserzählung und Reformation: Ein Handbuch zur Tradierung und Funktion von Erzählstoffen und Erzählliteratur im Protestantismus*, ed. Wolfgang Brückner, 124–77. Berlin: Erich Schmidt.

Derrida, Jacques. 1967. *Écriture et différance*. Paris: Le Seuil.

Dryander, Johannes Eichmann. 1527. *Ein new Artzney und Praeticyr Bèuchlein von allerley Kranckheiten, wie man die Erkent und Geheylet werden sèollen, auss den berumptesten und Erfarnesten zu unsernn Zeyten lebenden Medicis . . . in eyn Kurtze Summa zusamen gezogen*. Cologne: Apud Eucharium.

———. 1535. *Das Nocturnal oder Die nachtvhr* [The Evening device, or the Night time Clock]. Frankfurt am Main: Christian Egenolph.

———. 1536. *Anatomia capitis humani*. Marburg: Ex officina Eucharii Cervicorni Agrippinatis,

———. 1537a. *Anatomiae, hoc est, Corporis humani dissectionis pars prior: In qua singula quad caput spectant recensentur membra, atque singul partes, singulis suis ad vivum commodissime expressis figuris, deliniantur: Omnia recens nata / per Io. Dryandrum. Item Anatomia porci / ex traditione Cophonis. Anatomia infantis / ex Gabriele de Zebris*. Marpurgi: Apud Eucharium Cervicornum.

———. 1537b. *Abraam Iudaei—De nativitatibus: Hoc est, de duodecim domiciliorum caeli figurarum significatione, ad iudiciariam astrologiam, non solum utilis sed & necessarius plane liber / pristino suo nitori restitutus per Ioan. Dryandrum*. Marburg: Eucharium Cervicornum [Ibn Ezra, Abraham ben Meèir, 1092–1167. *De nativitatibus*].

———. 1539. *Spherae materialis, sive, Globi celestis: (das ist) Des Hymels Lauff grèundtliche Auszlegung, so vil zur Anleytung der Astronomie dienet . . . / durch Iohan Dryandern . . . von newen verdeèuscht . . . Getruckt zêu Marpurg: Sub rectoratu Ioannis Dryandri*. Frankfurt am Main: Christian Egenolph.

———. 1541. *Anatomia Mundini, ad vetustissimorum, eorundemque aliquot manu scriptorum, codicum fidem collata, iustoq; suo ordini restituta*. Marburg.

———. 1542. *Der gantzen Artzenei gemeyner Inhalt: Wes einem Artzt, bede in der Theoric und Practic zêusteht: Mit Anzeyge bewerter Artzneienn . . . Hiebei beneben des menschen cèorpers Anatomei, warhafft contrafeyt und beschriben . . . / Newlich in Truck verordnet durch Ioan*. Dryandrum. Frankfurt am Main: Christian Egenolph.

———. 1547. *Von rechtem christlichem Brauch des Artzes und der heylsamen Artzeney*. Franckfurt: Cyriacus Jacob zum Bartt.

———. 1557. *Artzenei Spiegel gemeyner Inhalt derselbigen, wes bede einem Leib unnd Wundtartzt, in der Theoric, Practic unnd Chirurgei zusteht, mit Anzeyne bewerter Artzmeien . . . Hiebei beneben des Menschen Cèorpers Anatomei, und chirurgischen Instru-*

menten, warhafft contrafeyt, und beschriben . . . Hie bevor durch D. Joan. Dryandrum, jtzt widerumb mit Verbesserung, ina Truck verordnet. Frankfurt am Main: Christian Egenolph.

Duchet, Michele, ed. 1987. *L'Amérique de Théodore de Bry: Une collection de voyages protestante du XVIᵉ siècle: Quatre études d'iconographie.* Paris: CNRS.

Duclos, D. 1998. *The Werewolf Complex: America's Fascination with Violence.* New York: Berg.

Ebersohl, Horst. 1965. *Hans Staden von Homberg als Vorläufer der modernen Geographie: Analyse seiner geographischen Auffassung (ungedruckte Zulassungsarbeit zum Staatsexamen für das Lehramt am Gymnasium).* Saarbrücken.

Ebersole, Gary L. 1995. *Captured by Texts: Puritan to Postmodern Images of Indian Captivity.* Charlottesville: University of Virginia Press.

Edgerton, Robert B. 1992. *Sick Societies: Challenging the Myth of Primitive Harmony.* New York: Maxwell Macmillan.

Evreux, Yves d.' 1985 [1615]. *Voyage dans le nord du Brésil, fait durant les années 1613 et 1614.* Paris: Payot.

Faber, Gustav, ed. 1982. *Hans Staden: Brasilien: Die wahrhaftige Historie der wilden, nacketen, grimmigen Menschenfresser-Leute.* Tübingen: Erdmann.

Fabian, Johannes. 1983. *Time and the Other: How Anthropology Makes Its Object.* New York: Columbia University Press.

Fausto, Carlo. 1999. "Of Enemies and Pets: Warfare and Shamanism in Amazonia." *American Ethnologist* 26(4): 933–56.

———. 2001. *Inimigos fiéis: História, guerra e xamanismo na Amazônia.* São Paulo: EDUSP.

Ferguson, R. B., and Neil L. Whitehead, eds. 1999. *War in the Tribal Zone: Expanding States and Indigenous Warfare,* 2nd ed. Santa Fe: School of American Research Press.

Fernandes, Florestan. 1948. *Organização social dos Tupinambá.* São Paulo: Instituto Progresso.

———. 1949. *A análise funcionalista da guerra: Possibilidades de aplicaçao à sociedade tupinambá; ensaio de análise crítica da contribuição etnográfica dos cronistas para o estudo sociológico da guerra entre populações aborígenes do Brasil quinhentista e seiscentista.* São Paulo: Museu Paulista.

———. 1952. "La guerre et le sacrifice humain chez les Tupinamba." *Journal de la Société des Américanistes* 41(1):139–220.

———. 1958. *A etnologia e a sociologia no Brasil: Ensaios sobre aspectos da formação e do desenvolvimento das ciencias sociais na sociedade brasileira.* São Paulo: Anhambi.

———. 1964. *Notas sôbre a educação na sociedade Tupinambá.* São Paulo: CRRE.

———. 1970 [1950]. *A função social da guerra na sociedade tupinambá.* São Paulo: Pioneira.

Forsyth, Donald W. 1985. "Three Cheers for Hans Staden: The Case for Brazilian Cannibalism." *Ethnohistory* 32(1):17–36.

Foucault, Michel. 1977. *Discipline and Punish: The Birth of the Prison*. New York: Pantheon.

Fouquet, Karl. 1941. *Hans Staden: Zwei reisen nach Brasilien; abenteuerliche Erlebnisse unter den Menschenfressern der neuen Welt im 16. Jahrhundert. In die Sprache der Gengenwart übertragen*. São Paulo: Hans Staden.

———. 1944. "Bibliografia da 'Verdadeira Historia' de Hans Staden." *Boletin Bibliográfico* 4:7–31.

———. 1956. "Hans Staden von Brasilien aus gesehen." *Hessische Heimat* 5: 7–11.

———. 1957. "Hans Staden und sein Reisewerk: Einige Bemerkungen anläßlich der Vierhundertjahrfeier." *Staden Jahrbuch* 5: 7–21.

———. 1963. *Hans Staden: Zwei reisen nach Brasilien*, 2nd ed. Marburg an der Lahn: Trautvetter.

———. 1964. "Die Ausgaben der 'Wahrhaftigen Historia' 1557—1964." In *Hans Stadens Wahrhaftige Historia: Herausgegeben und übertragen von Reinhard Maack und Karl Fouquet*, 211–31. Marburg: Trautvetter and Fischer.

Fox, Richard G., ed. 1991. *Recapturing Anthropolog: Working in the Present*. Santa Fe: School of American Research Press.

Frank, Erwin. 1987. "'Sie fressen Menschen, wie ihr scheussliches Aussehen beweist . . . 'Kritische Überlegungen zu Zeugen und Quellen der Menschenfresserei." In *Authentizität und Betrug in der Ethnologie*, ed. Hans Peter Duerr, 199–224. Frankfurt: Suhrkamp.

Gaffarel, Paul, ed. 1878. Introduction to *Les Singularitez de la France Antarctique*. Paris: Maisonneuve.

Gandavo, Pero de Magalhães. 1922. *History of the Province of Santa Cruz: The Histories of Brazil*. Volume 2. New York: Cortes Society.

Geertz, Clifford. 1973. *The Interpretation of Cultures*. New York: Basic Books.

Girard, René. 1977. *La violence et le sacré*. Paris: Grasset.

Goldman, Laurence R., ed. 1999. *The Anthropology of Cannibalism*. Westport, Conn.: Bergin and Garvey.

Gordon-Grube, Karen. 1988. "Anthropophagy in Post-Renaissance Europe: The Tradition of Medicinal Cannibalism." *American Anthropologist* 90: 405–9.

———. 1993. "Evidence of Medicinal Cannibalism in Puritan New England: 'Mummy' and Related Remedies in Edward Taylor's 'Dispensatory.'" *Early American Literature* 28(3): 195.

Greenblatt, S. 1991. *Marvelous Possessions: The Wonder of the New World*. Oxford: Clarendon.

———, ed. 1993. *New World Encounters*. Berkeley: University of California Press.

Hakluyt, Richard. 1582. *Divers voyages touching the discouerie of America, and the Ilands adiacent vnto the same, made first of all by our Englishmen, and afterward by the French-*

men and Britons: And certaine notes of aduertisements for obseruations, necessarie for such as shall heereafter make the like attempt, with two mappes annexed heereunto for the plainer understanding of the whole matter. London: T. Woodcocke.

———. 1589. The principall navigations, voiages and discoveries of the English nation . . . : made by sea or ouer land, to the most remote and farthest distant quarters of the earth at any time within the compasse of these 1500. yeeres: deuided into three seuerall parts, according to the positions of the regions whereunto they were directed . . . Whereunto is added the last most renowmed English nauigation, round about the whole globe of the earth. London: George Bishop and R. Newberie.

Handelsman, Alix. 1977. "Der gantzen Artzenei." Journal of the History of Medicine and Allied Sciences 32(1): 72–73.

Hanigan, William C., William Regen, and Reginald Foster. 1990. "Dryander of Marburg and the First Textbook of Anatomy." Neurosurgery 26: 489–98.

Harbsmeier, Michael. 1989. "Writing and the Other: Travellers' Literacy, or Towards an Archaeology of Orality." In Literacy and Society, ed. Mogens Trolle Larsen and Karen Schousboe, 197–228. Copenhagen: Akademisk Forlag.

———. 1993. "Buch, Magie und koloniale Situation: Zur Anthropologie von Buch und Schrift." In Das Buch als magisches und Repräsentationsobjekt, ed. Peter F. Ganz and Malcolm Parkes. Wolfenbüttel: Wolfenbüttel Mittelalter-Studien.

———. 1994. Wilde Völkerkunde: Andere Welten in deutschen reisebeerichten der Frühen Neuzeit. Frankfurt am Main: Campus.

———. 1997. "Spontaneous Ethnographies: Towards a Social History of Traveller's Tales." Studies in Travel Writing 1:216–38.

Hendricks, J. 1993. To Drink of Death: The Narrative of a Shuar Warrior. Tucson: University of Arizona Press.

Honor, Hugh. 1975. The New Golden Land: European Images of America from Discoveries to the Present Time. New York: Pantheon.

Hoskins, Janet, ed. 1996. Headhunting and the Social Imagination in Southeast Asia. Stanford: Stanford University Press.

Hulme, Peter. 1998. "Introduction: The Cannibal Scene." In Cannibalism and the Colonial World, ed. Francis Barker, Peter Hulme, and Margaret Iversen, 1–38. Cambridge: Cambridge University Press.

Hulme, Peter, and Neil L. Whitehead, eds. 1992. Wild Majesty: Encounters with Caribs from Columbus to the Present Day, an Anthology. Oxford: Oxford University Press.

Hulme, Peter, and Tim Youngs. 2002. The Cambridge Companion to Travel Writing. Cambridge: Cambridge University Press.

Keazor, Henry. 1998. "Theodore de Bry's Images for 'America.'" Print Quarterly 15(2): 131–49.

Keeley, Lawrence H. 1996. War before Civilization. New York: Oxford University Press.

Kiening, Christian. 2000. "Alterität und Mimesis: Repräsentation des Fremden in Hans Stadens Historia." In Nach der Sozialgeschichte: Konzepte für eine Literaturwissenschaft *zwischen Historischer Anthropologie, Kulturgeschichte und Medientheorie,* ed. Martin Huber and Gerhard Lauer, 483–510. Tübingen: Max Niemeyer.

Kingdon, Robert McCune. 1988. *Myths about the St. Bartholomew's Day Massacres, 1572–1576.* Cambridge: Harvard University Press.

Knivet, Anthony. 1625. "Anthony Knivet, his comming to the R. De janeiro and usage amongst the Portugals and Indians: his divers travels, throw divers Regions of those parts." In *Hakluytus posthumus, or, Purchas his Pilgrimes: Contayning a history of the world in sea voyages and lande travells by Englishmen and others,* ed. Samuel Purchas. Hakluyt Society, Extra series, no. 14–30. Glasgow: J. MacLehose and Sons.

Kyle, Donald G. 2001. *Spectacles of Death in Ancient Rome.* London: Routledge.

Leach, Edmund. 1977. *Custom, Law and Terrorist Violence.* Edinburgh: Edinburgh University Press.

Léry, Jean de. 1574. *Histoire memorable de la ville de Sancerre.* Geneva.

———. 1578. *Histoire d'un voyage faict en la terre du Brésil.* Geneva: Antoine Chuppin.

———. 1990. *History of a Voyage to the Land of Brazil.* Translated by Janet Whatley. Berkeley: University of California Press.

Lestringant, F. 1997. *Cannibals.* Berkeley: University of California Press.

———, ed. 1994. *Jean de Léry: Histoire d'un voyage faict en la terre du Brésil (1578)* Paris: Livre de Poche.

Letts, Malcolm Henry Ikin, ed. 1928. *Hans Staden: The True History of his Captivity, 1557.* London: G. Routledge and Sons.

———. 1929. *Hans Stade. The True History of His Captivity.* New York: Robert McBride.

———. 1933. *Nazi Germany: "I Lived with the Brown Shirts."* Privately published.

———. 2005 *Hans Stade. The True History of his Captivity, 1557.* London: Routledge.

Lévi-Strauss, Claude. 1992. *Tristes Tropiques.* New York: Penguin.

Linebaugh, Peter. 1975. "The Tyburn Riot against the Surgeons." In *Albion's Fatal Tree,* ed. Douglas Hay, 65–117. London: Allen Lane.

———. 2003. *The London Hanged: Crime and Civil Society in the Eighteenth Century.* 2nd ed. London: Verso.

Lobato, José Bento Monteiro. 1927. *Aventuras de Hans Staden, o homen que naufragou nas costas do Brasil em 1549 e esteve oito mezes prisioneiro dos indios tupinambás; narradas por dona Benta aos seus netos Narizinho e Pedrinho e redigidas.* São Paulo: Companhia Editora Nacional.

Lussagnet, Susan. 1953. *Les Français en Amérique.* Paris: Presses Universitaires de France.

Luther, Martin. 1961. *Luther's Works,* Volume 37, *Word and Sacrament.* Edited by Robert H. Fischer and Helmut Lehmann. Philadelphia: Fortress.

Maack, Reinhard, and Karl Fouquet, eds. 1964. *Hans Stadens Wahrhaftige Historia.* Marburg an der Lahn: Trautvetter and Fischer.

Madrueira, Luís. 1998. "Lapses in Taste: 'Cannibal-Tropicalist' Cinema and the Brazilian Aesthetic of Underdevelopment." In *Cannibalism and the Colonial World*, ed. Francis Barker, Peter Hulme, and Margaret Iversen, 110–25. Cambridge: Cambridge University Press.

———. 2005. *Cannibal Modernities: Postcoloniality and the Avant-Garde in Caribbean and Brazilian Literature*. Charlottesville: University of Virginia Press.

Marcus, George E., ed. 1992. *Rereading Cultural Anthropology*. Durham: Duke University Press.

Menk, Gerhard. 1989. "Die beiden Widmungsschreiben Hans Stadens an die Grafen von Waldeck und Hanau. Bildungs- und hilfswissenschaftliche Betrachtungen zur Stadenforschung." *Zeitschrift des Vereins für Hessische Geschichte und Landeskunde* 94: 63–70.

Menninger, Annerose. 1988. "Die Vermarktung des Indio: Eine rezeptionsgeschichtliche Untersuchung zu den Interessen der Autoren Staden und Schmidel und der Verleger an der Publikation ihrer Americana im deutschen Sprach und Kulturraum des 16. Jahrhunderts. In *Die neuen Welten in alten Büchern: Entdeckung und Eroberung in frühen deutschen Schrift und Bildzeugnissen*, ed. Ulrich Knefelkamp and Hans_Joachim König, 92–117. Bamberg: Staatsbibliothek.

———. 1992. "'Unter Menschenfressern?' Das Indiobild der Südamerika Reisenden Hans Staden und Ulrich Schmiedl zwischen Dichtung und Wahrheit." In *Kolumbus' Erben: Europäische Expansion und überseeische Ethnien im Ersten Kolonialzeitalter, 1415–1815*, ed. Thomas Beck, Annerose Menninger, and Thomas Schleich, 63–99. Darmstadt: Wissenschaftliche Buchgesellschaft.

———. 1995. *Die Macht der Augenzeuge: Neue Welt und Kannibalen-Mythos, 1492–1600*. Stuttgart: Franz Steiner.

———. 1996a. "Hans Stadens 'Wahrhaftige Historia': Zur Genese eines Bestsellers der Reiseliteratur." *Geschichte in Wissenschaft und Unterricht* 47(9): 509–525.

———. 1996b. "Die Kannibalen Amerikas und die Phantasien der Eroberer: Zum Problem der Wirklichkeitswahrnehmung außereuropäischer Kulturen durch europäische Reisende in der frühen Neuzeit. In *Kannibalismus und Europäische Kultur*, ed. Hedwig Röckelein, 115–41. Tübingen: Diskord.

Métraux, Alfred. 1948. "The Tupinamba." In *Handbook of South American Indians*, 3: 95–134. Bureau of American Ethnology Bulletin 143. Washington: Smithsonian Institution.

Milbradt, Hilmar. 1956. "Zu einem bisher unbekannten Brief des Hans Staden an von Homberg in Hessen an den Grafen Wolrad von Waldeck." *Hessische Heimat* 5: 27–29.

Montaigne, Michel de. 1580. *Essais*. Paris.

Monteiro, John M. 1999. "Destruction, Resistance, and Transformation: Southern, Coastal, and Northern Brazil, 1580–1890." In *The Cambridge History of Native American Peoples*, vol. 3, pt 2, ed. F. Salomon and S. Schwartz. Cambridge: Cambridge University Press.

———. 2000. "The Heathen Castes of Sixteenth-Century Portuguese America: Unity, Diversity, and the Invention of the Brazilian Indian." *Hispanic American Historical Review* 80(4): 697–719.

Moraes, Rubens Borba de. 1983. *Bibliographia brasiliana: Rare books about Brazil Published from 1504 to 1900 and Works by Brazilian Authors of the Colonial Period.* Los Angeles: UCLA Latin American Center Publications, University of California / Rio de Janeiro: Kosmos.

Münzel, Mark. 2001. "Hans Staden." In *Hauptwerke der Ethnologie*, ed. Christian Feest and Karl Heinz-Kohl, 437–41. Stuttgart: Kröner Verlag.

Neuber, Wolfgang. 1991. *Fremde Welt im europäischen Horizon:. Zur Topik der deutschen Amerika-Reiseberichte der Frühen Neuzeit.* Berlin: Erich Schmidt.

———. 1995. "Marburger Menschenfresser—Hans Stadens Brasilienbericht (1557). Über die Verbindung von Indianern und akademischer Anatomie." In *Marburg Bilder eine Ansichtssache: Zeugnisse aus fünf Jahrhunderten*, ed. Jörg Jochen Berns, 149–64. Marburg: Rathaus.

Nóbrega, M. da. 1988. "Informaçao das Terras do Brasil (1549)." In *Cartas do Brasil*, 97–102. São Paulo: Belo Horizonte / Editora Itatiaia / Editora da Universidade de São Paulo.

Nordstrom, Carolyn, and Antonius Robben. 1995. *Fieldwork under Fire: Contemporary Studies of Violence and Survival.* Berkeley: University of California Press.

Obermeier, Franz. 1999. "Die Rezeption von Hans Stadens 'Wahrhaftige Historia' und ihrer Ikonographie." *Jahrbuch Institut Martius Staden*: 133–51. São Paulo, 1999/2000.

———. 2000. *Brasilien in Illustrationen des 16. Jahrhunderts.* Americana Eystettensia. Series B, Monografías, estudios, ensayos 11. Frankfurt: Vervuert.

———. 2001. "Bilder von Kannibalen, Kannibalismus im Bild: Brasilianische Indios in Bildern und Texten des 16. Jahrhunderts." *Jahrbuch für Geschichte Lateinamerikas* 38: 49–72.

———. 2002. Hans Stadens Wahrhafftige Historia 1557 und die Literatur der Zeit. *Wolfenbütteler Notizen zur Buchgeschichte* 2:43–80.

Obermeier, Franz, Joachim Tiemann, and Guiomar Carvalho Franco, eds. 2006. *Hans Staden: Warhaftige Historia: Zwei Reisen nach Brasilien (1548–1555): História de Duas Viagems Ao Brasil.* São Paulo: Fontes Americanae l. Instituto Martius-Staden.

Oliveira, Jô. 2005. *Hans Staden: Um Aventureiro no Novo Mundo.* São Paulo: Conrad.

Parshall, Peter. 1993. "Imago Contrafacta: Images and Facts in the Northern Renaissance." *Art History* 16(4): 554–79.

Petrinovich, Lewis F. 2000. *The Cannibal Within.* New York: Aldine de Gruyter.

Pirsig, Wolfgang. 2002. "Early Depictions of the Nasal Turbinates." *Rhinology* 40(2): 104–6.

Pratt, Mary Louise. 1986. "Fieldwork in Common Places." In *Writing Culture: The Poet-*

ics and Politics of Ethnography, ed. James Clifford and George E. Marcus, 27–50. Berkeley: University of California Press.

———. 1992. *Imperial Eyes: Travel Writing and Transculturation*. London: Routledge.

Price, Merrall Llewelyn. 2003. *Consuming Passions: The Uses of Cannibalism in Late Medieval and Early Modern Europe*. New York: Routledge.

Rabasa, José. 2000. *Writing Violence on the Northern Frontier: The Historiography of Sixteenth-Century New Mexico and Florida and the Legacy of Conquest*. Durham: Duke University Press.

Ramos, Alcida Rita. 1998. *Indigenism: Ethnic Politics in Brazil*. Madison: University of Wisconsin Press.

Ratzel, F. 1893. "Staden, Hans." In *Allgemeine Deutsche Biographie*, 35: 364–66. Leipzig: Duncker and Humblot.

Rautmann, Albert E., and Todd W. Fenton. 2005. "A Case of Historic Cannibalism in the American West: Implications for Southwestern Archaeology." *American Antiquity*, 70(2): 321–41.

Ricoeur, Paul. 1971. "The Model of the Text: Meaningful Action Considered as a Text." *Social Research* 38(3).

Rival, Laura, and Neil L. Whitehead, eds. 2001. *Beyond the Visible and Material*. Oxford: Oxford University Press.

Rousseau, Jean-Jacques. 1755. *Discours sur l'origine et les fondements de l'inégalité parmi les hommes*. Amsterdam: Marc Michel Rey.

———. 1994. *Discourse on the Origin of Inequality*. Translated by Franklin Philip; edited by Patrick Coleman. Oxford: Oxford University Press.

Rubiés, Joan Pau. 2004. "Travel Writing and Humanistic Culture: A Blunted Impact." Paper presented at the conference "The Early Modern Travel Narrative: Production and Consumption," April–May 2004, University of Southern California.

Ruppel, Heinrich. 1956. "Lebens und Charakterbild Hans Stadens." *Hessische Heimat* 5: 2–7.

Salomon, Frank, and George L. Urioste, eds. 1991. *The Huarochirí Manuscript: A Testament of Ancient and Colonial Andean Religion*. Austin: University of Texas Press.

Sanday P. R. 1986. *Divine Hunger: Cannibalism as a Cultural System*. Cambridge: Cambridge University Press.

Sanborn, Geoffrey. 1998. *The Sign of the Cannibal: Melville and the Making of a Postcolonial Reader*. Durham: Duke University Press.

Scarry, Elaine. 1985. *The Body in Pain: The Making and Unmaking of the World*. New York: Oxford University Press.

Schachtner, Petra. 1999. "Johannes Dryander und die Aufwertung der angewandten Mathematik zur Universalwissenschaft." In *Melanchthon und die Marburger Professoren (1527–1627)*, vol. 2, ed. Barbara Bauer, 789–820. Marburg: Universitätsbibliothek Marburg.

Scheffler, Jürgen. 2003. "Karl Meier, Engelbert Kaempfer und die Erinnerungskultur in Lemgo 1933–45." In *Engelbert Kaempfer (1651–1716) und die kulturelle Begegnung zwischen Europa und Asien*, ed. Sabine Klocke-Daffa, Jürgen Scheffler, and Gisela Wilbertz, 305–42. Lemgo: Landesverband Lippe, Institut für Lippische Landeskunde.

Schlechtweg-Jahn, Ralph. 1997. "The Power of Cannibalisation: Hans Staden's American Travels Account of 1557." In *The Propagation of Power in the Medieval West*, ed. Martin Gosman, Arjo Vanderjagt, and Jan Veenstra, 1–14. Groningen: Egbert Forsten.

———. 1999. "Magie, Religion und Wissenschaft: Hans Stadens Brasilienreisebericht von 1557." In *Artes im Mittelalter*, ed. Ursula Schäfer, 263–82. Berlin: Akademie.

Seed, Patricia. 1995. *Ceremonies of Possession in Europe's Conquest of the New World 1492–1640*. Cambridge: Cambridge University Press.

Seltzer, Mark. 1998. *Serial Killers: Death and Life in America's Wound Culture*. New York: Routledge.

———. 2005. "True Crime." In *Violence*, ed. Neil Whitehead, 203–23. Santa Fe: School of American Research Press.

Sousa, Gabriel Soares de. 1974. *Notícia do Brasil*. São Paulo: Empresa Gráfica da Revista dos Tribunais.

Southey, Robert. 1819. *History of Brazil*. London: Longman, Hurst, Rees, and Orme.

Spix, Johann Baptist von, Karl Friedrich Philipp von Martius, and Hannibal Evans Lloyd. 1824. *Travels in Brazil, in the years 1817–1820: Undertaken by Command of His Majesty the King of Bavaria*. London: Longman, Hurst, Rees, Orme, Brown, and Green.

Staden, Hans. 1557. *Warhaftige Historia und Beschreibung eyner Landtschafft der wilden, nacketen, grimmigen Menschfresser Leuthen in der Newenwelt America gelege*. Marburg: Andres Kolben.

———. 1961. *Bankai yokuryåuki: Genshi Burajiru hyåoryåu kiroku*. Tokyo: Teikoku Shoin.

Stagl, Justin. 1995. *A History of Curiosity: The Theory of Travel, 1550–1800*. Chur: Harwood Academic.

Stewart, Pamela, and Andrew Strathern. 1999. "Feasting on My Enemy: Images of Violence and Change in the New Guinea Highlands." *Ethnohistory* 46(4):645–70.

Stodola, Kathryn Zabelle Derounian, and James Arthur Levernier. 1983. *The Indian Captivity Narrative, 1550–1900*. New York: Twayne.

Strauss, Walter L., ed. 1974. *The German Single-Leaf Woodcut, 1500–1550*. New York: Hacker Art Books.

———, ed. 1975. *The German Single-Leaf Woodcut, 1550–1600*. New York: Abaris.

Strong, Pauline. 1999. *Captive Selves, Captivating Others: The Politics and Poetics of Colonial American Captivity Narratives*. New York: Westview.

Sturtevant, William. 1976. "First Visual Images of Native America." In *First Images of America: The Impact of the New World on the Old*, ed. Fredi Chiappelli, 417–54. Berkeley: University of California Press.

Tanner, John. 1994. *The Falcon: A Narrative of the Captivity and Adventures of John Tanner*. New York: Penguin.

Taylor, Christopher. 1999. *Sacrifice as Terror: The Rwandan Genocide of 1994*. New York: Berg.

TenHuisen, Dwight E. R. 2005. "Providence and Passio in Hans Staden's Wahrhaftig Historia." *Daphnis* 34: 213–54.

Thevet, André. 1557. *Les Singularitez de la france Antarctique, autrement nommée Amerique: & de plusieurs Terres & Isles decouvertes de nostre temps*. Paris: Chez les Héritiers de Maurice de la Porte.

———. 1575. *La Cosmographie universelle*. Paris: Pierre L'Huillier and Guillaume Chaudière.

———. 1878. *Les Singularitez de la France Antarctique*. Edited by Paul Gaffarel. Paris: Maisonneuve.

———. 1928. "Histoire Thevet Angoumoisin, Cosmographe du Roy de deux voyages par luy aux Indes Australes et Occidentales etc., fol. 53–62v." In *La religion des Tupinamba, Appendix II: L'Anthropophagie rituelle des Tupinamba*, ed. Alfred Métraux, 239–52. Paris: Ernest Leroux.

Tithecott, Richard. 1997. *Of Men and Monsters: Jeffrey Dahmer and the Construction of the Serial Killer*. Madison: University of Wisconsin Press.

Todorov, Tzvetan. 1984. *The Conquest of America: The Question of the Other*. Translated by Richard Howard. New York: Harper and Row.

Turner, C. G. 1999. *Man Corn: Cannibalism and Violence in the Prehistoric American Southwest*. Provo: University of Utah Press.

Vaughan, Alden T., and Edward W. Clark, eds. 1981. *Puritans among the Indians: Accounts of Captivity and Redemption, 1676–1724*. Cambridge: Belknap.

Vespucci, Amerigo. 1894. *The Letters of Amerigo Vespucci and Other Documents Illustrative of his Career*. Translated by Clements R. Markham. London: Hakluyt Society.

Viveiros de Castro, E. 1992. *From the Enemy's Point of View: Humanity and Divinity in an Amazonian Society*. Chicago: University of Chicago Press.

Voigt, Lisa. 2001. "Sites of Captivity in Colonial Latin American Writing." Ph.D. dissertation, Brown University.

Wagner, Sabine. 1995. "Zwischen Paraíba und Acheron: Die Überlieferung der Reiseberichte des 16. Jahrhunderts im Barock." In *Von der Weltkarte zum Kuriositätenkabinett, Amerika im deutschen Humanismus und Barock*, ed. Karl Kohut, 58–77. Frankfurt: Vervuert.

Wandel, Lee Palmer. 1994. *Voracious Idols and Violent Hands: Iconoclasm in Reformation Zurich, Strasbourg, and Basel*. Cambridge: Cambridge University Press.

———. 2006. *The Eucharist in the Reformation: Incarnation and Liturgy*. Cambridge: Cambridge University Press.

Whatley, Janet, ed. 1990. Introduction to *Jean de Léry: History of a Voyage to the Land of Brazil*, xv–xxxviii. Berkeley: University of California Press.

Whitehead, Neil L. 1984. "Carib Cannibalism: The Historical Evidence." *Journal de la Société des Américanistes* 70(1): 69–88.

———. 1993a. "Native American Cultures along the Atlantic Littoral of South America, 1499–1650." *Proceedings of the British Academy* 81:197–231.

———. 1993b. "Deceptive Images of Tribal War." *Chronicle of Higher Education*, November 10, 1993.

———. 1995a. *Wolves from the Sea: Readings in the Archaeology and Anthropology of the Island Carib.* Leiden: KITLV.

———. 1995b. "The Historical Anthropology of Text: The Interpretation of Ralegh's *Discoverie.*" *Current Anthropology* 36:53–74.

———. 1997. "Monstrosity and Marvel: Symbolic Convergence and Mimetic Elaboration in Trans-Cultural Representation." *Studies in Travel Writing* 1: 72–96.

———, ed. 1998a. *The Discoverie of the Large, Rich and Bewtiful Empire of Guiana by Sir Walter Ralegh.* Manchester: Manchester University Press.

———. 1998b. "Yanomamology, Missiology, and Anthropology." *American Anthropologist* 100(2): 517–20.

———. 1999a. "The Crises and Transformations of Invaded Societies (1492–1580)—The Caribbean." In *The Cambridge History of Native American Peoples,* vol. 3, pt 1, ed. F. Salomon and S. Schwartz, 864–903. Cambridge: Cambridge University Press.

———. 1999b. "Lowland Peoples Confront Colonial Regimes in Northern South America, 1550–1900." In *The Cambridge History of Native American Peoples,* ed. F. Saloman and S. Schwartz, *III (2)*: 382–441. Cambridge: Cambridge University Press.

———. 1999c. "Native Society and the European Occupation of the Caribbean Islands and Coastal Tierra Firme, 1492–1650." In *A General History of the Caribbean,* vol. 3, ed. C. Damas and P. Emmer, 180–200. New York: UNESCO.

———. 2001. Review of *Álvar Núñez, Cabeza de Vaca: His Account, His Life, and the Expedition of Pánfilo de Narváez,* ed. Rolena Adorno and Patrick Charles Pautz. *Ethnohistory* 48(3): 525–27.

———. 2002a. *Dark Shamans: Kanaimà and the Poetics of Violent Death.* Durham: Duke University Press.

———. 2002b. "South America / The Amazon: The Forest of Marvels." In *The Cambridge Companion to Travel Writing,* ed. Peter Hulme and Tim Youngs, 122–38. Cambridge: Cambridge University Press.

———. 2002c. "Arawak Linguistic and Cultural Identity through Time—Contact, Colonialism, and Creolization." In *Comparative Arawakan Histories,* ed. F. Santos-Granero and J. Hill. Urbana: University of Illinois Press.

———. 2002d. "Magical Modernities and Occult Violence in South America." In *Violence, Globalisation and Localisation,* ed. M. Bax et al., 51–68. Amsterdam: Free University Press.

————, ed. 2003. *Histories and Historicities in Amazonia*. Lincoln: University of Nebraska Press.

————, ed. 2004a. *Violence*. Santa Fe: School of American Research Press.

————, ed. 2004b. *Nineteenth-Century Travels, Explorations, and Empires: Writings from the Era of Imperial Consolidation, 1835–1910*, vol. 8, *South America*. London: Chatto and Pickering.

————. 2005a. "Black Read as Red: Ethnic Transgression and Hybridity in Northeastern South America and the Caribbean." In *Black and Red: African-Native Relations in Colonial Latin America*, ed. Matthew Restall, 223–44. Albuquerque: University of New Mexico Press.

————. 2005b. "The Taste of Death." Afterword to *Terror, Violence and the Imagination*, ed. P. Stewart, A. Strathern, and N. L. Whitehead, 231–38. London: Pluto.

Whitehead, Neil L., and Laura Rival, eds. 2001. *Beyond the Visible and Material*. Oxford: Oxford University Press.

Whitehead, Neil L., and Robin Wright, eds. 2004. *In Darkness and Secrecy: The Anthropology of Assault Sorcery and Witchcraft in Amazonia*. Durham: Duke University Press.

Wilbert, Johannes. 2004. "The Order of Dark Shamans among the Warao." In *In Darkness and Secrecy: The Anthropology of Assault Sorcery and Witchcraft in Amazonia*, ed. Neil L. Whitehead and Robin Wright, 21–50. Durham: Duke University Press.

Wintroub, Michael. 1999. "Taking Stock at the End of the World: Rites of Distinction and Practices of Collecting in Early Modern Europe." *Studies in the History and Philosophy of Science* 30(3): 395–424.

Wynkelmann, Hans Just. 1664. *Der Amerikanischen Neuen Welt Beschreibung*. Oldenburg: Henrich-Conrad Zimmern.

Yue, G. 1999. *The Mouth That Begs: Hunger, Cannibalism and the Politics of Eating in Modern China*. Durham: Duke University Press.

Zamora, Margarita. 1988. *Language, Authority, and Indigenous History in the "Comentarios reales de los incas."* Cambridge: Cambridge University Press.

————. 1993. *Reading Columbus*. Berkeley: University of California Press.

Zheng, Yi. 1996. *Scarlet Memorial: Tales of Cannibalism in Modern China*. Boulder: Westview.

INDEX

abatí, 47

Abbati Bossange, lxxxiv, xciii–xciv, xcvi, 96–99, 122, 173

Abbeville, Claude de, 166

Abraham, 99, 103

Adorno, Giuseppe, 47

Africa, 164

Agudin, Antonio, 59

Aguirre, Lope de, 159

albatross, 40

Alcatrazes, Ilha de, 40

Aleman, Stephanie Weparu, 162

Algeria, 179

Alkindar, xlv, xlviii, lxx–lxxi, xciii–xciv, 55, 73, 75–76

allelophagy, lxiv

All Saints Day, 23

almonds, 23

Amazonia, xlvii, liii, xciv

Amazon River, xxiv, xxxi, xxxiii, 151, 156

Amazons, xxiv

Ambirem, xxviii

Amsterdam, xvi

Anasazi, 162–63

anatomy, lxiii–lxiv, 11, 154–55, 170

Anchieta, José, xxvi–xxviii, 157

Andrade, Oswald de, x, liv, 166

animals, lxxxii, lxxxviii, xcvii, 91, 107–9, 112, 116, 120, 128–29, 137–41, 176, 179

anteater, lxxxii

anthropology, x, xxvi, xxxi, xlii, xliv–xlvii, liii, lviii, lxxxvi–lxxxvii, 160

Antipodes, 12–13

Antonio, 91, 95

antropofagistas, x, xxxix–xl, li–lvi, lxxxiii, 166

Antwerp, xvi, 103, 144–45, 177

anus, xxxv, lxxviii, 137, 148

Arabs, 21, 23

arasoya, 57–58, 129–31, 147

Arawété, lxii, xciv, xcviii

archaeology, 155, 162–63, 177–78

Arens, William, xxxix, xliii–xliv, lvi, 162, 165

Argentina, 30

Ariró, 61

Arizona, 179

armadillo, 138, 152

arms, xxxiv, 108, 137, 148–49

arquebus, 17, 21, 37, 45–46, 50, 62

astronomy, 11–12, 16, 154–55, 169. *See also* celestial bodies; navigation
Asunción, 38–39
Atlantic, 151
Augustine, Saint, 12–13
Azores, 30
Aztec, 171

Babylonia, 171–72
Bahia, xxviii, 156
Bakhtin, Mikhail, lxvi
Balkans, lviii
Barbary, 21, 23
bats, 140
bees, 108, 140–41
Bellei, Sergio, li, liv, 166
Battle of Lepanto, 179
Bhaba, Homi, lii
Bilbao, 39
birds, 50, 55, 108, 112, 121, 141, 176
Biscay, 39, 77
Black Moors, 26, 32, 105
blood, xlvii, lxiv, lxvii, 80, 114, 149, 159, 176
body fat, xlvii, 161
body paint, xxxv, lxxxi, 113, 119–21, 123, 132, 137, 141, 148
body parts, xxx, xxxiv–xxxv, lxiii–lxv, lxvii–lxviii, 147–49
bones, lxx, lxxxi–lxxxii, 149, 176
Boorsch, Suzanne, lxxiii
Bouman, J. J., xvi
Bourgogne, lxxxvii
Boywassu kange, l, 86
Brabant, 144
Bradbury, Ray, 166
brain, 81, 137, 148, 160, 162
Brant, Heinrich, 22, 144
brazil wood, ix, lxxiii–lxxiv, 29, 50, 58, 82, 96
bread, 30, 114

Bremen, 21–22, 144, 177
Brikioka, xix, xlix, xcvi, 44–45, 47, 49–50, 59, 62–63, 67, 77–78, 84, 86–89
Bruckhausen, Hans von, 22, 144
Bucher, Bernadette, 174
Burgkmair, Hans, lxxiv
Burton, Richard, xvi, xlii–xliii, xlvii, 152, 154, 164
buttocks, 137

Cabeza de Vaca, Álvar Núñez, xcviii–c, 152, 179
Cabral, Pedro Alvares, xxiii
Cadiz, 156
caltraps, 108, 129
Calvin, Jean, xxxii, 160
Caminha, Pedro Vaz de, xxii–xxiv
Canadian Broadcasting Company, 168
Canarias, 31, 105
Cannibal Conqueror, lxxx
Cape Ghir, 22–23
Cape Verde, 31–32, 105–6
capybara, 139
Caraïbe, xl, 163
Carajás, 19, 109, 116
Cardim, Fernão, xcv, 159–60
Caribbean, xxiv, lii, lvii, 156, 159, 173
Carijó, lxxxi, lxxxviii, xcii, xcv–xcvii, 19, 34, 38, 44, 47, 67, 79–81, 107, 159, 162
cartography, 155–56. *See also* cosmography
Carvajal, Gaspar de, xxiv
castaways, ci–civ
Castile, 23, 30, 59, 144, 156
Catherine, Saint, 35, 37
Catherine de Medici, lxxiii
Catholics, xxxvii, xl, xliii, lv, lviii, lxiv–lxv, 160
Ceará, 164
celestial bodies, lxxi–lxxii, lxxvi, 11–12, 32. *See also* cosmology; navigation; weather

Cervantes, Miguel, c, 179

Charles V, 154

children, 71, 117, 119, 121–23, 157, 160: in captivity, xcvii–xcviii, 59, 67, 155; of chiefs, xxiv, 69, 122; sacrifice of, xxiii, lviii, xcvii–xcviii, 131, 157–58; in sacrificial killing and feasting, xxiv, xxx, lxi, lxvii, lxxvi, 54–55, 129, 131, 137, 147–49

Chile, cii

China, lviii

Christianity, lxi–lxii, 60, 88–89, 92–93, 95, 170–171: eucharistic cannibalism and, x, xxx, xxxii, xxxvii, xl, lvi, lviii, lxi, lxiii–lxvi, xciv, 159, 169; narrative of redemption in, xxi, xxvi, lix, lxxxiv–lxxxv, 143; religious conflict and, xxxii, xxxvii–xxxviii, xl, lxi–lxvi

Christopher, Saint, 15

cinema, lxxxii–lxxxiii

Clastres, Hélène, xli, xlvi, 157, 171

Clastres, Pierre, xli, xlvi, 170–71

clothing, xxvi, lxviii–lxix, lxxix, 14, 33, 37, 42, 60, 77, 82, 97, 119. See also nakedness

Coelho, Duarte, 26

Coelho, Gonzalo, 156

colonialism, ix–xi, ci–ciii, 162: colonial imagination, xxx–xxxi, xxxviii; indigenous society affected by, xxvii, xxx–xxxi, lxii–lxiii, lxxix; intercolonial conflict, xi, xxxi–xxxiii, lii, lxxix

Columbus, Cristobal, lv, lvii, cii, 156–57

Combès, Isabelle, xxxv, 153–54, 163, 169

combs, 58, 72, 99

commodities, 26, 38–39, 59, 76–77, 82–83, 86, 96–99, 102, 108, 113–14, 123, 171

Conklin, Beth, 165

Conrad, Joseph, lii

Cosa, Juan de la, 156

cosmography, 9, 13, 16, 34, 105–7. See also cartography

cosmology, xxxv–xxxvi, xlv, lxii–lxiii, lxv, lxxvi, lxxxi, lxxxvii, xciv–xcv, 13–14, 84, 119, 122, 125, 127, 155, 175

cotton, 58, 82, 96, 107, 142

Crockett, Davy, x

Cuba, lxi

Cubas, Braz, 78

Cunha, Manuela Carneiro de, xlvi

Cutia, lxxxviii, 38

Daniel, 103

Darien, Gulf of, 156

Darling, Andrew, 163

dates, 23

David, 7

de Bry, Theodor, xv–xvi, lxxvi–lxxix, lxxxiii, 153–54, 161, 174

deer, 137

Defoe, Daniel, c–cii

Devil (Anhanga), 112

Dieppe, 96, 101–3, 145, 177, 179

disease, xx–xxi, xxvii, xxxi, xlv, lxv, lxxvi, lxxviii–lxxix, lxxxix, xcii, xciv, 48, 61, 68–70, 73, 75–76, 79–81, 126, 152, 162

dismemberment, lxiii–lxxi, lxxviii, lxxxi–lxxxii, 45, 87, 108, 137, 148

Dracula, xxxvii

dreams, xlvii, xci, 70–71, 84, 86, 128. See also shamans

Dryander, Johannes, xi, xvii–xviii, xxi, lv, lvii, lix, lxiii–lxiv, lxxii, lxxxiv, lxxxviii, 5, 9, 154–56, 168–69, 172, 178

Dürer, Albrecht, lxxiv

ear piercing, 113, 121

Ebersole, Gary, ci

eggs, 40, 131, 147

Egypt, 170

Elmo, Saint, 25

Enguaguaçú, 43

Eoban of Hesse, 10, 47, 144

epistemology, lvii, lxxi–lxxiii, lxxxix,
 10–12, 174

Erasmus of Rotterdam, 15

Erfurt, 155

ethnography, xvii, xxi, xxvi, xxxiv, xxxvi,
 xli, xliv–xlv, xlvii, liii–lv, lvii, lxii, lxxv,
 lxxxiv–civ, 155, 160, 165, 177–78

ethnohistory, liii, lxii, xciii, ci, 167

ethnology, ix, xv–xvii, xxvi, xxx–xxxi,
 xxxvi, xxxix, xli–lvi, lxviii, lxxiii,
 lxxxvi, lxxxviii, 153, 163; of Tupí, 14,
 47, 51, 54, 55, 57–58, 61–62, 68, 73,
 79–80, 99, 105–42, 173

Evreux, Yves de, 166

eyebrows, lxix, 129

eyes, lxxxii, 75, 81, 129, 148

eyewitness observation, ix, xvii, xli–lvii,
 lix, lxiii–lxiv, lxxxv, 10–12, 154, 162

facial hair, xlv, lxix, lxxvi, xci, 37, 54, 56,
 71, 113, 173

facial piercing, xxiv, lxxvi, 113, 119–20

Fausto, Carlos, xlvii, 178

feathers, 58, 71, 96

feather work, xxiv, xxviii, xlvi, lxxiv, lxxvi,
 lxxix, 49–50, 113, 119–20, 123, 128–30

feet, lxxxii, 12, 60, 81

Ferdianado, Juan, 39

Fernandes, Florestran, xlvi–xlvii

Fernando VI, 156

Ferreira, Jorge, 88–89, 92

Finisterre (Dark Star), 13

fish, 23–24, 30, 47, 84–85, 92, 94–95,
 100, 103, 109, 112–13, 115–16, 121, 123,
 128–29, 176

fish flour, 47, 113, 115–16

fish hooks, 33, 39, 78

Flaubert, Gustave, xxxviii

flea, 140

flesh (mokaen), xxx, xlix, lvi, lxi–lxvi,

lxix–lxx, lxxvi, xciv, 7, 60–61, 71, 74–
 75, 81, 87, 91–92, 95–96, 104, 116, 125,
 127–28, 137, 148, 175

Florence, lxxiv, 156

Florida, xcix, 179

food, 39, 42

Ford, John, 176

Fouquet, Karl, x, 144, 151–53

France Antarctique, xxxii

Frankfurt, xv, 152, 154

Funchal, 22

Galicia, 59

Gandavo, Pero Magalhães de, xxxi

gender, xxxvii, xliii, lviii, lxvi, xcvi, 174

genipap, 141

Genoa, 47

Geneva, xxxvi

genitalia, xxx, lxxxi–lxxxii, 149

geometry, 12

Geronimo, 180

Girard, René, 163

Goitacás, 19, 109, 176

gold, 30

Goldtworm, Casparus, 13

Gottfried, Johann, xvi

gourds, 124–26, 128. See also tammaraka

Gregory IX (Pope), lxii

Guadalquivir, 31

Guanabara, Bay of, xxxii

Guantánamo, lxi

Guaymures (white cannibals), 159

Guianás, 19, 107–9, 156

Guinea, 105

gum, 23

Guyana, 161

hair, lxxvi, 108, 119, 121, 123

Hakluyt, Richard, xlii, 164

Hakluyt Society, xvi, xlii

hammock, 51, 54, 111–12

hands, lxxx, 81

Harbsmeier, Michael, lxxxiv
Harfleur, 145
heaven, 74
Heidelberg, 164
Heliodorus, 10, 47–48
Henri II, lxxiii, 163–64
herbal remedies, 129
Herzog, Werner, 159
Hesse, xvii, xix, 5, 7–10, 21, 107, 168
Hieronymus, 88–89, 92, 95
Hispaniola, cii
Hitler, Adolf, 166
Holland (region), 177
Homberg, xviii, 5, 8–9, 21, 177
Honfleur, xxi, 100–101, 177
honorifics, xxiii, xxix–xxx, xli, xlvi, xcv–
    xcvi, xcviii, 55, 75, 79, 119–22, 124, 137,
    148, 159
humanism, 155–56
Huston, John, 166

ibis, 50, 141
igá-ibira tree, 126–27
Igaraçu, 26
Imbeaçá-pe, 40, 42
India, 13, 21, 30
intestines, xlv, lvi, 81, 137, 148
Ipperu Wasu, xlviii, 55, 58, 67, 75
Iraçéma, 164
Iraq, lx
Isaac, 99, 103
Israel, 103
Itamaracá, 27
Itanhaem, 42
Ita Wu, 96
iwera pemme, lvii, lxxvi–lxxvii, 56, 226,
    131–32, 134, 147–48, 158

Jacob (biblical figure), 99, 103
Jacob (French trader), 82
jaguar, xxxix, lxxxii, 91, 108, 139
James, Saint, 13

Janzoon, B., xvi
Japan, 153, 174, 180
Java, 152
Jeppipo Wasu, xx, xlviii, 55, 66–70
Jeremiah, lxix, 60, 171
Jesuits, xliii
Jesus Christ, x, lviii, lxiii–lxvii, 5–7, 13, 55,
    88–89, 99, 103, 159, 169
Jews, 55
John, Saint, 13
Jurumirim, 37

Kampen, 21, 177
Kampfer, Hans, xviii
Karwattuware (French trader), xix–xxi,
    xlv, lx, xc, 60–61, 71–73, 177
Kassel, 168
Kenrimaku, xx, xlviii, 61, 70–71
Kiel, 167
kinship, xxvii–xxx, xxxii–xxxiv, xxxv,
    xlvi–xlvii, lxx, lxxvii, lxxxiii, lxxxvii,
    xciv, xcvi–xcviii, 9, 58, 67–71, 76–78,
    88–89, 92, 95–97, 99, 102–3, 108–9,
    121–23, 125–26, 158
Klüpfel, Karl, xvi
Knivet, Anthony, lxxxv, lxxxix, 176–77
Kolben, Andres, xv, 145
Konyan Bebe, xxvii, xxxiii, xxxix, xlix–li,
    lxxix, lxxxi–lxxxii, xc, xciii, 60–64, 84,
    86, 90, 117, 169–70, 173, 177
Kuntsmann map, lxxiv

Lactantius Firmianus, 12
La Margalle, lxxxvii
Latin, 153, 155
Leach, Edmund, lxi
legs, xxxix, lxx, 64, 75, 108, 137, 148–49
Le Havre, 101
Leiden, xvi
Lent, 170
Lepanto, Battle of, 179
Léry, Jean de, xxxii–xxxiv, xxxvi–xxxviii,

Léry, Jean de (*continued*)
xl–xlii, xliv–xlvi, li, liv, lviii, lxiii, lxv,
lxxxvi–lxxxix, xciii, 159–61, 166, 170,
174, 177

Lestringant, Frank, xxxv, xxxvii–xli, xlv,
lv, lxxxvi–lxxxvii, ci–ciii, 160–161,
163, 170

Letts, Malcolm, x, xlii, xlvii, 152–54,
164–65, 175, 180

Levant, xv, 152

Lévi-Strauss, Claude, xli, xlv, liv–lv,
lxxxvi–lxxxviii, 160

lions, 103, 139

lip plugs, xxiv, 62, 119–20, 123

lips, 148

Lisbon, xviii, lxxx, 21–23, 30, 105, 156

lizard, 39, 140

Lobato, Manuel, x

Locke, John, xxxi

Löfgren, Alberto, xvi

London, lx, 103, 145, 177

Louisiana, 179

Luther, Martin, lxv, 60

Lutheranism, lv, lix, lxiv, 154

Lyra, Nicholas, 13

macaguá, 131

Madeira, 22–23

Madrueira, Luis, lii–lv, lxxxiii, 166

Malinowski, Bronislaw, lxxxix, xcii–xciii,
178

Mambucabe, 67–69

Mameluke, 44, 87–90, 178

manioc, 27–29, 38, 47, 54, 73, 92, 114–15,
117–18, 122–23, 128

manioc flour, 76, 128

man-munching, 5

Manuel I of Portugal, 156

Maracaibo, 156

Marburg, xv, xviii, lxxi, 5, 10, 16, 145,
154–55, 175

Marckaya, xlviii, xcv, 19, 61, 71, 73–74,
99, 109

Marin, 28

Marquesas Islands, cii

Marxism, 166

mathematics, 9, 12, 155

Maximilian I, lxxiv

Maya, ciii, 171

medicine, 5, 170

Meiwes, Armin, 168

Melville, Herman, xliii, lii, lvi, lxxxiv,
cii, 165

Menk, Gerhard, xviii

Menninger, Annerose, lvii, 152, 165

Merck Pharmaceuticals, 170

metal tools, 33, 56, 58, 72–73, 76, 78, 99,
113–14, 119

Métraux, Alfred, xlii, xvli–xlvii

Mexico, 179

Meyen Bipe (São Sebastião), xcvi, 85,
87–89

Miller Atlas, lxxiv

miracles, 13, 15, 69. *See also* cosmology;
shamans

Mirando, Claudio, xcii, 76

mirrors, 58, 72, 99

missionaries, xxix, xxxi, xxxiv, xlv

Moby Dick (Melville), 166

modernism, x, xxxviii, li–lv, lxv, lxxi, lxxx,
lxxxvii

modernity, li–lv, lviii, lxii

Moner, Wilhelm de, 99, 145

Mongol, lxi

Monguape, 71

monkeys, 82, 96, 102, 112, 138, 161–62

moon, lxxvi, lxxviii, xc, 11–12, 65–67, 69,
106, 155

Montaigne, Michel de, x, xxxi, xxxviii, xl,
xlii, liii, lxiii, lxxxvi, 152

Morocco, 23

mosquito, 141

mummies, 170

mussels, 39

mussuruna, xcv, 55, 73, 128, 131–32, 147, 157–58

nakedness, xxiii–xxiv, xxvi, lxviii–lxx, lxxx–lxxxi, 14, 48–49, 77, 82, 107, 113, 141. *See also* clothing

navigation, lxxx, 17, 24–25, 32–34, 39–41, 95, 105–6, 126, 145. *See also* cosmography; mathematics

necklaces, 62, 119–20, 123

Neuber, Wolfgang, lxxxvii, 165, 176

New Mexico, 179

New World, xviii, xxii, xxiv, lxxiv, cii, 5, 13, 17, 30, 159

New York, lx

Nicholas, Saint, 15

Niteroi, xxxii, 71, 82, 167

Nóbrega, Manuel da, xxv–xxvi, 157, 160

Normandy, 100–101, 144

"Norman" traders, xxxii, xxxiv, xcii, 56, 60, 159

Noyes, lxxiii

Obermeier, Franz, 165

Ocaraçú, 90

Ojeda, Alonzo de, 156

Olinda, 26

Oliveira, Jó, 173, 175

Orellana, Fancisco de, xxiv

Orinoco River, ciii

ostrich, 120

Ouetaca, xxxvii, lviii, 159

Pacific, 165

Palestine, lx

palm, 36, 110, 113–14, 116

Palma, 31

Parakană, xlvii

Paraná, Rio, 30

Paria, Gulf of, 156

Paris, 15, 155

parrots, lxxxii, 82, 96, 175–76

Parshall, Peter, lxxii, 172–74

Parwaa, 88, 92, 94–95

peccary, lxxxii, 79–80, 114, 137–38

Penteado, 21, 144

pepper, 58–59, 71, 82, 96–98, 102, 116, 129, 142

Pereira, Luiz Alberto, x, lxxxii–lxxxiii, 175

Pernambuco, xviii, 26, 29, 129

Perot, 97, 145

Peru, 30

Philip Ludwig II, Landgrave of Hesse, xvii, xviii, lxxv, 5, 7, 9, 15–16, 154–55

philology, xlii

philosophy, xxxi, xli, lxiv, 12

pilgrimage, 14

pirates, 30

plants, 93, 107, 114, 121, 127, 141–42, 176

Polyphemus, 15

Portinari, Candido, x, lv, lxxx–lxxxii, 175

possum, 139, 152

postcolonial criticism, xxxix–xl, lii–liii, lxxxiii, 166

Postel, Guillaume, xxxvi, 152

Potiguar (Buttugaris), 19, 29, 151

Praga Brothers, 44, 87–91, 178

prayer, 14, 25, 35, 37, 42, 49, 52–54, 60, 66, 92, 95, 99, 103–4

prophecy. *See* shamans

Protestants, xxxii, xl, xlii, lviii, lxv, lxxii, lxxxv, 154–55, 159

psalms, xvii, 7, 51, 64, 143, 172

Purchas, Samuel, lxxxv

Puritans, 169

Rabelais, François, lxvi

Ralegh, Walter, xlii

rat, 39

Red Sea, 103

Reformation, lxv

Richard I, the Lionheart, 169

Rio de Janeiro, ix, xxviii, xxxii, xxxvii, 82, 96–97, 99–100, 105, 145, 167

Rio de la Plata, xviii, xcix, 30, 37–38, 40, 144, 156

Rio Jaguaripe, xxviii

Rio Paraibe, xlix, 29, 85, 109

Rio São Francisco, 35

ritual equipment, 173. *See also* tammaraka

Robinson Crusoe (Defoe), xl, c–cii, civ

Romans, 40–42

Rösel, Peter, 99, 144–45

Rotz, Jean, lxxiv

Rouen, lxxiii, 163

Rousseau, Jean Jacques, xxxi, xlii, liii

Rwanda, lviii

Sá, Mem de, lxxxiii

Sabbat, xxxiv

Saint Bartholomew's Day Massacre, 161

St. Elmo's fire, 25

saints, xxii, lxxxiv, 13, 14–15, 25, 37

Salazar, Captain, 38, 40

salt, 21, 116

Sampaio, Teodoro, xvi

Sanabria, Don Diego de, 30, 144

Sancerre, xxxvii

San Lucar, 31

Santa Catarina, Bay, lxxxviii, 37, 39

Santa Maria, Puerta de, 30

Santiago de Compostela, 13

Santos, Nelson Pereira dos, x, liv, lxxxii–lxxxiii

São Amaro, xix, 44–45, 47

São Paulo, 151, 167, 173

São Tome (Guinea), 31–32

São Vicente (Santos; Upaú-nema), xix, 34, 40–44, 47–48, 76, 78–79, 144–45

Saracens, 169

Saussure, Ferdinand de, lxxxvii

sea-snails, 93, 119–21

Sebastian, Saint, xxiv

Seine River, lxxiii

Selkirk, John, cii

Senchez, Johann, 77

Seville, 30–31, 144

sexuality, xxii–xxiii, xxvi–xxix, xxxii, lxxvii–lxxviii, lxxxi–lxxxiii, xcvii, 113, 122–23, 129–37

Scarry, Elaine, 168

Schantz, François de, 99, 145

Schetzen, Jaspar, 144–45

Schiriffi (sharif), 23

Schmalkaldic War (1546–47), xviii, 154

Setúbal, 21

shaman, shamans (pagé; karai), xxv, xxix, xxxv–xxxvi, lxxvii, 58, 66–67, 84–87, 119, 124–26, 178–79: dreaming and, xlvii, 86; healing and, xx, lxxvi, lxxxix–xc, 68–70; Staden as, xx, xlv, lxxii, lxxvi, lxxviii, xcvi–xcvii, c, 152; warfare and, xx, 63, 84–87, 12–26, 128; weather shamans, lxxii, 93–95, lxxxix–xc, 52–53, 74–75. *See also* tammaraka; weather; witchcraft

Shrove Tuesday, 145

signs, 13, 92, 94, 100. *See also* cosmology

skin, 80–81, 137, 148, 176

skins, 23, 30, 107, 129

skulls, xxviii, lxxvi, 12, 61, 64, 81, 137, 147, 160, 162, 176

slaves, xxvii, xli, xlv, lxxvi, lxxxi, xciv–xcvii, c, 26, 47–49, 59, 62, 64, 67, 71–76, 79–82, 84, 95, 97, 121–22, 125–26, 128, 157–58, 166, 171

Soderini, Piero, 156

Sousa, Gabriel Soares de, xxviii–xxxi, 137, 157

Southey, Robert, xlii, xlvii, 164–65

Souza, Tomé, 46

Sowarasu, 97

Staden Institute (Instituto Martius-
　Staden), 167
stars, lxxvi, 11, 13, 66
Strong, Pauline, ci
sugar, 22, 32, 43, 47–48, 76
suicide-bombers, lx
sun, lxix, lxxvi, lxxxi, 11–12, 32, 34–35, 54,
　60, 105–7, 142, 155
Supraway (Superaguí), 33–34
sweet potato, 142

Tabajarre, lxxiii, 44, 163
tammaraka (rattles), xlvi, l, lxvii, xciv,
　54–55, 57–58, 86, 89, 91, 108, 124–26,
　128. See also shamans
Tamoio, xxvii–xxviii, xxxvi, 151
Tanner, John (the Falcon), ci, 176
Tapuios, xxx, 159
Taquaraçú-tiba, 96–97
Tatamiri, 92
teeth, 61, 80, 108, 114, 149
Temimo, xxxv
Ten Huisen, Dwight, 171, 176
Terceira, 30
terrorism, lviii–lxii, 167
Texas, xcix, 179
theology, xvii, xxxiii, xl, lxiii–lxviii, lxxii,
　lxxxiv–lxxxv, xc–xciii, 10, 12–13, 60
Thevet, André, xxxii–xxxvi, xxxviii, xliv,
　xlvi, lxiii, lxxiv, lxxxvi–lxxxviii, 160,
　163, 166
Thomas, Saint, 16
thorn, 108, 129, 142
thunder, 35, 74, 94
Ticoaripe, 73
tobacco, 125
Todos os Santos, Bahia de, 107
tongue, 137, 148
Tootal, Albert, xvi
torture, lxi, lxvi–lxvii
travel accounts, xv, xxi, xliii, lii, lxxxiv–

lxxxv, lxxxvii, xciii, xcviii–c, 8–10, 16,
　144–45, 156, 177
Trobriand Islands, xciii
tunics (tipoí), 107
Tupí, ix–xi, xvi, xix–xxii, xxv–xxviii, xxxi,
　xxxiii–xxxiv, xxxvi–xxxviii, xli, lx,
　lxii–lxviii, lxx, lxxi–lxxv, lxxxviii–lxxix,
　lxxxi, lxxxii–lxxxv, lxxxviii–xc, xciv–
　xcvi, 152–53, 155–57, 159, 161, 163–64,
　167–68, 179; dances and feasts of,
　55–58, 90–91, 108, 117–19, 128–36;
　domestic architecture of, 109–10;
　ethnology of, 14, 47, 51, 54, 55, 57–58,
　61–62, 68, 73, 79–80, 99, 105–42, 173;
　kings and war-chiefs of, lxviii, 109,
　116–17, 123, 127, 131, 151; language of,
　xxxi, xlii, 52, 54, 60, 64, 72, 74, 77, 82,
　84, 97, 107
Tupí–Guaraní, xli
Tupina, xxix
Tupinambá, ix, xviii–xxii, xxix, xxxii,
　xxxv–xxxvi, lxxiii, lxxvi, lxxxiv, xcii,
　xcvii, c, 5, 19, 44, 59, 79, 85, 87, 105–6,
　109, 151, 157–58, 161, 163–64, 172, 176
Tupiniquin, xviii–xx, xxii, lxxxi, lxxxiii,
　xc, c, 17–19, 34, 43, 50, 59, 62–65, 67,
　77, 86–87, 99, 109, 151
Txiçao, xcviii
Typee (Melville), cii

United States, 162–64, 167, 180
uraçú-iba tree, 111
Uruguay, 30
Utrecht, xvi
Uwattibi (Ubatúba), xix, xlix, lxviii–lxix,
　lxxix, xciv, 54, 56, 64, 69, 85, 91, 98

Valencia, 23
Valero, Helena, 178
Varthema, Ludovico, 152
Vatierville, 144–45

Venezuela, 165

vengeance, xxviii, xxx, xxxii–xxxiv, xxxvii, xlv, xciii, 49, 54, 72, 91, 96, 121, 127, 137, 171

Vespucci, Amerigo, xxii–xxiv, xxvi, xxxi, lxxiv, 156–57, 159

Vienna, 10

Villeganon, Nicolas de, xxxi–xxxii, xxxvii, 159

violence, xix, xxi–xxiii, xxiv–xxx, xxxii–xxxiii, xxxviii, xli–lvii, lviii–lxii, lxxi, lxxiv, lxxvi–lxxvii, lxxix, xciv, xcvii, c, 17, 23, 48, 50–51, 61, 75, 117, 167–68

Virginia, 166

visual depictions, xv–xvi, lvi, lxiii, lxviii–lxix, lxx–lxxxiii, xc, 15, 152–55, 161, 172–73, 175

Viveiros de Castro, Eduardo, xlvi, lxii, xciv, 166

Voigt, Lisa, xcix

Vratinge Wasu, xx, xlviii, 55, 70, 80

Vufflens, lxxxvii

Waiwai, 161

Wandel, Lee, lxiv, 169–70

Wapishana, 161

warfare, 26–30, 43, 45–47, 50, 54, 58–59, 63–65, 67, 70, 76–79, 81–82, 84–85, 87, 90, 97, 99, 108–10, 120–21, 125–29, 145, 167, 171

Wari', 165

wax, 129, 137

weather, xlix, lxx, lxxvi, lxxxix–xc, xciv, xcviii, 7, 23–25, 30–35, 40–42, 52–53, 74–75, 84–85, 93–96, 100, 103, 106–7, 115. *See also* celestial bodies; shamans

Weilburg, 13

werewolf, lxxi

Wetter, xviii, 9

White Moors, 21, 23

wine, 22, 30

witchcraft, xxxiv–xxxvii, lxxvii, lxxxvi, lxxxix, 161, 163, 168. *See also* shamans

Wilbert, Johannes, 175

Wolfhagen, xviii, 8

Wolrad II, Count, xviii

women, xxxvii, lxxxi, lxxxii, 107, 117–18, 121–23, 157–58: in marriage, xxvii–xxviii, 109, 122–23; prophesy and, l–li, 126; sacrifice of, xxiii; in sacrificial killing and feasting, xxx, xxxiv, xlvi, lxi, lxvi, 54–58, 69, 71, 129–137, 147–49, 160, 162, 174; violence and, xxiv–xxv, 54, 160, 162

World War I, 178

World War II, lxxxvii, 167

Wynkelman, Johann, xvi, 153

Yanomami, 165, 178

Yucatan, ciii

Zebedee, 13

Zeeland, 103, 177

Zemeckis, Robert, civ

Zwingli, Huldrych, lxv

Neil L. Whitehead is a professor of anthropology at the University of Wisconsin.

Library of Congress Cataloging-in-Publication Data
Staden, Hans, ca. 1525–ca. 1576.
[Warhaftige Historia und Beschreibung eyner Landtschafft der wilden, nacketen, grimmigen Menschfresser Leuthen in der Newenwelt America gelegen. English]
Hans Staden's true history : an account of cannibal captivity in Brazil / Hans Staden ; edited and with an introduction by Neil L. Whitehead ; newly translated by Michael Harbsmeier.
p. cm. — (The cultures and practice of violence series)
Includes bibliographical references.
ISBN-13: 978-0-8223-4213-7 (cloth : alk. paper)
ISBN-13: 978-0-8223-4231-1 (pbk. : alk. paper)
1. Brazil—Description and travel—Early works to 1800. 2. Indians of South America—Brazil—Early works to 1800. 3. Tupinamba Indians—Early works to 1800. 4. Voyages and travels—Early works to 1800. I. Whitehead, Neil L. II. Harbsmeier, Michael. III. Title.
F2511.S8313 2008
394'.908109032—dc22   2007044903